DEATH TANGO

DEATH TANGO

Ariel Sharon, Yasser Arafat, and Three Fateful Days in March

YOSSI ALPHER

ROWMAN & LITTLEFIELD
Lanham • Boulder • New York • London

Published by Rowman & Littlefield
An imprint of The Rowman & Littlefield Publishing Group, Inc.
4501 Forbes Boulevard, Suite 200, Lanham, Maryland 20706
www.rowman.com

86-90 Paul Street, London EC2A 4NE

British Library Cataloguing in Publication Information Available

Library of Congress Cataloging-in-Publication Data
Names: Alpher, Joseph, author.
Title: Death tango : Ariel Sharon, Yasser Arafat, and three fateful days in
    March / Yossi Alpher.
Description: Lanham, Maryland : Rowman & Littlefield, [2021] | Includes
    bibliographical references and index.
Identifiers: LCCN 2021034048 (print) | LCCN 2021034049 (ebook) | ISBN
    9781538162071 (cloth) | ISBN 9781538162088 (epub)
Subjects: LCSH: Sharon, Ariel. | Arafat, Yasir, 1929-2004. | Arab-Israeli
    conflict—1993– | Arab-Israeli conflict—1993—Peace. | Palestinian
    Arabs—Politics and government—1993–
Classification: LCC DS119.76 .A44496 2021 (print) | LCC DS119.76 (ebook)
    | DDC 956.05/3—dc23
LC record available at https://lccn.loc.gov/2021034048
LC ebook record available at https://lccn.loc.gov/2021034049

CONTENTS

CYPRUS

Mediterranean Sea

LEBANON

Beirut

Damascus

SYRIA

Haifa

ISRAEL

Jenin

Netanya

Tulkarm

Nablus

Tel Aviv

Amman

Ramallah

WEST BANK

Jerusalem

JORDAN

GAZA STRIP

Hebron

Beersheba

SCALE

0   50 km

EGYPT

Israel, Palestinian Authority, and Neighboring States. (Shapiro Repro)

ACKNOWLEDGMENTS

I am indebted to the Rockefeller Brothers Fund (working through the Institute of International Education) and its president, Stephen Heintz, for their financial support for the traveling, interviewing, and public relations required in writing and publishing this book. This is not the first time Stephen has responded to my request for logistics support. I truly appreciate his faith in me.

I wish to thank all those Israelis, Arabs, Americans, and one Russian who agreed to speak with me and share their memories and insights for this book. I traveled far and wide to meet them and they responded with open hospitality and friendship. They are a primary source of the information and ideas I sought. They are listed after the book's second appendix. A special word of thanks is due Eric Cohen for hosting me at the Park Hotel in Netanya and walking me through the scene of Israel's worst terrorist tragedy. For him it was also a family tragedy.

I was warmly welcomed and assisted by Nava Reich, director of the Meir Amit Intelligence and Terrorism Information Center Library at the Israel Intelligence Heritage and Commemoration Center (IICC) in Ramat HaSharon, Israel. Similarly, the newspaper reading room of Bet Ariela, the Tel Aviv Central Library, proved a very friendly resource. Professor Tamar Hermann, senior fellow at the Israel Democracy Institute and academic director of the Guttman Center for Public Opinion and Policy Research, guided my effort to pinpoint Israeli public opinion data from 2002. And Nikolai Surkov of the Moscow State Institute of International Relations' Oriental Studies Department ably guided me through the contradictions in Russian Middle East policy in the early Putin years.

Gareth Smyth, who from 1996 reported from Beirut and was *Financial Times* correspondent there from 2000 to 2003 and chief correspondent in

Iran from 2003 to 2007, earned my sincere gratitude when he volunteered to share with me his personal archive of superb articles and diary notes from early 2002. In effect, Gareth gave me an on-the-scene journalist's-eye view of the Beirut Arab League summit and all that preceded and followed it.

Many thanks to three veteran colleagues who kindly agreed to read the manuscript at an early stage. All three offered truly valuable comments, insights, and criticism. Ambassador Fred Hof was chief of staff of the "Mitchell" Committee and is currently diplomat-in-residence at Bard College. The work of the Mitchell Committee regarding the Israeli-Palestinian conflict directly preceded the period in 2002 that constitutes the focus of this book.

Bruce Riedel is a senior fellow at the Brookings Institution and thirty-year veteran of the CIA with service in the White House advising four presidents on the Middle East. Our friendship goes back to the Iranian revolution of 1978–1979, when Bruce as CIA Iran-analyst and I as Mossad Iran-analyst dialogued day and night for months in an effort to comprehend a very different Middle East dynamic.

Professor Efraim Inbar is president of the Jerusalem Institute for Strategy and Security and a partner in the distant past in track-two talks with Palestinians and Jordanians regarding mutual security concerns. He is someone I can faithfully depend on for a smart, challenging, contrary set of views.

My wife, Irene, constantly challenged me to write plain English and to explain myself to the general reader while we weathered the corona pandemic together in isolation.

Finally, my gratitude is extended to my literary agent, Leslie Gardner of Artellus Ltd., London. Without her wisdom and guidance, this book would not have reached a publisher. Many thanks to Susan McEachern, Katelyn Turner, Alden Perkins, and Kate Hertzog at Rowman & Littlefield, who shepherded publication with admirable expertise and patience.

And last but by far not least, Rachel Gul of Over the River Public Relations undertook the daunting task of making the world aware of this book.

INTRODUCTORY NOTE

During three days at the end of March 2002, a fascinating confluence of strategic events in the Middle East took place. March 27 witnessed Israel's worst terrorist atrocity, perpetrated at the Park Hotel in the coastal city of Netanya on Passover eve, the Jewish people's holiday of national liberation. March 28 in Beirut, just 183 kilometers (115 miles) up the Mediterranean coast, introduced the Arab Peace Initiative (API). This historic document is seen to this day in many quarters as the defining formula for Arab-Israel peacemaking based on a successful resolution of the Israeli-Palestinian conflict. The next day, March 29, the Israel Defense Forces (IDF) launched Operation Defensive Shield, Israel's response not only to the Netanya atrocity but to all the suicide bombings that preceded it. The IDF reoccupied the entire West Bank and effectively ended progress in implementing the Oslo-based Israeli-Palestinian peace process.

This book is about those events. Israel, the Palestinians, the rest of the Middle East, and indeed the entire international community were affected by this dramatic sequence, which changed the course of the Palestinian-Israeli conflict and Arab-Israel relations. March 27, 28, and 29, 2002, set both of these dynamics on two new and parallel tracks.

The personalities, leadership strengths and weaknesses, and decision-making skills of Israeli prime minister Ariel Sharon and Palestinian leader Yasser Arafat in 2002 form a key dimension of this narrative. I met on several occasions with them both. Here and with regard to additional key figures and narratives, I have drawn on these experiences.

For years after 2002, all the relevant parties tried to reset the Middle East peace process, restart the Oslo process, and implement the API. Some are still trying. The conflict and the regional relationship maintained the same semi-frozen equilibrium until 2020, when four Arab states normalized relations with Israel despite the lack of progress toward a resolution of the Israeli-Palestinian conflict. Paradoxically, and cynically, they cited the Arab Peace Initiative as having granted them authority.

From my personal standpoint, it was only after multiple subsequent failures of the Israeli-Palestinian peace process, sometime around a decade ago, that I began to see the events of those three days as a kind of grand-strategic crossroads. That realization was enough to put those three days in March on my writing agenda. There they lingered until I realized that too much distance in time from 2002 would mean that a measure of natural attrition would take its toll on the principal actors of the day when I went looking for them for interviews. When I did, beginning in 2019, a few of the key Arab players, particularly participants in the Arab League summit of March 2002, would not agree to discuss that event with an Israeli. More ominously, it emerged that the atmosphere at the time of researching and writing in 2019–2021 was also a problem. As one former Arab foreign minister told me at the outset of our not-for-attribution interview about his role in formulating the API, "This whole issue about the peace process has become toxic in the Arab world. Just as people in Israel don't believe they have a partner on the other side, it's even worse here. So I understand the reluctance to talk about the issues."

That reluctance was demonstrated by a number of Israelis as well as Arabs. Among one or two fellow Israelis who had been active militarily or politically in the events of 2002, the response to my interview request was shaded by deep pessimism regarding the peace process then and now. It was as if they were saying, "What's the use in your inquiries, Yossi?" On the Arab side, reluctance was nourished by the wages and overflow of the Arab revolutions and state collapse that have plagued the Middle East region since 2011: from Iraq in the east to Tunisia in the west; from Syria in the north to Yemen and Sudan in the south. Several Arab acquaintances who were active in the events described here agreed to be interviewed, but only anonymously.

In sharp contrast, as I set off on those inquiries, interviews, and travels, I discovered new facts and insights and refreshed distant memories about the events of March 2002 to an extent that compelled me, happily, to reassess and restructure this book's narrative on a near-constant basis. Standing in the banquet hall of the Park Hotel in Netanya alongside the hotel manager (then and now) as he describes the Passover eve carnage of March 2002 is a sobering experience. So is discovering that Israeli prime minister Ariel Sharon, an object of fear and hatred among many Arabs, was secretly angling for an invitation to the Beirut Arab League summit weeks before it took place, then publicly soliciting a summons to visit Beirut ten days after the Park bombing.

Equally sobering is hearing from the chief Palestinian author of the Arab Peace Initiative that the whole "show" in Beirut was really not about peace. Rather, it involved little more than a Saudi leader trying to redeem his and his country's reputation half a year after the tragic terrorist attack of 9/11 on the United States. Lest we forget, that was an event in which Saudi ideology and Saudi manpower (fifteen of the nineteen bombers) were dominant. Tom Friedman, seen by some as the real "father" of the API, added yet another Saudi motive: a leader's drive to prevail in an internal power struggle in Riyadh.

One advantage of writing about compelling events in the Middle East nearly two decades after they transpired is hindsight. One can see where those events have led—where and how they fit into the grand thrust of the region's ensuing strategic evolution, particularly with regard to the Arab-Israel conflict and its Palestinian-Israeli expression.

Apropos Palestinians and Israelis, what was in 2002 still the very core of the overall conflict and of the malaise that affected and infected the entire region has today in many ways become a sideshow. The Palestinian issue now looms primarily as a threat, largely ignored or downplayed by Israel's current leadership, to the future nature and substance of the Israeli state. The rest of the Arab Middle East, while slowly but surely coming to terms with Israel's presence, is busy with its own fragmentation and disarray. And in Iran and the Islamic State, the Arab world confronts the simultaneously empowering yet crippling effects of its religion, Islam.

★   ★   ★

To weave together the diverse but interrelated threads of this narrative, I structured the book with interacting and overlapping themes. The narrative is broadly composed of two matrices. One is chronological. It centers on each of the three days of late March 2002 when the primary events transpired. The other is event-centered and also focuses on specific personalities who played a major role in those events. Woven together, these two currents explore in detail the pre-March backdrop and post-March consequences of the Park Hotel bombing in Netanya, Israel; Arab League approval of the Arab Peace Initiative in Beirut, Lebanon; and Israel's Operation Defensive Shield invasion and reoccupation of the entire West Bank part of the Palestinian Authority.

The United States, by far the principal concerned and involved external power, is present throughout.

The Passover Seder and suicide bombing described in chapter 1, "March 27, 2002: Netanya, Tulkarm, Beirut," draw on a multitude of contemporary Israeli media sources along with the author's conversations with relatives of the deceased and the Park Hotel manager. Chapter 15, "Behind the Events of March 2002," is based on a chapter in my 2016 book *No End of Conflict: Rethinking Israel-Palestine* (Rowman & Littlefield). The conversation with *New York Times* opinion columnist Thomas L. Friedman that comprises chapter 7 is reproduced verbatim. It was edited only for clarity and to omit irrelevant comments.

The title of this book, *Death Tango*, is part of a phrase used by Aaron Miller, who in 2002 was actively mediating on behalf of the United States, to describe the relationship between Ariel Sharon and Yasser Arafat. Seen with the benefit of hindsight, the term also describes the Israeli-Palestinian relationship, then and now. My thanks to Aaron.

Finally, wherever a source is not cited, I am the source. I have attempted throughout the narrative to maintain objectivity and stick to facts. But I am also responsible for any inaccuracies and mistakes.

Yossi Alpher
Ramat HaSharon, Israel
September 2021

GLOSSARY OF TERMS

API	The Arab Peace Initiative, ratified in Beirut on March 28, 2002.
Fateh (Arabic)	Literally, opening or victory; reversed as an acronym of Palestinian National Liberation Movement; founded by Yasser Arafat; the primary component of the PLO.
Hamas (Arabic)	Acronym of Islamic Resistance Movement, effectively the Palestinian branch of the Muslim Brotherhood. Since 2007 rules the Gaza Strip.
IDF	Israel Defense Forces, Israel's army.
Intifada (Arabic)	Rebellion, uprising, resistance movement. The first Intifada began in late 1987 and ended with the Oslo Accords of September 1993. The second Intifada transpired from September 2000 to 2004–2005.
Mossad (Hebrew)	Literally, institution. Israel's external intelligence agency.
Muqataa (Arabic)	Headquarters; in 2002, Arafat's West Bank headquarters and official seat of the PA, in Ramallah, West Bank.
Nakba (Arabic)	The Palestinian disaster of destruction and exile in 1948.
PA	Palestinian Authority, founded in 1994 in accordance with the Oslo Accords. The government of areas A and B of the West Bank. Technically the government of the Gaza Strip, though stripped of authority by Hamas since 2007. Dominated by the PLO.
PLO	Palestine Liberation Organization, comprising a number of Palestinian movements and dominated by Fateh.

Rais (Arabic)   Head, usually head of state; in this context, President Arafat of the Palestinian Authority.

Shabak   Acronym of the Hebrew letters shin-bet-kaf, Sherut Bitachon Klali, General Security Service, often represented as Shin-Bet. Responsible for internal security in Israel as well as (with the IDF) security in the West Bank and Gaza Strip.

UNRWA   United Nations Relief and Works Agency for Palestinian Refugees in the Near East, created in December 1949.

PROLOGUE: TIME AND HISTORY

Taking the long view, what if anything could three days change in the modern-day saga of Israelis, Palestinians, and the Arab world? Time is the critical dimension that challenges the narratives of the Arab-Israel and Israeli-Palestinian dynamic.

Many Arabs, and particularly Palestinians, argue that time is on their side. It took around two hundred years to expel the Christian crusaders from Palestine a millennium ago, but ultimately the Arabs triumphed over the crusader state. By extension, it is just a matter of time until the Jewish state is defeated and the Jews expelled. Or until a binational Arab-Jewish entity called "Israel" becomes a binational Arab-dominated entity called "Palestine." One way or another, according to this Arab narrative, the Jews will eventually lose the will to fight, because they are a foreign implant and not a genuine nation.

This take on time and the conflict is one key reason why Palestinian refugee status has been formed and molded so as to be multi-generational. The great-grandchildren of refugees who fled Haifa and Jaffa seventy-three years ago live in UNRWA camps in Lebanon and the Gaza Strip. Their vision of a home left behind by their ancestors in 1948 is largely imaginary. But it represents a key dimension of the Arab state of mind regarding Israel: *nakba*, victimhood, and return, generation-generation.

Never in history was there an Arab state of Palestine. Most Arab states as we know them today are recent colonial-era creations. In 2021, roughly half of them were wracked by mass civil unrest, revolution, and/or civil war, barely functioning as states. The Arab future looked grim. But of course, that could change.

The Israeli historical take on time is surprisingly complementary. In the course of three thousand years of Hebrew history in the Holy Land, no

Jewish state ever lasted even two hundred years, whether it was called Israel or Judea, whether it was ruled by Solomon or the Hasmoneans. The demise of more than one Hebrew kingdom was brought about by internal strife.

Apropos internal strife, Israel at age seventy-three (in 2021) is, despite the COVID-19 pandemic, an economically thriving state and a military (and reputedly a nuclear) power. Yet it has been described by its president in 2015, Reuven Rivlin, as fast becoming a tribal state composed of four groups: secular Jews, religious Zionist Jews, ultra-Orthodox or Haredi Jews, and Arabs. All, according to Rivlin, are fearful, hostile to one another, and even hostile to members of their own group. "There is no longer a clear majority, nor [are there] clear minority groups," Rivlin stated pessimistically.[1]

Israel, like the Palestinians, also cultivates a narrative of victimhood that is anchored in the Holocaust and in more than seventy years of conflict with the Arab world and lately with Iran.

Which side will best weather the vicissitudes of time and history? Long ago, God's commandments and Egyptian hieroglyphs were written in stone. Nothing is written in stone any longer in the Middle East.

1

MARCH 27, 2002: NETANYA, TULKARM, BEIRUT

The explosive belt usually consists of several cylinders filled with explosive (de facto pipe bombs), or in more sophisticated versions with plates of explosive. The explosive is surrounded by a fragmentation jacket that produces the shrapnel responsible for most of the bomb's lethality, effectively making the jacket a crude, body-worn, Claymore mine. Once the vest is detonated, the explosion resembles an omnidirectional shotgun blast. The most dangerous and the most widely used shrapnel are steel balls 3 to 7 millimeters (0.12 to 0.28 inches) in diameter. Other shrapnel material can be anything of suitable size and hardness, most often nails, screws, nuts, and thick wire. Shrapnel is responsible for about 90 percent of all casualties caused by this kind of device.

A "loaded" vest may weigh between 5 to 20 kilograms (11 to 44 pounds) and may be hidden under thick clothes, usually jackets or snow coats.

A suicide vest may cover the entire stomach and usually has shoulder straps.

The discovery of remains as well as incidentally unexploded belts or vests can offer forensic clues to the investigation after the attack.

Suicide bombers who wear the vests are often obliterated by the explosion; the best evidence of their identity is the head, which often survives because it is separated and thrown clear of the body by the explosion.

(from Wikipedia)

★   ★   ★

The world of 2002 was not all that different from the world of 2021. Some events still ring familiar.

In early March 2002, US and Afghan troops launched Operation Ana-
conda against al-Qaeda and Taliban fighters in Afghanistan. In May, East
Timor gained independence, while the United States and Russia reached
agreement to cut their nuclear arsenals by up to two-thirds. In July, Penn-
sylvania miners were rescued after spending days in a dark, flooded mine
shaft. In October, a terrorist bomb in Bali, Indonesia, killed hundreds. Also
in October, Jimmy Carter won the Nobel Peace Prize, while two snipers,
a man and a boy, killed ten in the suburbs of Washington, DC.

In 2002, New England won the Super Bowl, Brazil won the soc-
cer World Cup, and *A Beautiful Mind* won the Academy Award for best
picture.

On March 27, 2002, in the evening most Israelis, like Jews everywhere, celebrated the *Pesach* or Passover feast, or *Seder*, around the family
dinner table. With them were uncles and aunts, grandparents, friends, and
lots of children. Not a few had a different agenda: an escape abroad from
an unpleasant family confrontation; or camping out in Egyptian Sinai,
where the Children of Israel wandered for forty years and the Passover
story began.

Some celebrated at a hotel.

The latter option might reflect lack of room at home for all the relatives, or perhaps a reluctance on the part of busy and harried celebrants to
prepare the special dishes required for the Passover meal—the gefilte fish,
the chopped liver, the horseradish, the *charoset* with its dates, nuts, and dried
fruit that is eaten with *matza*, or unleavened bread. Each dish has a symbolic
significance. Each has its ethnic variants, originating in Poland or Romania,
Afghanistan or Morocco.

Another reason to move the celebration to a hotel can be loneliness—
the absence of family and friends to celebrate with. Some celebrants might
simply be tourists from abroad who have no family in Israel.

The Park Hotel on King David Street in Netanya is a modest,
medium-size structure in a medium-size city in the center of Israel. It is a
three-star family-owned hotel with few frills. Its only real attraction is that
it overlooks the city's beautiful Mediterranean beach. Netanya's beach is
reached by descending a steep drop from a corniche and park that are ac-
cessed directly from the hotel.

That Passover eve in 2002, Wednesday, March 27, the Park offered
competitive rates for its ceremonial dinner compared to fancier Tel Aviv
and Jerusalem hotels. It attracted more than three hundred guests. Some
came from a distance. Many were repeat families who over the years had
come to know the Cohens, who built and managed the hotel. Eric Cohen,

manager and son of the original founders, celebrated Pesach nearby at home that evening. But his mother was among the celebrants at the Park.

The Cohen clan took turns year after year managing the Seder. This meant mainly confirming that everyone who came had paid in advance for a seat at a numbered table, then making sure the food was served properly, then supervising the cleanup. That holiday eve the task fell to Eric Cohen's brother-in-law, Amiram Hamami. Security was entrusted to whoever would be sent by a local security agency; for this occasion the guard was a recent Russian immigrant, a burly fellow who manned a booth at the hotel entrance.

As the 7:30 p.m. start of the Seder neared, guests were crowding in off King David Street, the main north-south road that follows the coast and the corniche. It was raining—a light, intermittent spring shower, signifying the end of the winter rainy season on the eastern Mediterranean shore and the start of the region's long, dry summer.

Netanya has given its King David Street many names. Farther south it is Gad Machnes Street, named after a deceased municipal founding father and citrus farmer. Yet farther to the south come the national founding fathers: Jabotinsky Street, then Ben-Gurion Street. Jabotinsky is more central than Ben-Gurion, perhaps because Netanya was founded by right-wing followers of the Zionist revisionist leader. North of the Park Hotel, leading a mile up the coast to Laniado Hospital, the road following the drop to the beach becomes Nitsa Boulevard, then HaMlachim (Kings) Street. The Park Hotel is located at number seven King David Street.

Like the senior Cohens, many of the celebrants were elderly. Hannah Rogan, who had recently moved to Netanya, was ninety; she came with a childhood friend of the same age, Yulia Talmi. Alter and Frieda Britavich were in their late eighties. Juliette-Geula Ben-David, in her seventies, came with her second husband: The two were known to amused family members for their late-in-life romance and the stark contrast between her bulk and his matchstick figure.

Anna Fried came with children and grandchildren and her husband, George Yakobovich. The elderly couple were among the few who actually stayed at the Park Hotel for the holiday; George didn't want Anna to have to deal with Passover cooking, and the sanctity of the holiday—George was more religious than the family he married into late in life—required that they not return home by car on Passover.

Amos Saban, sixty-five, arrived from Holon, south of Tel Aviv, after accepting a last-minute invitation from friends who had a spare ticket. Zeev Vider arrived from the Israeli construction project he was working on in

Nigeria. Shalom and Nehama David came from Pardes Hanna, north of Netanya, with their two-and-a-half-year-old son, Aviel, because a hotel Seder would enable them to "get away from the pressure." Others came from Tel Aviv, Jerusalem, the northern Negev. Perla Armela was touring from Sweden.

Then there were the waiters: mostly Arab citizens of Israel from nearby Israeli Arab towns. Jewish waiters, like Jews in general, preferred not to work on a Jewish holiday. It is one of the ironies of a Pesach meal in an Israeli hotel that the ceremonial food is served by Palestinians—albeit Israeli Palestinians—who by and large do not particularly empathize with the Jews' holiday of national liberation.

★   ★   ★

Abd al-Basset Oudeh and his driver, Fathi Khatib, entered Israel earlier that afternoon from Tulkarm, located east of Netanya in the West Bank. Tulkarm sits on the green line boundary separating the West Bank from Israel. The boundary is called the green line because it is an armistice line rather than an international border, and armistice lines are marked in green on maps. To this day, Israel's boundaries with the West Bank and Gaza Strip are green lines, not international borders of the sort Israel has with Egypt and Jordan.

As the crow flies, Tulkarm is only sixteen kilometers (ten miles) from Netanya.

The Park's waiters came from Arab towns on the Israeli side of the green line. Oudeh and Khatib came from the Palestinian side.

The green line at Tulkarm was easy to cross that day in a beat-up Israeli-licensed Renault Express. Khatib had purchased it a year earlier with sixteen thousand shekels of Israeli money and a counterfeit Israeli ID. Oudeh, a local Hamas activist who was on the wanted list of the Israeli General Security Service, the Shabak, was cleanshaven, his head crowned with a long-haired wig. He shaved particularly closely just before joining Khatib in the Renault. He wore lady's blue jeans and women's shoes. He was twenty-five years old.

A jacket hid his explosive belt. It had ten kilograms (twenty-two pounds) of explosives sewn into it, along with metal shrapnel and a detonation cord. The belt had been supplied by a Hamas bomb-making workshop in Nablus, the largest city in the northern West Bank and a Hamas hub nourished by student activists at the city's an-Najah University. In fact, two belts for two bombers had been smuggled from Nablus and hidden until this day in the women's restroom of a new Tulkarm mosque. By 2002, after thirty-five years of Israeli occupation of the West Bank, the Palestinian resistance had accumulated lots of experience evading Israel's efforts to suppress its activities and unearth its arms caches.

Hamas is the Palestinian branch of the Muslim Brotherhood, an Islamic fundamentalist movement that originated in Egypt around a hundred years ago. In 2021 the Brotherhood was still a major social and political presence in Egypt, albeit an underground presence. It had governed Egypt briefly for a year in 2012–2013 after winning modern Egypt's only truly democratic election, until a military coup removed it from power. Turkey's president Recip Tayip Erdogan is a friend of the Brotherhood. It has a strong presence in war-torn Yemen. It is represented in Israeli politics by the Raam party, which in 2021 took the unprecedented step of joining a "Zionist" government under Prime Minister Naftali Bennet in order to deal with Arab economic and law-and-order issues.

The Muslim Brotherhood is strong among Palestinians in Jordan, too, where they comprise roughly half the population. But Jordan's powerful security services keep a close eye on it. Much of Sunni Islamist radicalism is a byproduct of the Muslim Brotherhood.

Hamas ostensibly has a political wing and a military wing. But on the whole the entire movement openly embraces the terrorist killing of Israeli civilians because they are living on what is deemed sacred Muslim soil. Therefore, they are aggressors and enemy soldiers of Zion. Since 2007, as rulers of the Gaza Strip, Hamas's leaders have been obliged to temper their militancy at least some of the time with a realpolitik approach. They have to find ways to coexist with a much stronger Israel to Gaza's east and north and an anti–Muslim Brotherhood regime in Egypt to the south, across the border with the Sinai Peninsula.

But in 2002, Hamas in the West Bank was violently hostile toward Israel. The Passover eve plan had been conceived, hatched, and shepherded over many months by Tulkarm's Hamas leader, Abbas as-Sayyid. It had gone into high gear the day before, March 26. As-Sayyid videoed Oudeh twice: once reading his will against a backdrop of a Hamas flag and again wielding an M-16 automatic rifle. As-Sayyid himself wrote the will with its ritual farewells, terrorist rationales, and Islamist prayers, and staged the entire scene in a safe house rented by Hamas in Tulkarm. The videos would feature in Hamas propaganda for months to come.

A second suicide bomber who had been readied for the same Passover mission, Nidal Qalaq, turned up ill, perhaps due to nerves, perhaps a genuine malady. Despite the availability of a second explosive belt, there would be only one suicide bombing that evening, not two.

Curiously, as-Sayyid decided at the last minute to pack Oudeh's suicide vest only with metal pellets and metal shreds. Ominously, he also had access, since delivery to Hamas by his pharmacologist nephew back in 1997, to four kilograms (ten pounds) of cyanide. Apparently, he backed off from using the poison due to lack of experience and fear of accidental leaks prior to detonation, despite the fact that as long ago as 1996 someone in Hamas had authored a twenty-three-page manual entitled "The Mujahedin [Jihadists'] Poisons Handbook."

Somewhere in the course of this prolonged process of preparations there was a leak concerning Oudeh's intent to carry out a suicide bombing at Passover. Palestinian Authority security, which answered to Fateh and the PLO, not Hamas, and worked in coordination with Israel under the provisions of the Oslo Accords reached in 1993–1994, actually got the warning months before Passover. Later it would claim that it had been unable to locate Oudeh.

As-Sayyid had studied medical engineering in Jordan, where he joined Hamas. From the early 1990s when he returned to Tulkarm and for the ensuing ten years, he was a Hamas activist. He was well built, with graying close-cropped hair and a mustache. Overtly, he propagandized and organized demonstrations, offenses for which he had spent three years in an Israeli jail. Covertly, he ran a clandestine operational cell in Tulkarm. It went into action when the second Intifada or Palestinian uprising began in September 2000.

The Passover eve operation in Netanya in late March 2002 was preceded by two earlier suicide bombings in Netanya, on a shopping street and at a mall. They, too, were organized by as-Sayyid. They killed eight Israelis and wounded more than one hundred. For many months prior to March 27, as-Sayyid, like Oudeh, had been in hiding in and around Tulkarm.

Oudeh, disguised as a woman, and his driver, Khatib, set off from Tulkarm in the early afternoon of Passover eve. They entered Israel in their Israel-licensed car without incident at a border crossing patrolled by the Israel Defense Forces. Arab citizens of Israel, some 20 percent of the population, enjoy free access to the West Bank, where many have family and business ties. So the Israeli soldiers at the green line checkpoint had no reason to suspect an Arab "couple" crossing back into Israel in their Israeli car.

The two Hamas operatives, though briefed by as-Sayyid, had no specific target in mind and no firm understanding of what Passover was all about. Their instructions were to find a Passover event featuring a large number of celebrants. Because Netanya was nearby—barely a twenty-minute drive directly west toward the Mediterranean—and well known to Khatib, they started there, driving around the main shopping streets and past the beachfront hotels. But prior to sundown on a holiday eve all commercial activity had ceased. People were at home preparing for the holiday. Stores were closed. So were malls. The cafes and restaurants decorating the broad plaza leading to the main descent to Netanya's beach were deserted. Netanya in a light drizzle looked to the two Palestinians like a ghost town.

They drove south for half an hour to Tel Aviv, where they encountered the same phenomenon of deserted streets. By now it was late afternoon. They returned to Netanya and renewed their search for a target. Sundown was approaching. Here is where the peculiar layout of the Park Hotel became a factor. The hotel's entrance placed visitors immediately in a relatively small lobby that, in turn, led directly into a bar vestibule, then the dining hall where the Seder was held. No winding corridors, no stairs, and no elevators confronted an attacker looking for a large crowd. In effect, from the road, and if your timing was right or you were just lucky, you could see a few hundred people filing into a Passover celebration. And if you got by the harried security guard outside in the rain, within seconds you could place yourself, explosive vest and all, in their midst.

★ ★ ★

Beirut, Lebanon, is barely two hours' drive north from Netanya along a coastal highway. Not that anyone makes the drive: Lebanon and Israel are not on friendly terms, nor were they in 2002. Technically and legally they have been in a state of war since 1948.

March 27 was a very different sort of day in Beirut. The city was hosting a major Arab gathering for the first time in decades. A prolonged civil war that broke out in 1975 had taken its toll on buildings such as the Phoenicia Intercontinental Hotel overlooking the Mediterranean, near Beirut's landmark Corniche. The twenty-one-story hotel, far grander than Netanya's Park to its south and overlooking the same eastern Mediterranean coast, had been rebuilt and had reopened for business a mere three years earlier. Behind it, the battle-scarred, never-finished geometric shell of the Murr Tower with its thirty-four stories overshadowed the Phoenicia.

Now the Phoenicia was hosting an Arab League summit meeting.

A mere four kilometers south down the coast were Beirut's Palestinian refugee camps. All told, Lebanon's refugee camps are home to at least 200,000 residents. The refugees are barred, for seventy-three years now and counting, from acquiring Lebanese citizenship and from working legally in most trades in Lebanon. That they were in many ways the catalyst and the subtext of this Arab summit went unspoken in Beirut in late March 2002.

Now all of the Phoenicia's 462 rooms and suites were rented to the Arab dignitaries who had arrived in the days before for the Arab League summit. The twenty-first floor Imperial Suite cost $8,000 a night. Because the Saudi-sponsored Arab Peace Initiative was heading the agenda, some 2,600 accredited journalists along with diplomatic observers had also come to Beirut, filling neighboring hotels too.

The city was in a holiday mood. The Lebanese TV station al-Mustaqbal, owned by Prime Minister Rafiq Hariri, set the scene for the summit by repeatedly broadcasting Bruce Springsteen's mid-1980s rendition of the pacifist 1969 anthem "War" with the station's added message, "Arabs want peace." The clip, rhyming war as a "heartbreaker" with "friend to the undertaker," offered a jarring backdrop of scenes of death in Palestinian refugee camps and in Israeli shopping malls. Only a few Western journalists noted the war-peace dissonance.

But, like in Netanya to the south, there were security worries in Beirut as well. Some eight thousand Lebanese Army soldiers lined the streets, with thousands more at the ready. Commercial flights had been cancelled the day before at Beirut International Airport. Schools were closed in Beirut in deference to the summit's security arrangements.

Fully half the twenty-two Arab leaders scheduled to arrive on March 26 did not show up. They sent underlings, usually their foreign ministers, who in any case had come early for preparatory meetings. Some of the leaders, such as Egypt's Hosni Mubarak and Jordan's King Abdullah, reportedly feared assassination. Rockets might be aimed at their incoming aircraft by Lebanon's pro-Iranian Shiite Islamist movement, Hezbollah, whose headquarters were in the Dahia quarter in southern Beirut. Then too, the absentee leaders may have had their reservations about the peace extravaganza orchestrated in Beirut by their rich rival and sometime benefactor, Saudi Crown Prince Abdullah.

Libya's Moammar Qaddafi was an obvious no-show. Hezbollah, backed by Iran, held him accountable for the disappearance in the late 1970s of a renowned emissary to Lebanon's Shiites, Moussa as-Sadr. It was far more likely that the charismatic as-Sadr, a Shiite activist, had been done in by the Shah of Iran during his final months in power before Ayatollah Khomeini deposed the Tehran regime and took power.

But Qaddafi had long since given up denying complicity. In the event, some in Beirut were disappointed by his absence. They had been hoping to see him pitch his Bedouin tent on the grounds of the Phoenicia and parade around with his entourage of sexy female bodyguards.

Palestinian leader Yasser Arafat, who in some quarters was also blamed for as-Sadr's mysterious death, remained in Ramallah in his West Bank headquarters, the Muqataa. It was under siege by Israeli troops due to the suicide bombings against Israeli civilians that had taken place earlier in March. Israel believed that Arafat encouraged the bombings; at a minimum, he was doing nothing to stop them.

Israel's prime minister Ariel Sharon, a battle-hardened foe, bowed to US president George W. Bush's request to allow Arafat to attend the summit. But Sharon, in a typical cynical flourish, refused to commit to allowing Arafat to return from Beirut to Ramallah. So Arafat refused to leave Ramallah. Accordingly, plans were made at the Phoenicia to host him by video hookup.

But Lebanese president Emile Lahoud, hedging his bets, vetoed the idea. He never said so explicitly, of course. Summit participants noted the large screen prepared for Arafat to speak immediately after Syria's Bashar Assad completed his remarks. Palestinian Liberation Organization foreign minister Farouk Kaddoumi raised his hand several times to get Lahoud's attention and remind him. Then Lahoud deliberately gave the floor to the president of Djibouti, and the Palestinian delegation walked out in a pique. Lebanese minister of culture Ghassan Salamé, the conference organizer and spokesman, explained to the press that Arafat had gone live on al-Jazeera rather than wait his turn as scheduled.[1]

Why did Lahoud so openly snub Arafat? Presumably because the latter had made life miserable for the Lebanese in the not-too-distant past. Arafat had run an ex-territorial fiefdom on southern Lebanese soil, a Fateh state-within-a-state stretching from the Palestinian refugee camps just south of Beirut down to the Lebanese-Israeli border and east to the Lebanese-Syrian border. Dubbed by Israel as "Fatehland," it had repeatedly launched terrorist attacks against Israel's Galilee region prior to 1982, provoking endless Israeli revenge raids.

When these failed to deter Fateh attacks, the Israel Defense Forces, exploiting the dubious rationale of responding to an assassination attempt in London against Israel's ambassador there, attacked and occupied southern Lebanon and briefly parts of Beirut. In 1982 Israel rid southern Lebanon of Fateh's armed occupation. But it ended up stuck in the role of occupier until its May 2000 withdrawal back to the two countries' international border.

Now, twenty years after Israel's invasion and occupation and two years after its withdrawal, Beirut was able to host a grand Arab convocation.

Many Arabs understood Israel's departure as a reflection of the vitality of Arab "resistance" against Israel, spearheaded not by Palestinians but by Lebanese Shiite Hezbollah. And yet here was an Arab summit dedicated to approving a plan for peace with Israel, with Hezbollah perceived as a threat to summit attendees.

If all these contradictions, intrigues, and machinations paint Beirut as a Byzantine wonderland, that, as most Lebanese will acknowledge, is not far from the truth. Yet Beirut also knows how to overcome adversity and prevail. Accordingly, March 26 was devoted to the arrival of those Arab leaders who did come, led by Saudi Arabia's Crown Prince Abdullah and Arab League secretary general Amr Moussa, an Egyptian.

All in all, the event at the Phoenicia was running smoothly. Minister of Culture Salamé had a year earlier earned his spurs by successfully mounting a Francophone summit in Beirut. Arab foreign ministers, who arrived at the Arab League summit a day or two earlier, could now brief their bosses on the progress registered toward turning Abdullah's surprise peace initiative, first publicized a month earlier, into a consensual document.

Completing last-minute negotiations among the Arab foreign ministers regarding the peace initiative was not an easy task. There were concerns over provisions regarding the 1948 Palestinian refugees, now allegedly four million strong (by 2021, more than five and a half million). There was controversy concerning the scope and nature of peace and normalization that the Arab Peace Initiative would offer Israel.

★   ★   ★

Meanwhile, back in Netanya the Hamas team of Oudeh and Khatib had found their mark.

2

MARCH 27, 2002: PASSOVER EVE
IN NETANYA AND JERUSALEM

Passover celebrates the liberation of the Children of Israel from slavery in Egypt and their journey to the Promised Land. The term "Passover" (Hebrew: *Pesach*) refers to the most brutal of the ten plagues that God visited upon Pharaoh and the Egyptians to persuade them to let the Hebrews leave. God slaughtered the firstborn of every Egyptian family but passed over, or spared, the Hebrews' firstborn after they smeared the blood of a lamb on their doorposts.

The Passover meal is preceded by the reading of the Haggadah, a 2,000-year-old ritual text of prayers, stories, questions, and songs. The format of the Haggadah, a Platonic-style dialogue symposium among learned rabbinic scholars, emerged in an era when the entire Levant was heavily influenced by Greek culture. The Last Supper celebrated by Jesus and his disciples in Jerusalem at a time of Roman rule was a Passover Seder.

Much of the Haggadah text is boring and convoluted. Yet it has defied all attempts by secular Israeli modernists, kibbutz farmers celebrating Spring, and American Jewish feminists and reformers to render its contents shorter, more modern, and to the point. Tradition still reigns. As do obscure deliberations. Rabbi Yoseh the Galilean and Rabbis Eliezer and Akiba still argue nonsensically whether God visited upon the Egyptians ten, forty, or fifty plagues, with five times as many at sea.

The Park's Haggadah reading was set to begin at 7:30 p.m., sundown. It is a peculiarity of Jewish holidays that they actually begin the previous evening and run from sundown to sundown.

The celebrants, dressed in their holiday finest, had almost all filed in past the security guard and through the cramped hotel lobby. At the entrance to the banquet hall, they showed their Seder tickets to Amiram Hamami. He identified them on his list and pointed them toward their numbered tables. The most expensive tickets placed celebrants in a sunken circle of four or five tables that fronted onto a stage. There the Seder leader—the man who would lead the reading of the Haggadah—was already seated. Privileged diners with the more expensive tickets had to step down about ten centimeters, or half a foot, into the circle.

The Park, hardly a luxury hotel, had little to offer by way of expensive carpets or paintings on the walls. The small lobby was "basic," with a few innocuous tables and a few comfortable chairs. The reception desk was unassuming. Then, as now, it dispensed real keys with real room numbers on them—no electronic key cards. The smaller bar vestibule linking the lobby to the banquet hall was dimly lit. The bar, closed that night for the holiday meal, was almost unnoticeable as celebrants moved from the lobby into the hall.

In contrast with these unassuming surroundings, the atmosphere in the Park banquet hall itself was festive. Families and old friends greeted one another noisily. Most of the celebrants were by now busy seating themselves at the smaller round and larger oval tables arranged in a semicircle facing the sunken area and the stage. Beyond the semicircle, a few tables were spaced along the walls of the banquet hall. Each place setting had a wineglass, a water glass, and a small bowl of salt water for the ceremonial hard-boiled egg or potato. Each table hosted a bottle of sweet wine for the four blessings and a plate of matza, unleavened bread, covered with a cloth napkin.

Not all the tables were filled at 7:30. A few guests were still outside the hotel looking for parking. One large oval-shaped family table emptied out at the last minute when the family convening there decided to go back outside to wait for a straggler. Nothing starts precisely on time at an Israeli holiday celebration.

Midst the pressure of the crowd and the search for the table with their number, one or two diners and stragglers noticed a strange figure. His or her appearance was later described by survivors as "different," "dressed in women's clothes," or "a homeless in strange clothes."

Abd al-Basset Oudeh had left the beat-up Renault Express driven by Fathi Khatib at the entrance to the Park Hotel. Khatib turned the car around and headed back east, through rapidly emptying Netanya streets straight to the green line and Tulkarm. It was important that he get back across the green line and into the West Bank before alarms were sounded and the border crossing closed.

Oudeh strode unnoticed in the rain past the lone security guard near the front door. By now the guard was worn out from scrutinizing around three hundred Seder participants. In any case, he had no reason to suspect a woman. Oudeh's disguise, however different and strange, was adequate to the task of entering the hotel unquestioned just as it had served him to traverse the Israel–PA green line near Tulkarm.

Oudeh followed the holiday stragglers. He crossed the lobby in about ten quick paces and the bar vestibule in four. At the entrance to the banquet hall, Amiram Hamami had just stepped aside to deal with an unpleasant disagreement among diners over who was supposed to be seated where. So no one challenged Oudeh in his bizarre female outfit to produce a ticket. He quickly placed himself, standing, at the most central spot in the dining hall, between tables numbered 9 and 10 on the outer ring of the semicircle, near the more expensive tables in the sunken area of the Passover site. Most of the seated celebrants did not see him. They were eyeing their Haggadah texts or looking toward the stage where the leader of the Passover service was seated, a bit like a caller in a bingo parlor.

The opening passage of the Haggadah was being recited: "Blessed art thou our God, King of the Universe, who chose us above all peoples." Oudeh, who had earlier that day made his peace with his own god, Allah, and knew he was bound for immortality, calmly detonated the vest.

The explosion was deafening. Ball bearings and metal shrapnel flew in all directions. Human beings and furniture were transported by the blast across the banquet hall. People were shredded. Body parts were severed. Blood flowed. Ears were ringing. Smoke and dust enveloped the dining hall and the lobby, briefly limiting visibility to barely a meter. Windows were shattered. So were tables and chairs, fragmented and scattered along with broken crockery.

The blast blew diners, some of whom had not yet even sat down, across the room. Some of the dead were twisted into anatomically impossible poses. One middle-aged man was bent backward at the waist onto a distant table, the upper half of his torso sprawled on the tabletop, arms spread, eyes on the ceiling, dead despite the absence of a noticeable wound. A dinner knife was transported from one of the tables deep into the ceiling. Shattered wineglasses, bottles, and dishes covered the floor, mixed with warm blood and body parts.

After a second or two, the screaming and moaning started. For many of those still alive and conscious, choking on smoke and dust, the urge to flee was overwhelming. Within seconds, the more lightly wounded straggled out of the dining hall in a daze and a heavy haze. So did a few of the mortally wounded. An injured young man collapsed on a parked car outside. One of the medics who was just arriving on the scene took one look and shouted to the others not to bother with him, he couldn't possibly survive.

Inside the Park banquet hall, celebrants knocked unconscious by the blast but still alive and lying on the floor of the sunken area by the stage were within minutes drowning in half a foot of water dumped on them by the hotel's sprinkler system. It was designed to put out a fire and it was working at full capacity.

Other celebrants, with no obvious wounds, were slumped against walls and upturned tables, eyes open and speechless, traumatized. The knee-jerk inclination of first responders was to pass over them in favor of the obviously wounded, the moaning, the screaming, the drowning.

By now, eighteen months into the second Intifada, Netanya's rescue crews had accumulated lots of experience at terror attack sites. But not on this scale, and not on Passover eve. Some were medics from Red Magen David (the Israeli equivalent of the Red Cross), some firefighters, a few volunteers as young as high school students.

The wounded whom first responders deemed savable were ambulanced to Netanya's only hospital, Laniado, which served a regional population of hundreds of thousands. But Laniado was at best a temporary solution for most of the badly wounded; it could function on a weekend or a holiday eve as little more than a triage center. It was managed by an ultra-Orthodox Jewish foundation that, for religious reasons, maintained a skeleton staff on Passover eve despite the general terrorism alert in effect.

In any case, Laniado was a provincial hospital that lacked the neurosurgery and cardiovascular departments vital for treating the Park wounded. It was located only three minutes up the coast from the hotel. Many of the ambulances summoned to the hotel found themselves transporting the wounded first to Laniado, then, after triage, on to hospitals in Tel Aviv that went on alert the moment they were informed of the attack. At least the roads were relatively empty on a holiday eve when most of the country was seated at the Seder table.

The Israel Police also went on higher alert. No one knew if this would be the night's only suicide bombing. No one knew whether one or more additional bombers had been launched upon Israel that afternoon by Hamas chieftains in Tulkarm or neighboring Qalqilya, or in Jenin or Nablus to the north. Were they also somehow evading army security at the green line and avoiding police and hired security guards at hotels hosting Passover feasts?

None of the triage and ambulance delays affected those killed instantly. Juliette Ben-David's skinny new husband was literally cut in half by the blast. But the wounded suffered. Juliette herself was saved by her ample bulk, though she was badly injured and would linger as an invalid for ten years until her death. Corinne Ben-Aroyo would wake up hours later in a Tel Aviv hospital with a broken rib, collapsed lung, and a chest full of blood. Her husband, Shimon, was killed and her three adult children badly wounded.

The family that abandoned their oval table at the last minute to wait for a straggler were unscathed. At the adjacent table three people were killed. Shalom and Nehama David and their little boy, Aviel, who came to the Park Seder to "get away from the pressure," survived. Ninety-year-old Hannah Rogan and Yulia Talmi were both killed. So was Zeev Vider, who had come from Nigeria. Alter and Frieda Britavich died within hours of each other in a Tel Aviv hospital.

Tom Fried and his sister, Shirly, arrived at the Park, luckily for them, a minute late. Once they understood what had happened, they tried to find their parents, their grandmother and her husband, George Yakobovich. Smoke and stench rendered this a difficult task. Fried's father didn't answer his phone. Could all four perhaps still be in the Yakobovich couple's hotel room? Only hours later did the two younger Frieds ascertain that their parents and step-grandfather were killed on the spot and taken directly to the morgue; their grandmother lingered for two weeks in the hospital before succumbing to her wounds.

Amiram Hamami, who abandoned his post at the entrance to the hall to deal with a problem farther inside, paid with his life. Someone phoned his brother-in-law Eric Cohen, the hotel manager, who left his Seder table at home and arrived within minutes. At first, Eric was led by whoever phoned him to believe that the problem at the Park was that all the emergency sprinklers had mysteriously opened and were pouring water on the guests. Only when he saw the ambulances crowding the parking area did he understand.

Within days the death total would reach thirty. The Park attack remains to this day the most devastating suicide bombing in Israel's history. Because it was Passover eve, this was also the most traumatic terrorist attack. It was far and away the low point of the second Intifada, which began in September 2000 and would continue through 2004.

The second Intifada was all about Palestinian suicide bombings. The first Intifada, back in the late 1980s and early 1990s, had been mild by comparison, featuring mainly Palestinian stone-throwing and Molotov cocktail attacks on Israelis.

★   ★   ★

No one seems to have blamed the Park's security guard for what happened that Passover eve. In general, suicide bombings in public places in

Israel during the second Intifada did not produce any sort of outcry against the guards who had failed to stop the bomber. Was the Park Hotel guard truly fooled by a disguise? Had he been inaccurately briefed as to what and whom to look for? Had he seen the bomber and, frozen by fear, preferred to do nothing and save his own skin?

On a few occasions during the second Intifada, a guard did stop a suspicious person trying to enter a mall or a movie theater. The bomber detonated on the spot, killing himself and the guard but usually no one else. The dead guard was briefly a hero for having done his job and saved many lives. Here and there a suicide bomber, petrified with fear, gave himself up to a surprised security guard.

Meanwhile, the Shabak's postmortem on each and every suicide bombing, whether successful or failed, sought to learn and apply lessons. The most important lesson appears to have been the need to intercept the bomber while still in the West Bank, at his or her base. Once on the loose inside Israel, a determined suicide bomber would always be able to kill someone—if only a security guard recently arrived from Russia.

★   ★   ★

Prime Minister Ariel Sharon, celebrating Passover with family at his ranch in southern Israel, immediately understood the meaning of the Park bombing. The month of March 2002 had witnessed a record series of fatal Palestinian suicide bombings even before the Park Hotel. Hamas, Islamic Jihad, and Fateh al-Aqsa Martyrs Brigade terrorists had been on a suicidal rampage. In addition to the Park attack, one or another of these extremist movements killed eleven and injured more than fifty in a March 2 suicide bombing in the center of Jerusalem. They killed one on a bus in Afula on March 5. They killed eleven and injured fifty-four in a suicide attack on March 9 at the Moment Café in Jerusalem, around the corner from the prime minister's official residence. On March 20 they killed seven and wounded thirty on a bus traveling from Tel Aviv to Nazareth. The next day three were killed and eighty-six injured on King George Street in Jerusalem.

Nor did the Park bombing end the March suicide wave. Two days after Park, two were killed and twenty-eight injured when a female suicide bomber blew herself up in the Kiryat Yovel supermarket in Jerusalem. On March 30 one person was killed and thirty injured in a suicide bombing in a cafe on the corner of Allenby and Bialik Streets in Tel Aviv. The next day fifteen were killed and forty injured at the Matza restaurant in Haifa. That

Matza belonged to Arab citizens of Israel and was frequented by Jews and Arabs alike was apparently of no significance to the bombers.

This list ignores occasional attacks against Israeli settlers in the West Bank. For the attackers as well as for the vast majority of Israelis, Park and the other attacks were not about the Oslo process or the occupation or the two-state solution.[1] They were aimed at the Israeli mainstream inside Israel. These attacks were existential in aspiration.

By the time the smoke cleared at the Park Hotel, more than four hundred Israelis, nearly all civilians, had been killed by Palestinians since the second Intifada erupted in mid-September 2000. The June 2001 Dolphinarium suicide bombing in Tel Aviv had been almost as destructive as the Park casualty count. Including the Park Hotel dead, 122 died in Israel in March, now the bloodiest month on record.

By the days approaching Passover, the atmosphere on the Israeli street had become somber, reminiscent of wartime. Some feared to board buses or even drive near them. Cafe crowds were thinning. Yet a majority of Israelis polled a few days before Passover agreed with the proposition that staying away from public places would constitute a victory for the terrorists. They indicated they would spend this Passover no differently than in previous years[2]—at the Park Hotel in Netanya, for example.

Security guards for commercial enterprises and public transportation were being recruited and trained at an accelerated rate. Unemployed Russian Jewish immigrants now found a new profession patrolling the entrances to malls, hotels, and cafes. Some were aging World War II veterans who knew little Hebrew but knew how to use a gun.

The second Intifada suicide bombings took a heavy economic toll. By March 2002, Israel's remarkable annual growth rate of 7 percent had dropped to -2 percent. Augmented budgetary allocations for the IDF and the Israel Police cost billions. Tourism collapsed. Commerce was crippled.

There was one curious economic development. The suicide bombings proved a boon for Israel's emerging malls and hurt the business of traditional main-street stores accessible from the sidewalk. After all, a mall offered the public a large protected space featuring everything from cinemas and cafes to shops, grocery stores, and clean restrooms, all for the inconvenience of a single security check at the entrance. The alternative was driving near buses and walking on sidewalks to individual shops and cafes, accompanied by a sense of constant, lurking danger.

A particular cause for alarm in Israel during recent months had been the Israel Navy's interception in the Red Sea on January 3, 2002, of the *Karine A*, a small cargo ship bearing sophisticated weaponry for the PLO.

Israeli intelligence quickly determined that the arms shipment had been sponsored by Iran, with Yasser Arafat's direct knowledge. The immediate planning for the shipment had been managed by the Iranian ambassador in Moscow.

The *Karine A* had intended to traverse the Suez Canal to the Mediterranean and offload its lethal cargo along the desolate northern Sinai coast of Egypt. From there the arms and ammunition would be moved in small fishing boats to the Gaza Strip. Some of the weapons and explosives would remain in Gaza. The rest would be smuggled from Gaza across forty-one kilometers (twenty-five miles) of Israeli territory to the West Bank, for use by Hamas in towns such as Tulkarm.

Were there additional arms shipments that Israel had not detected? Were smuggling operations like the *Karine A* fueling the second Intifada? The IDF had since 2001 carried out a number of deep punitive penetrations into autonomous Palestinian territory in the West Bank. It had laid siege to Arafat's Muqataa headquarters in Ramallah. Still, it was allowing entry to the Muqataa to various Western emissaries who were charged with persuading Arafat to exert himself to stop the violence. The emissaries were regularly reassured publicly by Prime Minister Sharon that Israel would respond to a week's peace and quiet with a negotiated cease-fire. Sometimes Sharon, inconsistently, specified two weeks of peace and quiet.

Such a pause in the violence did seem to be unfolding following a particularly moderate speech by Arafat to his fellow Palestinians. On December 16, 2001, Arafat warned that "in the aftermath of the terrorist attacks in New York and Washington [the '9/11 attacks,' on September 11, 2001] . . . we face deliberate distortion and incitement against us." He then proceeded to outlaw "bodies that carry out terrorist activities . . . including the suicidal attacks." He insisted he could "only allow one authority" in the Palestinian Authority.[3]

Arafat went on to praise US president Bush's commitment at the United Nations to a Palestinian state, and he suggested renewing negotiations with Israel. A few Israeli security officials chose to see this as a valid gesture of peace. But a more belligerent Arafat speech two days later, followed by the *Karine A* capture two weeks later, ended the illusion: Arafat was preparing for more violence against Israelis.

This was typical of Arafat's modus operandi. Offer both peace and violence. He had famously done this in his first, highly contested address to the United Nations General Assembly in 1974 when he stated, "Today I have come bearing an olive branch and a freedom-fighter's gun."[4]

Still, it was Israel that preempted and renewed the violence. It followed up on the *Karine A* capture on January 12 with the targeted assassination of Raed Karmi, a militant Fateh leader from Tulkarm who had plenty of Israeli blood on his hands but had been observing the cease-fire in and around his town. For some Israeli experts on the Palestinians, in retrospect the Karmi assassination was a mistake.[5] It would launch another round of violence culminating in the Park Hotel attack—not coincidentally planned in Tulkarm. For others, indeed for most of those involved in security affairs in Israel and the United States, *Karine A* had given Arafat's game away.

One of the emissaries visiting Arafat almost daily on behalf of the European Union was Alastair Crooke, formerly of Britain's MI6 external intelligence agency. Crooke was posted in Israel and the Palestinian Authority by the EU to develop ties with the Palestinian leadership. Controversially, he interpreted his mandate to include contacts with Hamas, which violently contested the Oslo peace process, as well as with Arafat. But trying to mediate between Israel and the Palestinians at the height of the second Intifada suicide bombings was a frustrating business. Arafat would deny any and all links to the bombings despite the hard intelligence Israel possessed regarding his connection to arms shipments and attacks on Israelis.

Sharon, meeting almost daily with his security team, was losing patience: The IDF, he argued, wasn't aggressive enough. The public was angry and Sharon knew he had to deliver results. Israel's targeted killings of Palestinian terrorist leaders in the West Bank and Gaza such as Raed Karmi neither deterred the enemy nor satisfied Israel's citizenry. "I singlehandedly eliminated all traces of terrorism in the Gaza Strip," Sharon more than once chided Lieutenant General Shaul Mofaz, IDF commander in chief. Indeed, in 1971 when still an IDF general, Sharon had reduced Palestinian attacks in Gaza from thirty-four in June to one in December.

"I once singlehandedly, yes, eliminated all the terrorists in Gaza, yes?" The roly-poly, white-haired Sharon, now well into his seventies and projecting an electable, grandfatherly image, had the habit of adding the Hebrew *ken* (yes) to many of his sentences and even interjecting it into the middle of sentences. Many of his aides and advisers gleefully imitated this quirk of speech privately, away from Sharon's ears.

But Sharon's days in charge of the Gaza Strip in 1971 were different days. Back then, he bulldozed entire Gazan neighborhoods to open up streets for Israel's tanks and no one objected. Since then, Israel had itself negotiated and shepherded the creation of the Palestinian Authority in the mid-1990s. It had welcomed Arafat's arrival from exile, first to Gaza and then to Ramallah, where he presided over the autonomous Palestinian Authority from the Muqataa.

Sharon was obligated by an international agreement, the Oslo Accords, to respect Palestinian autonomy and, when necessary, work with Palestinian security forces. Oslo also prescribed a menu of interim and final status talks with the PLO that Sharon, Arafat, and the United States were bound by. The international community was watching much more closely than during the pre-Oslo period. Sharon, in keeping with his support for the settlements and opposition to any contact with the PLO, had opposed Oslo bitterly in the mid-1990s as an opposition member of the Knesset (Israel's parliament). He was keenly aware that, some eighteen months into the second Intifada with its suicide attacks on civilians, a majority of Israelis were souring on the Oslo Accords.[6] Yet as prime minister he was obligated to implement Oslo.

That meant restraint. As one IDF company commander soon to be involved in the invasion of the West Bank testified: "Infantry entry [by Israeli forces] into the PA (Area A) was still the exception. . . . The dominant spirit among the senior command echelon was to prevent breakdown . . . to exercise restraint in order to avoid escalation."[7]

An American mediation presence led by a series of emissaries served as an additional constraint. EU mediators such as Alistair Crooke less so; they were generally scorned by Israelis and Palestinians for whom the EU was little more than a cash cow to keep the PA financially afloat. "The US plays, the EU pays, and the Arabs pray" was the sardonic slogan bandied about in the Israeli security community back then.

Israeli-Palestinian security coordination meetings were convened by the US Central Intelligence Agency. The CIA's close ties to the Mossad meant that any disruption by Israel of security ties with the Palestinians had immediate bilateral Israeli-American reverberations. To the chagrin of the EU and the UN, the Americans insisted on exclusivity in their role as mediator and facilitator between Israelis and Palestinians. Israel preferred it this way, while the Palestinians tended to believe the Europeans and the UN would prove more sympathetic.

The balding, olive-skinned Mofaz, like Sharon, was a former commando. The two talked the same language, and on a first-name basis. In response to Sharon's goading, Mofaz had prepared operational plans for a major invasion and reoccupation of the West Bank. The objective would be to root out and eliminate Palestinian terrorists anywhere and everywhere in the territory. Sharon approved the plans but hesitated to give a green light prior to Passover. In any case, such an operation had to be discussed by Sharon with his security staff and senior ministers. And it had to be explainable and justifiable to the international community and to Israel's Arab state neighbors. Sharon and Mofaz needed a convincing casus belli that no one could quibble with.

Mofaz telephoned Sharon shortly after the Park bombing and the two agreed to request ministerial approval the next evening.[8]

3

ZINNI

One reason for delay of an Israeli military operation in the West Bank prior to March 28 had been American pressure for some sort of a truce with the Palestinians rather than a fight. Vice President Dick Cheney had visited Sharon on March 18. Cheney offered, conditionally, to meet with Palestinian leader Yasser Arafat at his headquarters in Ramallah, which by then was besieged by Israeli tanks (no meeting took place). Secretary of State Colin Powell's emissaries, General Tony Zinni, former head of US Central Command (CENTCOM), and veteran diplomat and negotiator Aaron Miller were in the country looking for an agreed cease-fire opening.

Zinni had no previous experience with the Palestinians but was a quick learner. Along with the CIA, he had already informed the European Union and the United Nations that he insisted on American exclusivity in trying to arrange a cease-fire. Zinni only recently had retired from the US Marine Corps with the rank of four-star general. His CENTCOM posting had covered most of the Arab world but not the Israel-Palestine complex. He had an advanced degree in conflict resolution. He took pride in having been sent by US presidents to spearhead twelve different peace initiatives globally, from Mogadishu to the Philippines.

As US peace facilitator in the Palestinian arena, Zinni succeeded George Tenet. CIA director Tenet had been sent twice by President George W. Bush to try to effect a Palestinian-Israeli cease-fire as a prelude to an end to the second Intifada. He failed, which put him in good company with a long list of Americans sent over the years to make peace in the Middle East. After 9/11, Tenet was too busy with al-Qaeda to deal with the Israelis and Palestinians.

In conversations seventeen years later, Zinni is still the crew cut, burly, informally dressed, and blunt ex-Marine general. And Miller still presents a striking contrast. Tall, lean, with a mop of dark hair, Miller in 2002 already embodied twenty-five years of State Department institutional memory of futile efforts to resolve the Israeli-Palestinian conflict. Back when he had signed up with State, Miller had helped pioneer the successful entry of American Jews into a thoroughly "Arabist" State Department. Until around 1967, State had treated Israel as an anomaly in the region.

Zinni and Miller, both very smart straight-talkers, collaborated for a few short months back then. Zinni moved on to other conflict-resolution missions, while Miller began a successful career at Washington think tanks and as a CNN global affairs analyst. His 2008 book, *The Much Too Promised Land*, is a no-nonsense account of the Israeli-Palestinian conflict, from the title on down.

Zinni relates that Powell recruited him for the Israeli-Palestinian cease-fire mediation job essentially because the secretary of state wanted to prevent the US invasion of Iraq. Invading Iraq was the project Cheney and the administration's neoconservatives, or "neocons," were pushing in the aftermath of 9/11.

The neocons basically opposed any Israeli territorial peace concessions. They supported an uncompromising Israeli stand. And they advocated occupying and "democratizing" Iraq as a way of westernizing the Middle East and cementing US military power and economic influence there. They gave the Arabs short shrift. They bought the fabrications of Iraqi exiles who harbored transparent grudges against Baghdad dictator Saddam Hussein.

Powell was not a neocon. He opposed the Iraq operation and believed in the power of American peace facilitation. Powell, himself a former chief of staff of US armed forces, had good reason to fear that an Iraq occupation would backfire on the United States. A Palestinian-Israeli cease-fire that introduced a new peace process would, Powell reportedly reasoned, keep the administration on a more productive Middle East track.

But in early 2002 Powell, ever the disciplined general who respected the chain of command, had to accept strict limits on his mandate. This meant bowing to the wishes of a democratically elected president and particularly of his highly influential and activist vice president, Dick Cheney. Accordingly, Powell's emissaries to the Israelis and Palestinians would seek only a cease-fire. Thanks to neocon involvement, they would not try to launch a full-fledged peace process that would inevitably involve US pressure on Israel. Scarcely a year later Powell would, out of the same sense of disciplined obligation toward Bush and despite heavy misgivings, appear before the United Nations Security Council to knowingly present fabricated and faulty intelligence shaped to justify a US-led invasion of Iraq.

Powell knew the neocons were hostile to his policy outlook and that Cheney, neocon-in-chief, usually had the ultimate say with Bush. Yet Powell never spoke his mind in private to Bush. The president's total lack of experience with foreign and strategic affairs prior to taking office rendered him a relatively easy target for Cheney and his entourage to influence.

"Try something different," Powell now instructed Zinni. "Stick to one issue we can implement. I don't need another damn plan. Find a focal issue."[1] Zinni, accompanied by the experienced Miller, began meeting with Sharon and Arafat in February of 2002.

These high-level encounters were not a particularly productive track. Sharon, Zinni relates, was doubtful from the start. The Israeli prime minister had a direct line to Bush in the White House via Arieh Ganger, a well-connected hawkish Israeli-American businessman. The Sharon-Ganger-Bush channel negatively affected Zinni's profile, clout, and leverage. Zinni tried to persuade Sharon to drop his demand for a week or two-week Palestinian abstention from terrorist attacks as a condition for a cease-fire that might ultimately facilitate renewed peace talks. "You're simply giving Hamas the opportunity to sabotage progress," Zinni told Sharon.

As for Arafat, Zinni quickly perceived that the Palestinian leader shied away from the sort of confrontation with the extremist Islamist Hamas that a serious move toward a cease-fire and peace with Israel would inevitably engender. "He knew that signing a peace agreement is signing a death sentence. I didn't think his heart was in this like his security guys' were. [Egypt's president] Mubarak and [Jordan's King] Abdullah, who knew me from my CENTCOM days, called Arafat to urge him to get serious. Arafat told me, 'They won't walk behind my funeral like [they did for] Rabin and Sadat.'"

Indeed, Arafat knew Mubarak detested him. The world heard Mubarak's audible admonition to an obstructionist Arafat, "Sign, you dog," on a stage in Cairo during the Oslo phase II negotiations in September 1995. "Dog" is a particularly strong insult in Arabic because under Islam canines are considered ritually impure. This was a telling reminder of the enmity between Arafat and most Arab state leaders. The latter resented Arafat's plots and machinations on their territory and at the expense of their interests. They resented his endless fabrications and failed commitments.

In the event, Mubarak encouraged not only Arafat to get serious about a cease-fire with Israel. Amid all his unproductive conversations in Jerusalem and Ramallah, Zinni popped over to Cairo to meet with the Egyptian leader. "Just get an Israeli-Palestinian confidence-building measure" was Mubarak's exasperated and minimalist exhortation.

For Zinni, talking to the security commanders on both sides was far more productive than talking to Sharon and Arafat. Zinni met with IDF chief of planning general Giora Eyland on the Israeli side and Jibril Rajoub (West Bank security chief) and Mohammad Dahlan (Gaza Strip security czar) on the PLO side. He saw an advantage in the mutual acquaintance of his Israeli and Palestinian interlocutors from their years of post-Oslo security cooperation prior to 2002. The Palestinians clearly understood they needed both the Israelis and the Americans if the Palestinian independence project was to succeed.

Eyland was busy not only with the Zinni mission. He had also taken upon himself the task of putting together a proposal to appoint a Palestinian prime minister. Creating this new office in the Palestinian Authority would, Eyland hoped, make it possible to install a Palestinian official able to deal more rationally and forthrightly with Hamas terrorists than President Arafat, the *Rais* ("Head"). Eyland was working in parallel with Mossad head Efraim Halevy (see chapter 12).

Technically, manipulating the structure of the Palestinian Authority should have been a task for Shabak head Avi Dichter rather than for the Mossad and the IDF. But the division of labor among Sharon's advisers left plenty of room for overlap and flexibility. And for creativity, an attribute of both Eyland and Halevy.

Rajoub and Dahlan had both begun their security careers in the ranks of Fateh well before the Oslo Accords. They had fought the Israeli occupation, spent years in Israeli jails for doing so, then joined Arafat in his post-Beirut and pre-Oslo (1982–1994) Tunis exile. Now they had graduated, thanks to the Oslo Accords, to positions of power in the Palestinian Authority security establishment. They were cooperating closely with Israel, the CIA, MI6, and anyone else who would help train and organize proper PA security forces.

Dahlan and Rajoub both spoke fluent Hebrew, learned in jail. Their meetings with Israelis such as Eyland were often jovial and relaxed social occasions in addition to their professional agenda. That light touch, security veterans on both sides will confirm, is characteristic of get-togethers between these neighbors. They share not only a lot of history but also a certain respect for each other. This clearly impressed Zinni as a promising beginning to the cease-fire talks he was charged with facilitating.

The two Palestinian security chiefs were also a study in contrasts. Rajoub, glowering, heavyset, balding, mustached, spoke in a low, barely audible passive-aggressive growl that appeared to radiate enmity and suspicion. He seemed impenetrable.

Dahlan, younger, lean and cleanshaven, open and smiling, enjoyed social smoking breaks with his Israeli counterparts. He was intensely curious and harbored few inhibitions. He had no problem asking the Israelis whether specific office accessories such as compactus mobile shelving on rollers could be useful to him in outfitting his Gaza City intelligence headquarters. After a few hours with Dahlan, a former Israeli intelligence official might have felt like a good friend if he didn't remind himself that he was dealing with a former terrorist enemy. The Israeli heard Dahlan's compactus inquiry and mischievously imagined a Dahlan-administered Gaza torture chamber with its case files loaded on compactus shelves.[2]

Zinni tasked his Israeli and Palestinian interlocutors with forming a working group on security: "Give me your security issues" was his first request. The Palestinians soon agreed to a whittled-down Israeli list of thirty-one "wanted" Palestinian terrorists. Israel had thirteen additional demands, paralleled by a Palestinian list of requested Israeli concessions concerning freedom of movement, release of prisoners, and the like. IDF chief of staff Mofaz persuaded Sharon to "trust Zinni" and okay the Palestinian menu, even without a week of quiet. It was late March.

Now, with Arafat's possible departure for the Beirut Arab League summit in the offing, Zinni needed the Palestinian leader's agreement to the emerging cease-fire plan. It would, Zinni believed, mesh beautifully with the anticipated Arab Peace Initiative.

Zinni desperately needed to see Arafat in person and hear from him that he concurred about the cease-fire. The fact that fully three out of four Israelis thought Zinni's mission was doomed to failure[3] rendered the mission all the more urgent and Arafat's obfuscating all the more frustrating. Yet Arafat kept postponing this crucial meeting with Zinni.

On Passover eve, while the Park Hotel Seder in Netanya was still getting organized, Zinni and Miller were attending a Seder at the home of Shalom Lipner. Lipner was Prime Minister Sharon's deputy foreign policy adviser and Zinni's PoC, or "point of contact," with the Prime Minister's Office. Lipner and Zinni had become friendly during the months of Zinni's mission. At one point, on December 2, 2001, Lipner had even accompanied Zinni to the scene of a terrorist suicide bombing on the Ben Yehuda pedestrian street in central Jerusalem in which 11 Israelis had been killed and 180 injured.

The evening of March 27 at the Lipners began pleasantly. Zinni, at his first Seder, was engaged. He read the evening's text from a Hebrew-English Haggadah. The Lipner family Seder began a bit earlier than the Park's Seder and was progressing through the ritual reading and the ritual food. The celebrants spread horseradish on matza, unleavened bread with little taste and the consistency of crunchy cardboard. They were reciting the accompanying prayer, "Blessed art Thou O Lord our God, King of the Universe who commanded us to eat bitter herbs."

The phone rang. Within seconds Lipner's hospitality and domestic tranquility, Palestinian terrorism, Zinni's mission, and Israeli anger would all interact jarringly and unexpectedly.

"We were in the middle of dinner," Lipner relates, "when word first came to the [American] entourage of what had transpired in Netanya. Everyone was concerned and we waited for more details, while trying not to alarm the children. The Americans did not rush out the door immediately. Phone calls came . . . mostly from members of Zinni's team, who relayed data to him. . . . Zinni left a short while later, after which we finished eating dinner and the reading of the latter part of the Haggadah."[4]

Not all of Sharon's aides and advisers were as single-minded about Passover that evening as Lipner. One of the first phone calls to Zinni was from Giora Eyland, his Israeli negotiating counterpart.

"This is different," Eyland bluntly informed Zinni.

4

ON SUICIDE BOMBINGS
AS A STRATEGY

Palestinian suicide bombings like the Park Hotel attack of March 27, 2002, were a major feature of the second Intifada. Many Palestinians considered these attacks an appropriate strategic response to far superior Israeli technology and airpower. It was deemed appropriate regardless of the fact that most of the Israelis killed and injured in the suicide bombings were civilians.

The second Intifada took a heavy toll on Israelis. Between October 26, 2000, and July 12, 2005, 138 Palestinian suicide attacks killed 509 and injured 3,682.[1] Most of these casualties were civilians; a small proportion were IDF soldiers. These totals constituted the majority of Israelis killed and wounded during the second Intifada. Others were the targets of shootings and vehicle ramming attacks.

An earlier suicide bombing wave between 1993 and 1997, corresponding to the initial Oslo period during which Israel was transferring West Bank and Gazan territory to the Palestinian Authority, had featured 20 attacks and claimed 154 Israeli victims. Yet another set of statistics counts 250 suicide bombings between April 16, 1993, and April 2003.[2] The April 1993 date is when the first such Palestinian attack, a truck bombing in the Jordan Valley, was recorded. These statistics, incidentally, do not count the dead suicide bombers.

Perhaps more of interest is the fact that, of these 250 attacks in the course of a decade, 205 were perpetrated by Palestinian Islamists, primarily from Hamas but also from Palestinian Islamic Jihad (PIJ). This preponderance of Islamist bombers underlines the religious fanatic motive of most suicide attacks on Israelis. Hamas and PIJ opposed the Oslo Accords from their inception.

Against the backdrop of these bloody statistics, two questions are relevant to our narrative. First, in what context do individual Palestinians agree to sacrifice their lives in the act of killing Israelis? And second, how did the suicide bombings affect Israeli attitudes and motivation?

As to the first question, it is important to note that Palestinians opposing Israel did not invent suicide operations. These are as old as warfare itself. World War II gave us the Japanese Kamikaze pilots and Russian defenders of Moscow and Stalingrad who threw themselves, grenade in hand, under German tanks. And there were Shiite and other Lebanese suicide attacks against Israeli and American military targets in Lebanon in the 1980s. Those were essentially military operations that did not target civilians to achieve a political goal, thereby technically disqualifying them as terrorist attacks in the eyes of many terrorism experts.[3]

It was the Tamil Tigers of Sri Lanka who turned suicide into a frequent terror weapon against civilians. During the Sri Lankan civil war beginning in 1983, the Tigers perpetrated some 275 attacks. The Tamil Tigers also invented the suicide vest and made heavy use of this weapon as a force multiplier.

The Tamil Tigers (officially: Liberation Tigers of Tamil Eelam) facilitated recruitment of suicide candidates by nurturing a culture of martyrdom. Suicide bombing was "giving yourself" to the cause espoused by the Tamil minority in Sri Lanka. This had nothing to do with the Middle East: The Tamils are primarily Hindus and Sinhalese Buddhists.

Islam, particularly Shiite Islam, also glorifies martyrdom, though this can be any form of dying for the cause; in battle, for example. The Quran promises paradise to martyrs but actually prohibits suicide. Prohibited or not by Islam, since the first suicide bombings in Lebanon in the 1980s, this form of attack has become a fixture of Muslim conflicts with non-Muslims, or "heretics." Here we refer not only to the Palestinian context but to jihadists serving al-Qaeda, the Islamic State (ISIS), and other extremist Sunni and Shiite Muslim movements. After 2015 it was the Islamic State and its affiliates that carried out the most suicide bombings. The military defeat of ISIS led to a sharp decline in Muslim suicide bombings in 2018–2019.[4]

Endless academic and military studies seek to understand the motivation of the Arab Muslim suicide bomber in the hope of finding ways to curtail the phenomenon. For our purposes, Palestinian suicide bombers can generally be characterized as devout believers in a euphoric Muslim afterlife, fervent opponents of Israeli occupation, and/or Islamist opponents of Israel's very existence. They are usually young and male. One research team cites the narrative of a twenty-seven-year-old Hamas bomber who, "when asked how he felt when he was chosen for a suicide operation, . . . responded: . . . 'by pushing a button, you can immediately open the gate to heaven. It's the quickest way there. . . . [The days of preparation] were the happiest days of my life. . . . We floated and swam in a feeling that we were going to enter eternity. We had no doubt. We swore an oath on the Koran, in the presence of Allah.'"[5]

In addition to the predominant Islamic fanatic motive, a minority of Palestinian suicide bombers have been characterized as extreme nationalists and revenge seekers. A suicide attack offers the perpetrator glory because it strikes at the Zionist enemy, who allegedly understands only force, in a manner that Israeli security forces often are incapable of preventing. To this day, mainstream PLO/Fateh propaganda aimed at the West Bank and Gazan Palestinian population glorifies martyrdom for the cause of Palestinian independence with ultra-nationalist quasi-Islamist exhortations like (mother to son) "My son, we were not created for happiness. In my eyes, you are meant for Martyrdom!" and "Jerusalem is ours, our weapon is our Islam, and our ammunition is our children. And you, O my son, are meant for Martyrdom."[6]

Then too, some Palestinian suicide bombers are just troubled personalities harboring a problematic past or home situation. They may be exploited by extremists seeking suicide "volunteers." Among economically deprived Palestinian suicide-bombing candidates, the promise of financial reward for their families can also be a factor. In recent years, Israel's General Security Service (GSS) has been successful at intercepting potential Palestinian suicide and other attackers by analyzing their disturbed or threatening internet posts and profiling them.

For example, a twenty-two-year-old Palestinian from a village near Jerusalem posts, "Ten commandments for every *Shahid* [martyr]." This document was written by Bahaa Alian before carrying out a knife attack in Jerusalem in October 2015. Recycled photos of weapons and posters inciting to carry out attacks are another typical giveaway. So is the admonition, in a dialogue between two young men, "O Allah, forgive me, I shall repent and cleanse myself of all evil," repeated fifteen times the day before a terrorist attack by the two.[7] In all such cases, the warning lights go on in the GSS.

The effect of Palestinian suicide bombings on the Israeli population they target is easier to discern thanks to opinion polls and Knesset elections. Second Intifada suicide bombings were a major factor in moving the Israeli mainstream public away from the optimistic support for a compromise two-state solution that characterized the early Oslo years. The suicide bombings hardened Israeli resolve, weakened support for compromise solutions, and pushed a growing segment of the public to abandon hope and faith in a bilateral peace process and move politically to the right, where the Oslo Accords are to this day vilified as a failure not to be repeated.[8]

The second Intifada specter of Palestinian mothers publicly celebrating their sons' martyrdom by deadly suicide attacks shocked and troubled Israelis. The inability to comprehend the mindset of a suicide bomber targeting civilians, or for that matter the mindset of that suicide bomber's mother, was testimony to the deep perceptual gap separating the two increasingly interwoven societies. Perhaps the bomber's mother did grieve deep down inside. Perhaps patriotism and Islam prohibited her from acknowledging this openly. Justifiably or not from an objective standpoint, the Israeli public increasingly concluded that the Palestinians as a people were not candidates for peaceful coexistence.

One reflection of the Israeli mood was the West Bank fence. Its construction was radically accelerated by the Park Hotel bombing. The rationale for building it trumpeted in the preceding years by the Israeli political left was Ehud Barak's 1999 election slogan "We're here and they're there." In other words, in its original concept the fence could define the borders of a two-state solution between "here," Israel, and "there," the West Bank and Gaza Strip after withdrawal of Israeli settlements.

By March 2002 (see chapter 13, "The Fence"), the rationale was preventing entry of West Bank suicide bombers into Israel proper. Eventually, to the chagrin of the Israeli left, the bombings helped generate majority support for right, religious, and messianic parties that reject the two-state solution. The right-messianics covet the West Bank with or without a fence. Between the suicide bombings and Israel's military and political response, extremists on both sides gained ground.

A second Israeli security byproduct of the suicide bombings was a technological quantum leap in terrorist detection by the Shabak. It used cell phone signals to track down the enablers of suicide bombings. In February 2002, a month before the Park attack, the Knesset passed a "Shabak law" that codifies and legalizes Shabak access to the data banks of Israel's cellular operators. This was easily extended to Palestinian cellular operators, which are linked to Israel's operators in a single electromagnetic sphere controlled by Israel.

This intrusive and sensitive Shabak capability helped enable the rapid identification and apprehension of the Park bombing team in Tulkarm. That it also had other, possibly more sinister ramifications for the privacy rights of ordinary Israelis was a risk the politicians and the courts were prepared to take. Besides, in a country that has been preoccupied with security since its inception, most Israelis simply trusted the Shabak.

★　　★　　★

Ariel Sharon was elected to the office of prime minister in a direct two-man race against incumbent Ehud Barak in early 2001. Sharon's triumph was a byproduct of a cascade of security and political developments that had swept the country in the past two years. These included the failed Oslo process, increasing Palestinian terror attacks, an Israeli public perception of failed governance on Barak's part, and the abortive Camp David summit of July 2000.

US president Clinton convened an Israeli-Palestinian summit meeting at Camp David in July 2000 against the counsel of many, including his own advisers and Yasser Arafat himself. All believed the summit would not succeed. Inevitably, the failure at Camp David to produce a final status agreement helped trigger, within months, the second Intifada with its suicide bombings, followed by Sharon's election to replace Barak.

Yet the policies Sharon proceeded to pursue were anathema to his core right-wing electorate. The West Bank fence, unilateral removal of all settlements from the Gaza Strip, and endorsement of the "dovish" two-state solution were not at all what Israeli rightists had bargained for when they elected Sharon. The Palestinians' suicide-bombing strategy was a decisive factor in Sharon's elevation to the highest office in the state of Israel.

5

MARCH 28, 2002, JERUSALEM: ISRAEL PRIME MINISTER'S OFFICE

Unlike the earlier suicide bombings that month, the Park atrocity was understood in Israel as a "strategic" attack. It was a game-changer at the level of the overall Arab-Israel conflict. That was obvious very quickly to Prime Minister Ariel Sharon and the Israeli security community.

Sharon convened the security cabinet for a strategy meeting in the Cabinet Room of the Prime Minister's Office in Jerusalem on March 28 in the evening. The discussion commenced after sundown to avoid criticism from Orthodox and ultra-Orthodox politicians over meeting on Passover day. All heads of security were present, alongside relevant government ministers and advisers. Around the big conference table and between it and the walls of the room, participants were seated two- and three-deep. Refreshments, in view of the Passover stricture to eat only unleavened bread for a week, did not include the usual pastries Sharon favored.

Sharon loathed Palestinian leader Arafat. He had no faith whatsoever in the very concept of peace with the Palestinians. Now the Park Hotel attack provided the casus belli that mandated a new and far angrier attitude than the atmosphere that had characterized earlier meetings that month. Mossad head Efraim Halevy and National Security Adviser Uzi Dayan both recall the key operational phrase at the meeting, which lasted until five the next morning: "It's impossible not to respond."[1]

IDF chief of staff Shaul Mofaz assumed he would now present his plan for invading and occupying the West Bank. The plan focused particularly on the refugee camps with their hardline population. It was there that the suicide bombings were conceived and the explosive vests were made. Palestinian security autonomy had failed monstrously, the Israeli security community believed, and Israel had to clean up the mess. Mofaz planned to tighten the already-existing IDF siege of Arafat's Ramallah headquarters,

the Muqataa. Israel's forces would generally purge the Palestinian population of terrorists and terrorist ordnance.

Some twenty thousand IDF reservists were being called up as the
meeting began. This did not necessarily reflect the IDF's need for reinforce-
ments for the coming operation. Rather, Sharon believed that an overnight
reserve call-up was the best way to signal the public that the country was
facing an emergency. By the by, his own popularity ratings would benefit
enormously.[2]

Sharon, however, wanted first to talk not about Mofaz's plan but
about Yasser Arafat. Specifically, Sharon wanted to exile the veteran Fateh
leader, chairman of the Palestinian Liberation Organization, and democratically elected president of the Palestinian Authority. "We won't kill him,
yes? We'll get him out of the region. We'll put him in a helicopter."

Sharon was clearly identifiable on one end of a political spectrum that
defined Israeli leaders' attitudes toward Arafat and, more broadly, toward
the attempt to negotiate anything with him. The right extreme of the
spectrum was peopled by those who viewed Arafat as the personification of
evil—a man with the blood of thousands of Israelis and other Jews on his
hands. They saw the Oslo Accords as a tragic mistake. Some were secular
Jews devoid of territorial ambitions who had simply concluded that the
Palestinian national movement would never agree to end the conflict by
implementing a genuine territorial compromise. But many others were settlers influenced by the religious-messianic belief that all of the land of the
West Bank must belong to Israel. They believed it was a sin to negotiate
this issue with anyone, Palestinian or American. It was a sympathizer with
this view, Yigal Amir, egged on by influential settlers and far-right rabbis
of this persuasion, who had assassinated Prime Minister Yitzhak Rabin in
Tel Aviv in November 1995.

The far-left extreme of the spectrum was characterized by Israelis who
actually believed in Arafat as a peace partner with good intentions. So dedicated were they to peace with the Palestinians that they could rationalize all
Arafat's lies. They could minimize or otherwise excuse Arafat's denials of
ties to extremist elements and acts like importing weaponry from Iran on
the *Karine A*. For these Israelis, the end justified ignoring the more ignoble
means.

Then there was the moderate left and center that in 1993 entered into
the Oslo Accords with the PLO. It comprised most of those who negotiated Oslo and tried to implement the agreement, Rabin included. They
acknowledged Oslo's flaws, such as the failure to specifically prevent Israeli
settlement spread and to specify a Palestinian state as the desired end result

of the peace process. Nor were they blind to the Palestinians' violations, particularly incitement at the leadership level and the failure to prevent terrorist attacks on Israeli civilians. The moderate leftists had few illusions regarding Arafat. But they also recognized that in Palestinian eyes Israel was at fault too: Delays in transferring West Bank territory were understood by the PLO as Israeli violations of the Oslo Accords.

Israeli moderate leftists and centrists did not like the negative ramifications of prolonged occupation of millions of Palestinians. The occupation affected both the morale and the morals of Israeli society, and particularly the IDF. They wanted to end the occupation—but safely. The moderates worried that the occupation and settlements in the West Bank and Gaza Strip would eventuate in a binational state, apartheid, and Israel's demise as a democratic, Jewish state.

Yet this same moderate leadership tolerated the settlements and the settlers. Left-led governments even provided the settlers budgets and services and IDF protection in the hope of avoiding more internal divides of the sort that led to the Rabin assassination. The very rabbis who had incited the messianic right to assassinate Yitzhak Rabin were left alone, neither interrogated nor incarcerated. Ehud Barak, who preceded Sharon as prime minister and briefly led the center-left Labor Party, quite typically allowed considerable new settlement construction in an effort to buy right-wing tolerance for his peace efforts with both the PLO and Syria.

In retrospect, acquiescence in settlement expansion and even material support for the settlements could hardly facilitate a sincere peace process. But at the time, Israel's politics seemed to render this the only nonviolent option for an Israeli leader bent on a two-state solution that would preserve the country's Jewish and democratic status.

The Israeli moderate left hoped that Arafat, warts and all, would cooperate in providing Israel an opportunity to separate itself from the Palestinian population that had fallen under Israeli occupation in 1967. The Palestinians threatened the long-term future of the Jewish state demographically. Finding a modus vivendi with them was also the key to peaceful coexistence with the rest of the Arab world.

And Palestinian violence? Suicide bombings? Without a dedicated effort by Arafat to rein in Palestinian extremists, nothing would work and there would be no progress. Yitzhak Rabin's famous quip that the Palestinians under Arafat could handle terrorists better than Israel because unlike the IDF and Shabak they could operate *"bli bagatz uvli betzelem"* (without recourse to Israel's High Court or to Betzelem, a primary human rights advocacy organization) summed up, perversely, his cynical view of

Arafat. Then, too, Rabin, in accepting the 1993 Oslo framework negotiated behind his back by Foreign Minister Shimon Peres and his deputy,
Yossi Beilin, was outspokenly and prophetically concerned that Israel must
resolve the Palestinian issue in order to clear the agenda for dealing with a
looming threat from Islamist Iran.

Sharon, to be sure, had no faith in either Arab intentions or Arab capabilities when it came to peace agreements. For years he had masterminded
many aspects of Israel's settlement program in the West Bank and Gaza. He
had opposed Oslo. He scorned Arafat.

But he was not a messianic-ideological right-winger. It was Sharon
who undertook in 1979 to remove every last Israeli settler from the Sinai
Peninsula in order to enable Prime Minister Menachem Begin's peace deal
with Egypt's Anwar Sadat. It was Sharon who, shortly after his election
to the premiership in early 2001, sent his son and confidant, Omri, twice
to meet with Arafat on his behalf. And as we shall see, it was Sharon who
within barely a year after the Park Hotel atrocity would begin to contemplate, then execute, evacuation of Israeli settlers from the Gaza Strip. He
would preach compromise with the Palestinians and advocate to his fellow
Israelis that additional withdrawals from the West Bank be undertaken.

Now, meeting at the Prime Minister's Office in Jerusalem twenty-
four hours after the Park bombing, Mossad head Halevy, Shabak head Avi
Dichter, and Brigadier-General Yossi Kuperwasser, head of IDF Military
Intelligence Research Division, were all opposed to expelling Arafat. In
other words, Sharon's intelligence chiefs and advisers told him not to "put
Arafat on a helicopter."

After all, the PLO leader was a democratically elected figure who had
signed the internationally recognized Oslo Accords with Yitzhak Rabin in
1993. Arafat's security services observed at least a modicum of cooperation
with the IDF and the Shabak. Bush's emissaries from Washington considered Arafat to be Sharon's partner in ending the violence and moving
toward peace. It was argued that without Arafat around, things could get
worse, not better. As the security chiefs made their case, Sharon listened
respectfully. His ministers, seated around the table, listened impatiently as
the meeting entered the early hours of March 29.

Sharon indeed confronted a problematic reality. Prior to Oslo, the
Palestinian leader had been Israel's bitter enemy for more than three decades. He had led the Fateh movement he founded, eventually under the
umbrella Palestine Liberation Organization, in numerous terrorist attacks
against Israeli civilians. An engineer born in Egypt who had lived most of
his life there and in Kuwait, the near-mythological figure of Arafat became

a flesh-and-blood peace partner to Israel with the successful conclusion in September 1993 of the Oslo behind-the-scenes negotiation.

Yet the more implicated Arafat was by Israel's intelligence establishment in presiding over terrorism from the Muqataa in Ramallah, the easier it was to distrust and even hate the man. The discussion about Arafat's fate went on for hours. Just days before, Bush had been pressuring Sharon to allow Arafat to attend the Beirut Arab League summit and Sharon was refusing to commit to allowing Arafat to return. Sharon, who later regretted not having encouraged Arafat to leave for good without discussing it first with Bush, was now stuck with the Palestinian leader he detested. Arafat would have to remain in his besieged Muqataa office in Ramallah.

It was well past midnight in the Prime Minister's Office. Mofaz interrupted the discussion of Arafat's fate: "Hold on, Prime Minister. There's a military operation waiting. Our forces are deploying. We have to decide we're doing it." Mofaz and Sharon had in past weeks thoroughly discussed and refined the IDF operation. Defense Minister Binyamin "Fuad" ben-Eliezer from the Labor Party coalition contingent was of little consequence here. Sharon, who had been barred from officially holding the post himself in the aftermath of the September 1982 massacre of Palestinian refugees in Lebanon, was for all intents and purposes his own minister of defense.

Now it took all of three minutes for the cabinet to approve Operation Defensive Shield and send Mofaz on his way. The assembled ministers would not apprise themselves of the details regarding timetable, order of battle, and operational objectives.

One related item remained. The gravel-voiced Kuperwasser was, at brigadier rank, the most junior of the security figures seated at the table. He was filling in for his superior, IDF head of intelligence Aharon Ze'evi-Farkash, who had celebrated Pesach in the Galilee and had not reached Jerusalem in time. Now "Kuper" suggested to Sharon that the Americans be informed in advance of the unfolding IDF invasion of the West Bank. Sharon absolutely refused, apparently fearing a last-minute attempt by Powell's emissary Tony Zinni to delay Israel's response to the Park bombing.

Discussion of Arafat's fate was then renewed at the cabinet meeting until dawn. Finally, Sharon told the exhausted ministers and security chiefs, "Okay, I see that all intelligence service heads are against expelling him. I want to do it but I won't go against this unanimous front."[3]

Sharon then proceeded to deliver an early morning announcement to the public defining the objectives of what would be called Operation Defensive Shield. "The government," he stated, "held a special session last night against the backdrop of a sharp escalation in Palestinian terrorism.

The government approved in principle the objectives of a broad operational plan against Palestinian terrorism. . . . Israel will act to decisively eliminate all components of the Palestinian terrorist infrastructure. To that end it will engage in widespread operations until the goal is achieved. Arafat, who set up a terrorist coalition against Israel, is an enemy and will at this stage be isolated."[4]

★   ★   ★

Throughout the meeting with Sharon, no one mentioned the Arab Peace Initiative. Yet it had been approved that same day, March 28, by the Arab League summit convened in Beirut. In the course of time, it would emerge that the API, whether by design or by chance, reflected a revolution in Arab thinking about Israel. In parallel, the Park attack would come to represent a revolution in Israel's approach to the notion of a Palestinian territorial entity capable of policing itself and not harming Israel. Surprisingly, the years ahead would prove these two seemingly conflicted revolutions broadly capable of coexisting.

6

MARCH 28, 2002, BEIRUT:
THE ARAB PEACE INITIATIVE I

The chronicle of the Arab Peace Initiative spans several years and more than one author or sponsor. An understanding of its origins helps explain why and when the initiative was deemed necessary by the assembled leaders of the Arab League.

The API was ratified in Beirut on March 28, 2002, by all twenty-two Arab states. The final version differed considerably from the very simple and straightforward proposal made public earlier that month by Saudi Crown Prince Abdullah, who was Saudi Arabia's de facto ruler.

And earlier drafts, before Abdullah? The very idea of such an undertaking? According to Jordan's former foreign minister, Marwan Muasher, the origins of the API can be traced back to 1998. It was then that the initiative was conceived by King Hussein of Jordan, albeit more in terms of generalities than details. A sick and dying man, the king was unhappy with Israel's leadership under new Prime Minister Benjamin Netanyahu. "Bibi" was at best lukewarm to the Oslo process for Israeli-Palestinian peace that was inaugurated with Hussein's blessing in 1993.

Netanyahu had launched his relationship with Hussein in 1996, shortly after winning election for the first time in Israel, with elaborate promises to the effect that "I will surprise you" regarding Oslo and resolving the Palestinian issue. At the time, Netanyahu made this statement to a number of Arab and European leaders. He never delivered.

Two years later, Hussein was tired of waiting for Netanyahu's surprise. The only way out of the impasse, the king suggested to his advisers, was to abandon Israeli-Palestinian bilateralism. It was necessary to expand the process to the entire Arab world and appeal to the desire for peace of the Israeli mainstream, which deeply feared and suspected Palestinian motives.

After all, Hussein had successfully tested that desire when Jordan itself made its peace with Israel in 1994.

Hussein wanted to propose that, in return for Israeli agreement to establish a Palestinian state and resolve all border issues and the Jerusalem and refugee issues, all twenty-two Arab states would establish full diplomatic, security, and trade relations with Israel. That spectacular payoff would, Hussein believed, be sufficient to persuade Israelis to make the necessary sacrifices and take the requisite risks for peace.

Hussein seemed to believe that, because Israel had earlier trusted him and endorsed the two countries' international border in exchange for a bilateral peace, it would do something similar with the Palestinians and with Syria. This reasoning ignored certain glaring lacunae. For one, the Palestinians had never had a state of their own and their territorial demands contradicted Israel's. In other words, for Israelis there was no compelling historical narrative or strategic symmetry at work here as with Jordan. Then too, Hussein's initiative offered no details as to how the refugee and Jerusalem issues might be resolved.

Hussein understood that Jordan alone was not a central enough Arab player to sponsor the proposal. Muasher, in 1998 Jordan's ambassador to the United States, relates that initial attempts to persuade Egypt as the preeminent Arab country to market the idea had to be set aside. Egypt's president Mubarak had instead accepted an ultimately abortive US initiative pushed by then secretary of state Madeleine Albright.[1]

In the next two years, Muasher would repeatedly broach the initiative in conversations in Washington. He spoke with Saudi ambassador Prince Bandar bin Sultan and Egyptian ambassador Nabil Fahmy, as well as with President Clinton's national security adviser on Middle East affairs, Bruce Riedel.

The issue arose in conversations Clinton held at Camp David in 1999 with Israel's Ehud Barak, who had succeeded Netanyahu as prime minister. The Israeli leader was poised to pursue peace first with Syria, then with the PLO—one after the other; not simultaneously. Israeli governments have traditionally feared both multilateral peace processes and multilateral Arab complications. Coordinated Arab pressure could in turn generate United Nations or even US pressure to undertake security and other concessions toward peace that Israel did not want to make, judging them dangerous and unwise. Accordingly, Barak insisted that Clinton not consult with additional Arab leaders regarding Barak's peace initiatives. This scuttled any likelihood that Clinton would embrace King Hussein's precursor to the Arab Peace Initiative.[2]

Barak's own peace initiatives failed. The Clinton administration failed spectacularly in July 2000 at Camp David and in the following months at Taba in Egyptian Sinai to produce a bilateral Israeli-Palestinian settlement. The transition to the Bush administration that took office in January 2001 was a major explanation for further delay in any new peace initiatives. In any event, Bush's treatment of the Palestinian issue would be inconsistent to say the least. Conservative Republican lobbying against pressure on Israel to offer territorial concessions usually won the day in the Bush White House.

The inclination in Bush's Washington in 2001 was to see the peace process President Clinton had invested in so heavily and emotionally as a dangerous and hopeless waste of time. This is particularly ironic insofar as many Arab countries at the time anticipated that Bush would be more forthcoming on Israel-related peace issues than had Clinton. Ironic, in view of the exaggerated significance these same Arabs attached to the fact that a Republican like Bush was less beholden to American Jewish voters and more closely linked to Arab energy interests than Clinton the Democrat.

Saudi ambassador to Washington Bandar bin Sultan, for example, reassured Saudi Crown Prince (and acting ruler) Abdullah that Bush 43, George W. Bush, was like his father, Bush 41, George H. W. Bush, and would come up with a better plan than the January 2001 Clinton Parameters. In fact, it was Bush 43 who reportedly said privately that the West Bank was comparable to Texas and California and could be annexed by Israel by right of conquest.[3]

Indeed, George W. Bush's Middle East policies were influenced from the start by the neoconservative approach of Vice President Richard Cheney and his advisers. Essentially, neocon advocates of this approach (see chapter 3) opposed Israeli territorial concessions for peace with the Palestinians. They did not believe Israeli-Palestinian peace would help stabilize the Middle East. And they favored a muscular American approach to the region and particularly toward such brutal oil-rich dictators as Saddam Hussein.

There was no diplomatic movement on the Middle East until mid-2001. Meanwhile the second Intifada had erupted. Arab concern over both Palestinian-Israeli violence and Bush's seeming indifference to the peace issue generated renewed efforts. As the fateful day of September 11, 2001, approached, Bush received a letter from Jordan's new king, Abdullah II, advocating his late father's proposal.

The American president also received a somber letter from Saudi Crown Prince Abdullah. Riyadh's Abdullah warned that the United States was working against Arab interests regarding both the peace process and oil prices. He threatened to reciprocate by pursuing Saudi interests unilaterally.

For all of Bush's relative ignorance of foreign affairs, as former governor of Texas, an oil state, he was fully aware of the Saudi capacity to influence energy prices and, by extension, the American economy.

All of these Arab efforts were interrupted by the spectacular al-Qaeda attacks on the United States on September 11, 2001, known as "9/11." Fifteen of the nineteen Arabs who hijacked American passenger jets and flew them as suicide bombs into Manhattan's Twin Towers and Washington's Pentagon were young Saudi men ostensibly studying in the United States. This cast US–Arab relations and particularly US–Saudi ties in an entirely new light. The United States embarked on a military campaign against al-Qaeda and its Taliban supporters in Afghanistan, and elements within the Bush administration began to lay the foundations for the 2003 invasion of Iraq.

Bush's attitude toward the Arabs now became more complex. On the one hand, the administration was angry with the Saudis over their extremist Wahabi version of Islam, and angry with Islamists in general. On the other, US military operations in Afghanistan and later Iraq would require a high degree of understanding and acquiescence on the part of the Saudis and other usually pro–American Arab leaders.

Israeli prime minister Ariel Sharon was quick to equate PLO leader Yasser Arafat with al-Qaeda's Osama bin-Laden in the hope of recruiting Bush's support for a move to expel Arafat from the Palestinian Authority. Intelligence linking Arafat to Palestinian suicide bombings against Israelis helped win Bush's sympathy. So did the Israel Navy's interception of the Palestinian arms-smuggling ship *Karine A*, which linked Arafat to Palestinian smuggling of arms from Iran.

Yet September 11, 2001, also set in motion a dynamic of US interaction with both Arabs and Israelis and with escalating Palestinian-Israeli violence that within half a year would produce the Arab Peace Initiative. Bush, while planning an extensive armed response to 9/11, was also susceptible to moderate Arab admonitions, particularly from the Saudi Abdullah. And Abdullah was committed to the Palestinian issue. Riyadh's de facto ruler insisted that the administration deal seriously with Israeli-Palestinian violence and get the peace process back on track. Otherwise, the American response to 9/11 would aggravate Arab and Muslim attitudes toward the United States even further than what was demonstrated by 9/11.

Besides, even the neocons in Bush's entourage favored a positive approach to the Saudi leadership, regardless of 9/11. This reflected both ideology and energy-related business interests, which not coincidentally were related. Incredibly, the very same Bush 43 administration had allowed the Saudis to airlift Saudi royals and members of the bin-Laden clan from the

United States to Saudi Arabia before the sun went down on September 11, 2001, even as all other aircraft were grounded. Equally incredibly, at this unprecedented juncture in US-Saudi relations, Crown Prince Abdullah was emotional and insistent about one particular issue: the plight of Palestinian children. The Bush administration would look for at least minor and symbolic ways to appear accommodating.

By late 2001 the United States was at war in Afghanistan. The 9/11 attacks and their aftermath were now the administration's principal focus of concern in the Greater Middle East. Indeed, one would have thought that al-Qaeda's attack on the Twin Towers and the Pentagon, by far the worst terrorist aggression the United States had ever experienced, would have shunted all other Middle East issues completely aside.

But because so many Middle East challenges are linked and interactive, Washington's involvement in trying to quell the second Intifada was maintained, albeit at a far lower level of priority. It was confined largely to setting in motion an incremental dynamic of security- and confidence-building measures that might somehow eventuate in renewal of an Israeli-Palestinian peace process.

The Mitchell Report, an initiative carried over from the Clinton administration, sought to facilitate an immediate cease-fire, confidence-building measures, and the resumption of negotiations. CIA director George Tenet, followed by Tony Zinni, were dispatched to the region to achieve an Israeli-Palestinian security plan.

Suicide bombings raged, and Israel under Sharon was responding with targeted assassinations. Israeli tanks tore up Palestinian roads and an Israeli siege confined Arafat to his Muqataa compound in Ramallah. If the American response to all this was low key, at least one Arab actor was proactive.

Marwan Muasher, by now Jordan's foreign minister, had not given up on the peace initiative championed privately by King Hussein in 1998 and again by himself among Arab circles in Washington in 2001. Late that year, the ever-youthful-looking Muasher briefed *New York Times* columnist Tom Friedman regarding the idea that the Arab states offer Israel a multilateral peace deal under which it would withdraw from all the territories captured in 1967. In exchange, Israel would be granted comprehensive peace and security agreements with the entire Arab world.

Friedman was fully aware of the Arabs' need not only for an Israeli-Palestinian settlement but also for a vehicle to make amends to the United States for the terrorist atrocity of 9/11. He proceeded to publish, on February 6, 2002, a "Memo to: President Hosni Mubarak, Crown Prince Abdullah, King Abdullah, President Bashar al-Assad and the rest of the Arab

League, From: President Bush." Speaking as Bush, he explained to the leaders of Egypt, Saudi Arabia, Jordan, and Syria that it was not America's job to pressure Israel into making peace:

> We're just bystanders. You're the ones with the power to really reshape the diplomacy . . . You have an Arab League summit set for March in Lebanon. I suggest your summit issue one simple resolution: The 22 members of the Arab League say to Israel that in return for a complete Israeli withdrawal to the June 4, 1967, lines—in the West Bank, Gaza, Jerusalem and on the Golan Heights—we offer full recognition of Israel, diplomatic relations, normalized trade and security guarantees. Full peace with all 22 Arab states for full withdrawal. . . . This is how to bury Osama bin Laden and define for the world who the Arabs really are. . . . Now is the time for an Arab peace plan. . . . you all need this as much as Israelis and Palestinians do.

This Friedman column was followed by another, on February 17, based on an interview in Riyadh. Here Friedman coyly contrived to explain that by coincidence he and Saudi Crown Prince Abdullah had the same peace initiative for the Arab League summit. The interview even produced a lame apology from Abdullah for 9/11: "It is never too late to express our regrets."

Here we recall that the second Palestinian Intifada, whose brutal violence was ostensibly the trigger for these interventions by Bush, King Abdullah, and Crown Prince Abdullah, erupted barely two months after the failure of Clinton's peace summit at Camp David in July 2000. The Arab Peace Initiative of March 28, 2002, arrived about six months after 9/11 and one day after the Park Hotel suicide attack. The interplay between Arab Islamist violence, Israeli and American military responses, and initiatives to resolve the Israeli-Palestinian conflict remains a constant theme.

Friedman's account of his involvement with the Arab Peace Initiative is particularly instructive for the light it sheds on the Saudi political motives behind the entire API project.

7

THE ARAB PEACE INITIATIVE II: A CONVERSATION WITH THOMAS L. FRIEDMAN

Yossi Alpher: I'm speaking with Tom Friedman, October 23, 2019, in the office of the *New York Times* in Washington, DC.

Tom Friedman: I will tell you the whole story. This came entirely out of my head, okay? The back story is, during the Clinton administration I became a columnist for the *New York Times*. January 1995. And during the Clinton years, I began using a columnist conceit of writing letters on behalf of the US president to different leaders around the world. It's something I had fun with: memo from Bill Clinton to x, y, and z.

And they started to get a big reaction. Like I did a letter from Clinton to [Syrian president] Hafez al-Assad. And jokingly, in the middle of it, said, "Whenever we meet the chairs are facing out, both of our chairs, and I've got a crick in my neck from looking at you like that." And the next time [Secretary of State] Warren Christopher came to Damascus the chairs were facing each other, okay?

Then I did a letter from Clinton to Mubarak. These were informed letters, so the leaders all assumed, in their conspiratorial mind, they all assumed they were dictated by the president to me. And I wrote one to Mubarak from Clinton that enraged Mubarak so much Clinton had to stop in Cairo on his way home from a trip from Africa because one of the things I had in there was "as I told you on the phone." So that is the back story of the conceit.

Alpher: Right. And this brings us to the 9/11 attacks and the ensuing Arab Peace Initiative.

Friedman: Now 9/11 happens. It had a big impact on me. I was really shaken by it, and my initial reaction was to declare war on Saudi Arabia. I basically put Saudi Arabia in the dock. I said it's your ideology, it's ideology that made this happen.

I'll say one immodest thing. I won a Pulitzer Prize for commentary on 9/11. There were a lot of people commenting on 9/11, so for me it's the proudest achievement of my career that I got singled out.

I would go to Davos every year for their [World Economic Forum] meeting. It was always in January. In 2002 they decided that instead of having Davos in Davos, in honor of 9/11 they would have it at the Waldorf Astoria in New York. So I was thinking, what constructive thing can I offer up? Maybe I should write a letter from the new president, George W. Bush. It just jumped into my head: I think I'll write a letter from George W. Bush to the Arab League. And I was thinking I should say something really simple, full peace for full withdrawal, normalization, trade, etc.

So I tried it on different people. I went to Davos and had coffee with [Arab League secretary general] Amr Moussa. I said I'm thinking of writing this letter from Bush to the leaders of the Arab League, what do you think? He said [whispers], "Do it, do it." And then I run into the Moroccan Jewish adviser [Andre Azoulay] to the king [of Morocco]. I said, I'm thinking of doing this, what do you think? He said [whispers], "Do it, do it."

Alpher: They all said do it but implied, don't quote me?

Friedman: Amr [Moussa] takes credit for telling me to do it. He's very proud of this. So I do it. I published the letter in February 2002.

Alpher: There are other Arab leaders at the time who take credit for having input.

Friedman: I completely invented this. I mean it just came out of my head.

Alpher: And the main engine for this was 9/11?

Friedman: It was totally 9/11. I wanted to do something constructive. But meanwhile I'm beating the shit out of Saudi Arabia. So the spokesman for the Saudi Embassy [Adel Jubeir] out of the blue calls me and says, "Have you ever been to Saudi Arabia?" I'd been there, but only stopping with [Secretary of State James] Baker. Adel says, "We'd like you to come."

Alpher: This is after the Bush letter?

Friedman: No, I believe this was before the Bush letter. The Bush letter came out between when he invited me and when I went to Saudi Arabia.

So I go to Saudi Arabia. Now the column is out, the Bush letter is out. The oil minister, Naimi, takes me down to the Empty Quarter.

They lay out the red carpet. I meet with all kinds of editors, women's groups, doctors. Some are really tough. I walk out of one meeting after a guy insults me as being Jewish. I don't remember the exact context, but I don't take shit from these guys at all and they know that. I'm there for a week and at the end of the week, Adel says, Crown Prince Abdullah would like to see you. So I'd been to Jedda and I came back and we went to his horse farm outside of Riyadh.

We're sitting in his diwan, he's got a gigantic buffet, he's sitting in a chair, everyone sort of around him. And Adel says, "We should go up." I brought a book for him, I brought the Arabic edition of *The Lexus and the Olive Tree* [by Friedman, published 1999]. Dan Kurtzer, when he was the ambassador in Egypt, sponsored the Arabic translation. So I brought [Abdullah] a copy, autographed to him. They said it would break the ice, nice chat, and he said I look forward to talking to you later.

Then they sat me next to him at dinner. It was a big horseshoe table and a giant endless buffet and gigantic TV screen in front of us. And we basically watched TV and ate, me next to him, and people went back and forth, these are all kings and princes and what-not.

Alpher: Watching local TV?

Friedman: No, CNN. They're watching news, maybe it was al-Jazeera, I don't remember. It was sort of bizarre, a horseshoe table, people are eating, coming in. Walid bin Talal was there, the investor. I eat and we were making small talk. They started late because everything starts late.

Comes close to midnight, he invites me to come over to his house. So the three of us, the crown prince, Adel, and myself, go and sit in his den. It was like a small desk, he sat over here, I sat here and Adel translated in the middle. And he began by saying, "You broke into my drawer." I said Your Highness, I'm sorry, I don't know what you're talking about. "You broke into my drawer. That plan you put out, that was my plan."

I said well, that's really interesting, let's talk about it. And so for three hours we went back and forth on that. And we discussed other issues, too, like I said when are you going to apologize for 9/11? And he said something very general [see chapter 6].

This was my thing. I was at war, you know? But he keeps going back to this. So we talked for about three hours. It was about two or three in the morning. I said, you know, Your Highness, this is so important and we need to put this out, we need to share this, your idea, with the world. He said, you just put it out yourself, that Saudi officials endorse whatever.

Alpher: Publish it under your name?

Friedman: I said no, no, you put it out. He said no, no, you put it out. And Adel is translating in between, okay? We're going back and forth like this. Finally Adel says, write it up as a column, as you would write it up as an interview and send it to us and we'll consider it. So I thought, it's not my usual modus operandi, but this is big enough that I'm ready to do that. So anyway I go back to my hotel, I sleep, I type it up as an interview with him. But there is one thing.

Alpher: He never pulled anything out of a drawer to show you.

Friedman: No.

Alpher: So this was his conceit?

Friedman: This was his conceit: to hitchhike on my thing as a way of deflecting attention from Saudi Arabia. We'll get to that in a second. Adel, when we're talking, is laying out his version of my plan. He says, in return for the West Bank and Jerusalem, and I said, Your Highness, you mean East Jerusalem. It was pretty clear to me that he actually didn't know the geography of Jerusalem. So I said, you mean East Jerusalem and he said, yeah, yeah, East, whatever.

So I made that edit. I faxed it to Adel and a few hours later they called back and said to go with it, just like that. So now I know I got something big but it's Wednesday and I don't have a column until Sunday. So they ask me if I'd meet with some of his [the crown prince's] brothers and other officials. I meet with his brother, Nayef, who's minister of interior. Muhammad bin Nayef was standing behind him. He says, "This is my son." So I go see Muhammad bin Nayef [later a key security minister and crown prince].

This is God's truth.

Alpher: This is what?

Friedman: What I'm about to say is God's truth. I sit down in front of his desk at the Ministry of Interior and the first thing he says to me, the first thing, is, "Is it true the Jews control all the banks and big corporations in America?" Now I wanted to say [whispers mischievously], "You mean you know? You know? We thought it was a secret, you know?" My mind is spinning now. And I parry something: of course that's not true, you have to understand, blah blah. Anyway, I didn't walk out.

But I'm very careful. I don't tell him what his brother said and it quickly becomes apparent that he doesn't know that his brother just put out the biggest peace initiative. His brother has not discussed it. I never say anything, like what did you think of your brother's plan. We talked about security issues post 9/11. Then I went to see the minister of information. Once again it's clear to me this is nowhere. So now I start to realize this is a coup d'etat.

Alpher: A coup d'etat?

Friedman: Remember, he's crown prince. [King] Fahd is still alive but he's incapacitated. So this is [Abdullah's] stepping out, okay? He hasn't told any of his brothers. So comes Saturday, my column is in New York, they give me extra space. I tell Adel I'm staying here until Monday. I just care about one thing, how you translate this into Arabic at the Saudi Press Agency [SPA]. And if you fuck me, I have a column on Wednesday and I will fuck you back. I was not going to be out there in the *New York Times* and have them say, oh, oh no, no, no. So we agreed what time that thing was going to appear in both places, and I'm pretty sure Adel went down to SPA and did the translation himself. Because it was perfect.

Saturday night Adel calls me and says, "Do you have Ari Fleischer's phone number?" [Fleischer was President Bush's press secretary.] I say, Adel, you don't have an embassy in Washington? He says [whispers], "We're not using the embassy."

Now I know this is a coup d'etat. Because the ambassador was Bandar bin Sultan. And who is defense minister and maybe deputy crown prince at that point, his father [Prince Sultan], you know? It comes out the next day, and overnight Abdullah has become a world historical figure. I mean it goes everywhere. People had never heard of him, basically, and it just goes everywhere.

Including to Israel. I leave on Monday or Tuesday. I fly to London. I call Nachum Barnea [senior *Yedioth Ahronoth* columnist], who's my best friend in Israel. And I give him an interview, it's the only one. I give it to *Yedioth* because I just want them to know this is from me to you and this is real. And then I stepped out of it, because my view was it's only going to go as far as the Saudis and the Arabs take it. So I never went to the Beirut summit even though I set the ball rolling. It had to be their baby.

Now, once it was out, it may have been Marwan [Muasher] or somebody who told me that the king of Jordan had been pushing the same thing. I was just not aware of it.

Alpher: Marwan Muasher remembered what King Hussein had said to him in 1998. He tried to push it when he was ambassador in Washington and didn't get anywhere because 9/11 came along.

Friedman: Context is everything for these things, you know?

Alpher: Indeed. Regarding Crown Prince Abdullah, how did you understand his motive?

Friedman: There is always a mix of motives. Clearly one was to rebrand Saudi Arabia, and with the guy [Friedman himself] who's destroying their brand, okay? I'm doing everything I can to destroy their brand. So I was keenly aware that there were ulterior motives here and my view is, hey, this is a trade, putting this on the record is a trade I'm happy to make. That didn't stop me from continuing to write what I was writing about [Saudi Arabia]. But it was, this is a trade I'll make. So you want to change the subject and rebrand Saudi Arabia. For all I know this came out of their PR people. Adel was very PR savvy. One day I'll ask him the real truth: Did you just say we've got to change the subject with the guy who is doing the most damage to us?

Alpher: But how do you understand what comes out of Beirut, which is very different?

Friedman: I knew that once it got translated into diplomatese it was never going to survive as the original thing, because then you go through a Palestinian filter, which is where Nabil [Shaath, PA planning minister] comes in.

Alpher: And the Syrians.

Friedman: And the Syrians, exactly right, because it's the Arab League.

Alpher: And Jordan's Marwan Muasher.

Friedman: Let me say one other thing. If you google [Saudi ambassador to the United States] Bandar bin Sultan and Abdullah's peace initiative you will find zero matches. So one of the things that was undermined in Washington was the Saudi Embassy, which never pushed it with the Bush administration. [Secretary of State] Colin Powell never asked, why aren't you running with this. This is internal Saudi politics because it's Sultan, the defense minister [and father of Bandar] looking at his rival Abdullah.

Alpher: It's about rebranding Saudi Arabia and it's about Abdullah and his rivals.

Friedman: It was about a rivalry between him and his brothers, you know? Sultan in particular, and that's why Bandar never sold it, never pressed it. And the Bush people. Colin Powell was very uncreative. My view was the details don't matter, this is Saudi Arabia representing the Islamic world. Saudi Arabia meant the Gulf. If you look at the history of Gulf-Israel relations, suddenly there is a very different umbrella, you know? After that, I was critical of Abdullah. I wrote columns about this, I said you need to go to Israel. Just like Sadat did. And you need to go pray in the al-Aqsa Mosque and go to Ramallah. I kept saying you can't just fax it to the Israelis.

Just to finish my part of the story, Shimon [Peres] calls me and says would you connect me with King Abdullah?

Alpher: By now he's king?

Friedman: Now he's king. This was five years ago. [Abdullah was king from 2005 until his death in 2015. Peres was president of Israel from 2007 to 2014.] I said, it's tricky for me, Shimon. I'm a journalist. He said, well let's do an interview. And I did actually quote him. His dream was that the two of them revive the thing. Shimon wanted to revive it with him, and I was the carrier of that message. But the Saudis just were not ready to play, this was the end of Abdullah's life. I had to be very careful. I'm a journalist. It's okay to do these interviews but I don't want to be a go-between.

Alpher: Now, did you know that [Israeli prime minister Ariel] Sharon, from February 2002 on, is aware of all that's going on and tries to get himself invited to Beirut to the summit? He doesn't succeed. Nobody is biting because his image in the Arab world, and especially in Lebanon since 1982, is so negative.

Friedman: Several people wanted to ride this thing to rebrand themselves, you know what I mean?

Alpher: Then on April 8, ten days after the Park bombing, Sharon tells the Knesset there are some positive aspects to the Arab Peace Initiative and he's prepared to go to Beirut to talk to the Arab leaders about it. Nobody takes him seriously. But he understood, he feared this would bring about some kind of pressure on him that would be hard to deal with. [For more on Sharon's Beirut initiative, see chapter 9, "Ariel Sharon and the Arab Peace Initiative."]

Friedman: This is very important because I always asked myself afterwards, what happened (spoken in Hebrew: "ma kara")? Why isn't this energizing things more? I know this is important. But it wasn't in Washington or in Israel. In Israel it was because Sharon was afraid of it and in Washington it's because the Israel Embassy wasn't pushing it and Powell wasn't pushing it. I blame Powell a lot.

Alpher: But Powell was under pressure from the neocons. They want to go into Iraq.

Friedman: And little Tommy Friedman, Jewish kid from St. Louis Park, Minnesota. I really wanted to have peace, you know?

Alpher: Still, the Arab Peace Initiative has survived as a ritual, with annual reaffirmation: We'll coexist with you but we've still got conditions that we know you can't meet. We'll reapprove it every March.

Friedman: Right, and what I say is, it was not just true for the Arabs, this paved the way for Muslims. It was about the world of Islam coming to terms with Israel, not just the Arab world. Because it came out of Saudi Arabia.

Alpher: You still had all kinds of dissenters [in Beirut and thereafter], like Moammar Qaddafi.

Friedman: I watched this with great entertainment, you know what I mean? But that's where it came about. And that, by the way, is just a sidelight. You won't understand my views of MbS [Saudi Crown Prince Mohammad bin Salman] if you don't go back again to 9/11, okay. And I've taken a huge amount of shit for that and my attitude before, during, and today is, fuck you all. I knew just what I was doing, I'm not the least bit apologetic.

Of course I'm appalled by what happened to Jamal [Khashoggi, murdered in Istanbul in 2018 by security personnel sent by MbS]. But this goes back to my view of the Arab world. I believe that America treated the Arab world, where 9/11 came from, as a collection of big gas stations. Our message to them was: Keep your pumps open, your prices low, and don't bother the Yehudis [Jews] too much and you can do whatever you want. This was the social contract between America and the Arab world. You can treat your women however you like. You can preach intolerance in your mosques.

And my view is that in 9/11 we got hit with the distillation of all the pathologies that were going on. And that's why I supported the Iraq War. Not for WMD [weapons of mass destruction] reasons. I was part of that group of liberal hawks who said, if we don't find a way to bring multisectarian consensual politics to the Arab world, it's going to die.

They write the Arab Human Development Report, which comes out in 2002. And no Arab country will host its issuing. So they leak it to me, because Amr [Moussa] won't provide an Arab League venue in Cairo for it to be released.

Alpher: The annual Arab Human Development Reports paint a devastating picture of the Arab world.

Friedman: So when people said why do you support the Iraq War, I said this is why. There's the charge sheet against me. You support the Iraq War, you support MbS and you're way too excited about the Arab Spring. What do you have to say for yourself?

The logic of what I'm doing is very simple. Perfect is not on the menu in that part of the world. And it is my belief, after 9/11, that unless gender pluralism, education pluralism, Arab human development pluralism, political pluralism, and religious pluralism come to the Arab world, that we don't find a way to partner with people, we can't impose. It's going to go over a cliff.

Alpher: And you are on the record.

Friedman: Yeah, it's all yours.

8

THE ARAB PEACE INITIATIVE III:
THE DOCUMENT IS WRITTEN
AND APPROVED

Crown Prince Abdullah's February 2002 version of the API was, as reported by Friedman on February 17, the epitome of simplicity and symmetry: "full withdrawal from all the occupied territories, in accord with U.N. resolutions, including in Jerusalem, for full normalization of relations." This was a straightforward one-on-one trade-off equation. Its 1998 precursor, as conceived by Jordan's King Hussein and delivered to Muasher, had been somewhat more explicit and narrowly focused, describing a Palestinian state "with mutually agreed borders, a formula for Jerusalem, and a solution to the refugee problem." Saudi Arabia's Abdullah also called for Israel to return to the 1967 borders with Syria ("all the occupied territories") and deliver minor disputed territories to Lebanon. The Arab League states would reciprocate for Israel's withdrawal on all fronts with full diplomatic, commercial, and security relations with Israel, including a "mutual, comprehensive, defense/security pact."

One important substantive difference between these two seminal versions is Hussein's 1998 insistence on solving the issue of the 1948 Palestinian refugees. How, he did not say. The Palestinian leadership is more explicit. To this day the PLO demands that Israel acknowledge the refugees' "right of return." It must agree at least in principle to repatriate all of them, meaning more than five million of the original refugees (of whom few are still alive) and their diaspora-born children and grandchildren.

Here it is appropriate to note that the Palestinian refugee issue is truly unique at the global level. It is unique in terms of numbers, generations, and the creation of a dedicated and exclusive international institution, UNRWA, to deal with it. It is unique in view of the many decades of cynical Arab state exploitation that have rendered it so tragic and so destructive.

The refugee issue is discussed in greater depth in chapter 15, "Behind the Events of March 2002."

In 2002, in co-opting Friedman, the Saudi Abdullah ignored the refugees, perhaps because there were no Palestinian refugee camps in Saudi Arabia and the issue was not prominent on the Saudi agenda. In contrast, the Hashemite monarch's motivation obviously stemmed from the demographic reality in Jordan, where more than half the population at the time was Palestinian, mostly refugees whose loyalty to Hussein was doubtful. Jordan needs the issue to be resolved so it can normalize the status of its citizens of Palestinian descent, remain a "Hashemite kingdom," and not become an alternate Palestinian state. Still, even Hussein avoided offering a concrete formula for dealing with the refugees, presumably because he understood that no one had ever come up with a refugee plan that would be acceptable to both the Palestinians and the Israelis.

The Saudi version could not constitute an Arab peace proposal without official and unanimous Arab League approval. That meant, in the days leading up to March 28 in Beirut, a lot of bargaining, horse-trading, and out-and-out threats among the assembled Arab leaders. These would seriously affect the content and tenor of the ultimate League resolution. The final product that emerged from the Beirut conclave and bore the title Arab Peace Initiative was a different creature once the Levant states of Lebanon and Syria were done with it.

Even before Beirut, as Jordan's Muasher, the PLO's head negotiator Saeb Erekat, PA planning minister Nabil Shaath, and Arab League secretary general Amr Moussa made the rounds of Arab leaders throughout March, they encountered seemingly impossible demands. Thus, in Damascus, young and inexperienced Syrian president Bashar Assad, who had succeeded his deceased father, Hafez, in June 2000, was taking no chances with innovation. He demanded that the Palestinian right of return to homes abandoned in Israel in 1948 be mentioned explicitly and that Israel be rewarded with "normal relations" rather than "full normalization."

The first demand reflected the priorities of neighboring Lebanon, whose population of 3.5 million lived under Syria's large shadow. Lebanon's very existence is predicated on a delicate ethno-religious balance among Sunnis, Shiites, Maronite and Orthodox Christians, Druze, and other minorities. That equilibrium would be violated if Lebanon's predominantly Sunni Muslim Palestinian refugees, legally confined to camps and stateless since 1948, remained there and were absorbed once peace was achieved. They had to leave or at least remain disenfranchised.

Lebanon claimed in 2002 that its Palestinian refugees numbered around 400,000. The number was more likely just more than 200,000. So sensitive are its ethnic issues that Lebanon has for decades refused to carry out a census. But many Palestinian refugees are known to have migrated to other Arab countries and to Europe, particularly Germany, where they are eligible for citizenship.

Assad's second demand reflected the fact that even among Arab countries, very few had then or have now what we might call full normalization with one another. There is no Arab common market, there are no open borders, and there is little inter-Arab commerce and tourism. The closest the Arab world has come to normalized inter-Arab relations is the Gulf Cooperation Council (GCC), which unites Saudi Arabia, the United Arab Emirates, Kuwait, Bahrain, Oman, and Qatar.

Yet the GCC, an imperfect economic union, is plagued by internal rivalries. By 2020 three of its members had for several years been boycotting a fourth, Qatar. They only made amends in late 2020 in order to present a united and tranquil profile to the incoming Biden administration, which was expected to take a tough line toward the Saudis in particular.

As pre-summit contacts continued in March 2002, Syrian foreign minister Farouk al-Sharaa won Saudi agreement to replace the term "full peace" with "normal peaceful relations." Conceivably, Arab "normal" could legitimately mean vastly different levels of relations to different Arab states. Yet Israel could justifiably be expected to be rewarded for its territorial and other peace concessions with truly normalized relations with the entire Arab world. What was it to make of this dodgy wordplay?

Syria, like many Arab countries, could not respond to what had become a Saudi initiative with an outright "no." Riyadh, after all, held both important purse strings and trusteeship over the two most important sites of Islam, Mecca and Medina. Instead, Damascus and others mounted objections and insisted on convoluted language that Israel would easily find fault with. In a briefing to journalists in Beirut, Assad expressed reservations about the API, calling it no more than "a first step" in need of a mechanism for implementation. This, despite the resolution's demand for "full Israeli withdrawal from all the territories" to satisfy the Syrians.

In Libya, "Brother Leader" Moammar Qaddafi told League secretary general Moussa he would not agree to security guarantees and normalization for Israel. Libya and Israel had no common border, therefore had no need for these formalities. Iraq addressed the API from the same geographic point of departure. Whenever Crown Prince Abdullah encountered these sorts of objections, he would demand that they be recorded officially. Then the Syrians or Libyans or Iraqis would back off enough to enable some sort of compromise formulation.

In Egypt, President Mubarak, having missed his chance to lead the pack when approached in 1998 by Jordan's ailing King Hussein, was grumpy that the emerging API was sponsored by Saudi Arabia rather than Egypt. In contrast, the other Arab states preferred Saudi to Egyptian sponsorship, although they were all generally uneasy about this new and innovative departure.

Egypt, whose population in 2021 numbered more than one hundred million, may be the demographic heavyweight of the Arab world. But in 2002 it was still held to account by its neighbors for initiating a peace process with Israel in 1977 and breaking an Arab taboo. At least on paper, the Egyptian-Israeli peace treaty of 1979 comprised all the elements of normalization advocated by the Saudi initiative twenty-three years later. That an Arab grudge against Egypt resurfaced in the course of discussions of an Arab peace initiative was not the only anomaly. Even Arab states that had held overt (and abortive) peace negotiations with Israel, such as Syria twice in the 1990s and Lebanon in 1982, were troubled by the Saudi idea of a collective Arab peace initiative.

Following upon Syria's advocacy on Lebanon's behalf regarding the Palestinian refugees, the most significant opposition to the API's language was evinced by Lebanon itself. Lebanon's Shiite and Christian leaders, fearing ultimate enfranchisement of hundreds of thousands of Sunni Palestinian refugees, insisted that any end-of-conflict agreement with Israel must state explicitly that all Palestinian refugees leave Lebanon. They demanded adding a clause that would "award special attention to Lebanon's position which rejects Palestinian patriation (Arabic: *tawteen*)." From the standpoint of the API drafters, there was a concession here. The refugees would have to leave Lebanon, but they would not necessarily have to be absorbed by Israel.

By the time the Arab foreign ministers convened in Beirut on March 24, a more generalized "no tawteen" clause was agreed, the only question being whether fulfillment of the clause should be an Israeli or an Arab obligation. This was important. Lebanon's Palestinian refugee population might really be 400,000 or it might be closer to 200,000. But once all Arab states agreed that the Palestinians would have to leave Lebanon as a condition for peace with Israel, who would be charged by the API with accomplishing this?

Lebanese sectarian politics were then, as now, Byzantine. There was a lot of "deep state" control by the security services. And there was significant Syrian influence within those services. Consequently, Director of

Public Security Jamil El-Sayyed was then the ultimate Lebanese decision-maker. At a meeting between him and Muasher, it was agreed that "no patriation," meaning removing all Palestinians from Lebanon, would be the obligation of the international community, to which the Arab Peace Initiative resolution ultimately directs its appeal. The API's final wording can at least be construed to mean that Lebanon's Palestinian refugees would be absorbed by immigration-welcoming countries such as Canada and Australia. The Arabs, including the Palestinians, were ostensibly dropping the "right of return" demand that Israel absorb them. Were that to happen in reality, it would be an earthshaking departure from traditional Palestinian refugee policy.

On the other hand, the Arabs convening in Beirut designed their "just solution" to the refugee issue around UN General Assembly Resolution (UNGAR) 194. They willfully ignored the fact that their interpretation—that 194 mandates the "right of return"—has no basis in the General Assembly's language. UNGAR 194 refers only to the original refugees, not their descendants, and stipulates they should be willing to "live at peace with their neighbors." Needless to say, Israel, mindful of the Arab gloss on 194, rejects it. UNGAR 194 is not a Security Council resolution of the sort that is binding on relevant member states.

Little by little, what had begun as a straightforward Saudi initiative became complex and overnuanced. The Saudis had to go along with the objections because, in the Arab League, consensus is an absolute necessity. The resolution's drafters watered down whatever extreme demands they could, then relented. By March 28, the operative paragraphs of the API read as follows:

The Council of Arab States at the Summit Level at its 14th Ordinary Session:

1. Requests Israel to reconsider its policies and declare that a just peace is its strategic option as well.
2. Further calls upon Israel to affirm:
   I   Full Israeli withdrawal from all the territories occupied since 1967, including the Syrian Golan Heights, to the June 4, 1967, lines as well as the remaining occupied Lebanese territories in the south of Lebanon.
   II Achievement of a just solution to the Palestinian refugee problem to be agreed upon in accordance with UN General Assembly Resolution 194.

III The acceptance of the establishment of a sovereign independent Palestinian state on the Palestinian territories occupied since June 4, 1967, in the West Bank and Gaza Strip, with East Jerusalem as its capital.

3. Consequently, the Arab countries affirm the following:
   I   Consider the Arab-Israeli conflict ended, and enter into a peace agreement with Israel, and provide security for all the states of the region.
   II Establish normal relations with Israel in the context of this comprehensive peace.

4. Assures the rejection of all forms of Palestinian patriation which conflict with the special circumstances of the Arab host countries.

5. Calls upon the government of Israel and all Israelis to accept this initiative in order to safeguard the prospects for peace and stop the further shedding of blood, enabling the Arab countries and Israel to live in peace and good neighborliness and provide future generations with security, stability, and prosperity.

6. Invites the international community and all countries and organizations to support this initiative.

7. Requests the chairman of the summit to form a special committee composed of some of its concerned member states and the secretary general of the League of Arab States to pursue the necessary contacts to gain support for this initiative at all levels, particularly from the United Nations, the Security Council, the United States of America, the Russian Federation, the Muslim states, and the European Union.

Conceptually it is in clause 7, the Arab appeal to the entire international community for support, that "lies the rub" of the API. The busy Arab diplomats who frantically crisscrossed the Arab world to put together a compromise Arab League resolution never consulted Israel. Lebanese prime minister Rafik Hariri's pre-summit declaration that "We are speaking . . . to all Israeli leaders and to Israeli public opinion"[1] was not echoed in the final text of the API.

The meaning of paragraph 7 is that the API is not up for negotiation. The Arab League was announcing that the API was not intended to be the basis for discussions with Israel. The League ignored Tom Friedman's admonition to Adel Jubeir: "You can't just fax it to the Israelis." The Arabs didn't even fax it. It was a take-it-or-leave-it proposal. "We are giving Israel an end to all claims and a collective peace and security treaty and it still wants to negotiate?" remarked one Arab foreign minister years later. "We cannot, after we've given all these compromises, still have to negotiate over occupied territories. That was basically the Arab mindset."

And he added, when prompted to address the Park attack, "That was also our collective and conscious response to the Park Hotel suicide bombing of the previous day."[2] A colleague of his, Nabil Shaath, PA planning minister and a principal drafter of the API final version, echoed this sentiment: "[We resolved in Beirut that] we will not allow [Hamas] to stop us."[3] Yet no one in Beirut openly mentioned Hamas's Sheikh Yassin or addressed the Park atrocity in specific language.

To muddy the waters even further, the assembled Arab heads of state in Beirut in 2002 proceeded to reaffirm in a separate resolution the very "right of return" of all the millions of 1948 Palestinian refugees and their descendants—a demand that for tactical reasons had not been mentioned specifically in the API. Indeed, both the API and the right of return, side by side, have been reaffirmed at every Arab League summit ever since. (In fairness, it should be noted that every annual Arab League summit robotically reaffirms some thirty resolutions that nobody gives any thought to or does anything about. These include, for example, ritual and useless calls for Iran to transfer Persian Gulf islands to the United Arab Emirates. Something similar happens at every United Nations General Assembly meeting.)

The API was approved in Beirut without the participation not only of half the Arab leaders, but also without the entire Palestine Liberation Organization delegation, which walked out in a huff to protest the lack of participation by their leader, Yasser Arafat. Israel wasn't the only country in the region with a grudge against Arafat. Ariel Sharon prevented Arafat from attending the Beirut summit because he blamed the Palestinian leader for terrorist attacks against Israeli civilians. Lebanese president Emil Lahoud, with backing from Syria's Bashar Assad, prevented Arafat from speaking to the summit by video hookup because Lebanon and Syria considered the PLO leader a traitor. In 1970–1971 the PLO he led had caused mayhem in Jordan; in the late 1970s and early 1980s, in Lebanon. (See chapter 10, "A Kind of Death Tango: Sharon and Arafat.")

One British media correspondent in Beirut that day summed up in Shakespearean terms the delicate issue of attendance at the summit: "The Arab summit in Beirut was Macbeth's dinner party without Macbeth or Banquo's ghost—or even Lady Macbeth."[4] Overall, the atmosphere in Beirut was less than tranquil, even if a significant facade of rare Arab unanimity had been presented.

Who, ultimately, "invented" the Arab Peace Initiative? The Jordanians credit the late King Hussein. Tom Friedman credits himself. The principal Palestinian official involved in developing and polishing the API, Nabil Shaath, also credits Friedman. Shaath's Palestinian version of the API narrative minimizes the Jordanian contribution. That position is generally characteristic of the attitude of the PLO, which nurses long-held grudges against the Hashemite Kingdom, where a large Palestinian demographic is subject to strict monarchical and non-Palestinian rule. Crown Prince Abdullah of Saudi Arabia credited himself.

One relatively independent observer of the goings-on at the Phoenicia Hotel in Beirut during those days at the end of March 2002 was Ezzedine Choukri Fishere. An Egyptian diplomat attached to the United Nations political office in Jerusalem, Fishere had earlier represented Egypt at its Tel Aviv embassy. A UN presence at the Arab League's annual summit, led in 2002 by Secretary General Kofi Annan, was standard practice.

Fishere is also an accomplished writer of fiction with an eye for detail and nuance that many of his fellow Arab diplomats in Beirut seemingly lacked. "I . . . wandered among Arab diplomats," he relates.

> I asked friends and former colleagues why Arab leaders bother at all coming up with an initiative if their assessment of the situation is so bleak. Some trivialized the whole affair: "The initiative says nothing new; we have been saying mutual recognition and 1967 borders for 30 years. . . ." Others speculated that the Saudi initiative was not meant to resolve the Arab-Israel conflict but to salvage Saudi-American relations, which were on the rocks since 9/11. Many spoke of irritation and suspicion among Arab leaders at the initiative: "Look who is present and who is absent." After pushing and pulling, the crafty Arab League chief drafted a compromise text while, ominously, a senior Saudi official had a heart attack and was carried out of the meeting on a stretcher.[5]

Ominously, indeed. The summit gossip mill quickly spread the rumor that the Saudi, allegedly Prince Nawaf bin Abdulaziz, and his friends had summoned Lebanese call girls to their hotel rooms. Prince Nawaf, in readying himself for a rousing session of sex, took an overdose of Viagra! Some versions of what followed allege he suffered a brain hemorrhage rather than a heart attack.

According to Fishere, one key theme of the API drama was Egyptian president Mubarak's opposition to what he perceived as Saudi meddling in Egypt's business: the peace process. The Saudis, Mubarak believed, were conniving via Friedman with Israel. In 2005 Fishere found himself back in Cairo at the Foreign Ministry. There, paradoxically, he was tasked with downplaying the API at Mubarak's behest, despite the desire of Arab League secretary general (and former Egyptian foreign minister) Amr Moussa to "relaunch" the API initiative.

Meanwhile, in Beirut, the UN team had tried in vain to persuade Syrian foreign minister Farouk al-Sharaa to drop any mention in the API of "the Palestinian refugee problem" so as to render the resolution more acceptable to Israel. Still, Muasher and other moderate Arab diplomats at the Beirut summit somehow convinced themselves that there was enough reasonableness in the API to enable and encourage Israel to address it positively. "If Israel wants security and seeks peace, this is the way to security," stated Saudi foreign minister Saud al-Faisal after the summit. "It cannot keep the land and demand peace."[6]

Was that indeed what the API was all about? An open offer of peace and security that Israel could easily address? Or did Arab actors such as the PLO, Syria, Lebanon, and particularly Saudi Arabia simply find the API very useful from an internal Arab standpoint. Fishere believes the main innovation of the API was introducing the element of normalized relations to the peace process, along with a "lighter version of the refugee issue."[7]

The Beirut Arab League summit of March 28, 2002, never mentioned the Park Hotel bombing or Yassin's defiant message regarding its objective. Retrospective references in 2019–2020 by Nabil Shaath and an Arab former foreign minister to the effect that the API had constituted an appropriate Arab response to that atrocity ring hollow. It is doubtful that they reflect sentiments actually felt and expressed in Beirut in 2002. Fishere relates that in Beirut "people weren't even paying attention to the fact it was Passover." The strongest reaction he detected to the Park bombing in the Phoenicia Hotel summit meeting hall was something like "Oh, shit."[8]

Stopping terrorism against Israel or even responding to it was not on the Arab agenda on March 28, 2002. Syria's Assad, asked about the Park bombing at a press conference in Beirut, dismissed it as "a detail in a broader picture. . . . Violence breeds counter-violence." Lebanon's Lahoud, fearing lest the API be manipulated to end the second Intifada, stated, "The big threat lies in our acceptance of international pressure to replace the Intifada simply with the end of violence and not with stopping occupation and recovering rights."[9]

If it did not address terrorism—against Israel or any other country— what did the API stand for? For the PLO, according to Nabil Shaath, drafting the API offered an opportunity to clarify the Palestinian position regarding the 1967 borders, the status of Jerusalem, and the 1948 refugee right of return and obtain unanimous Arab backing for it. For Syria, the challenge of the API was to line up the Arab world behind the demand that Israel return the Golan Heights, conquered in the 1967 Six-Day War. Also for Syria but especially for Lebanon, it was about getting rid of their

Palestinian refugee population. For Saudi Crown Prince Abdullah, according to Friedman, one key motive was a naked power play: outmaneuvering fellow princes seeking to unseat him.

This dovetails with Shaath's view that the real purpose of the API was to restore Saudi prestige that had been so sorely damaged by 9/11 and to establish Saudi Arabia as the unchallenged leader of the Arab world. "It was their proposal. . . . It looked like an attempt by an important leader of the Arab world who is seeking support from everybody, to be involved. In a way, Abdullah was eager to play a leading role in the Arab world . . . like Nasser in his day. . . . I was very close to [Abdullah]. I was sitting beside him [in Beirut]. The Arab leaders would come and tell him today you are the Arab leader." In Palestinian eyes, the Beirut summit did not in any way constitute a breakthrough toward peace with Israel. It was a breakthrough for the post-9/11 Saudis, who would now seek to be identified regionally and globally with the API and Arab-Israel peace.

Small wonder, then, that Riyadh withdrew its ambassador to Qatar, Hamad al-Tuaimi, within months of the Beirut summit. Qatar's provocative al-Jazeera satellite channel had aired strong criticism of the Saudi royal family in a June debate on the Arab Peace Initiative. Five years would pass before Crown Prince Abdullah would permit the posting of a new ambassador in Doha.[10]

Here we confront another explanation for the absence in Beirut of fully half the Arab leaders. Egypt's Mubarak and Jordan's King Abdullah may have stayed home not only due to fear of assassination by Hezbollah's violent Shiite Islamist militants. They may also have been motivated by reservations regarding the power play of the Saudi crown prince. They may have been piqued at Abdullah's success in sponsoring a pan-Arab peace initiative that they themselves had refused or failed to promote.

Then too, having made and successfully routinized their own peace with Israel, the Egyptian and Jordanian leaders may conceivably have been indifferent to the API itself.

9

ARIEL SHARON AND THE
ARAB PEACE INITIATIVE

In Jerusalem, Prime Minister Ariel Sharon did indeed take note of the API, not at the last minute but from the moment Tom Friedman "suggested" it. Considering how cynical Sharon was regarding Israel's Arab neighbors, his approach to the API requires some background elucidation.

Sharon's approach to all things Arab was very much molded by his experience as a young IDF combat officer in the 1950s. He led commando raids against Palestinian villages and refugee camps across the green line armistice boundaries with the West Bank and Gaza Strip.

The raids were a response to cross-border attacks against Israelis by Palestinian refugees who fled or had been forcibly expelled in the 1948 fighting. The refugees sought either to return to the villages they had abandoned or to make Israel pay for the *nakba*, the Palestinian disaster of destruction and exile.

The young Ariel Sharon's objective was to deter and punish the Palestinian *fedayeen*, or fighters. When Arab civilians got caught in the crossfire, Sharon seemed unconcerned with the niceties of the laws of war. That was the case in October 1953 when Sharon, heading IDF commando unit 101, led a revenge operation in the village of Qibya in the (then) Jordanian West Bank. Dozens of innocent Palestinian civilians were killed. It was the case in 1971 when Sharon, now a general, briefly cleansed the Gaza Strip of terrorists, in part by bulldozing entire Palestinian neighborhoods in the Gazan refugee camps. The objective was to make way for roads that Israeli tanks and armored vehicles could traverse.

Something worse happened in June 1982 when Sharon, now minister of defense under Prime Minister Menachem Begin, led an invasion of Lebanon. The aim, ostensibly, was to expel the PLO from that country and install a friendly Christian Maronite regime in Beirut. Operation Peace for Galilee culminated three and a half months later in a massacre of many hundreds of Palestinian civilians at the Sabra and Shatila refugee camps near Beirut. The perpetrators were Lebanese Christian forces allied with Israel. Following that horrific incident, an Israeli commission of inquiry barred Sharon from ever again serving as minister of defense.

That explains why in 2002 Sharon could be prime minister but not prime minister and defense minister, a double ministry held in the past by a number of Israeli leaders, such as Ben-Gurion, Rabin, and Barak. And Sabra and Shatila, preceded by Kibya and Gaza, in turn explain why Egyptian strategic scholar Abdel monem Said Aly refers to "Sharon, whose reputation in the Arab world . . . was at the level of Genghis Khan."[1] Yet less than twenty years after Sabra and Shatila, at the height of the second Intifada with its gruesome Palestinian suicide bombings, Israelis elected Sharon prime minister.

Sharon was a dynamic fighter, whether in 1950s border raids or leading the Israeli charge across the Suez Canal during the Yom Kippur War in 1973. He was charismatic, and soldiers who served under him tended to worship him. But from the 1950s to Sabra and Shatila, he was also brutal. Nor, for that matter, was he ever a strategic thinker. Rather, he thought tactically, without necessarily appraising the long-term consequences of his ideas and actions.

When asked once to explain the strategic underpinnings of his advocacy of building Jewish settlements in the West Bank and Gaza Strip—a project he championed as a minister in a number of Israeli governing coalitions—he took out a detailed map of the southern West Bank and pointed to a wadi, or narrow valley. "You see this wadi," he said. "This is where a Bedouin tribe lives (he named the tribe; he was familiar with every detail of West Bank demography and geography). Now do you see the next wadi over here? This is where a related tribe lives (he named that tribe too). Now look at the hilltop separating the wadis. I put a settlement there to keep the two tribes apart."

Applying this divide-and-rule pseudo-strategy to a far larger territory and population, Sharon went on to describe proudly how he had located settlement blocs in the Gaza Strip with the objective of fragmenting more than 1.5 million Gazan Palestinians. A few thousand settlers and their IDF protectors, tactically located, would ostensibly divide the Strip into three separate and more controllable population concentrations.[2]

Thus, "divide and settle" every wadi and every hilltop was Sharon's "strategic" approach to the West Bank and Gaza Strip. And not only his approach: Between the Oslo signing in 1993 and the outbreak of the second Intifada, the number of Jewish settlers in the territories doubled from 120,000 to 240,000. That took place primarily under Labor governments, with Sharon usually in the political opposition. This unbridled settlement spread undoubtedly provided a major catalyst for Palestinian dissatisfaction with the Oslo process leading up to the second Intifada.

Whether exploiting loopholes in the law and using political trickery to establish new West Bank and Gaza settlements or leading the Israeli counterattack against Egypt in October 1973, Sharon lived up to his reputation as a "bulldozer." In politics, too, he never quit. In 2001, when asked to explain his political recovery and elevation to the premiership after being condemned and forced to resign following the 1982 Sabra and Shatila massacre in Lebanon, he explained, "Politics is a giant Ferris wheel: you're on top, then you're on the bottom. The main thing is never to abandon the wheel."[3]

Clearly, then, Sharon was a believer in taking the offensive. He distrusted defensive thinking. As we shall see, when in the aftermath of the Park Hotel bombing Sharon's security staff advised erecting a fence and wall barrier to keep West Bank suicide bombers out of Israel, he agreed only reluctantly to such a "defensive" measure.

Sharon had a deep-seated conviction that Arabs could not be trusted as peace partners for Israel. He did not vote in the Knesset in favor of Israel's peace agreements with Egypt (1979) and Jordan (1994) and did not vote for the 1993 Oslo Accords with the PLO. He was absolutely convinced—not without reason, according to many Israeli intelligence sources—that Yasser Arafat conceived of the 1993–1994 Oslo Accords as little more than a tactic for undermining Israel through deceit and violence. Arafat's mysterious death in 2004 is attributed by some to a highly sophisticated poisoning operation engineered by Israel's intelligence community under Sharon's command.

But Sharon was also a pragmatist, relatively devoid of ideology. After opposing the peace process with Egypt that commenced in 1977, he volunteered to take responsibility for removing all Israeli settlements from the Sinai Peninsula in order to facilitate Israel's withdrawal in accordance with the 1979 peace treaty. In 2005, under pressure from President Bush to enter into peace negotiations with the Palestinians, Sharon went to great lengths to find an alternative. He preferred to withdraw unilaterally from the Gaza Strip and a small part of the West Bank rather than enter into a direct confrontation with Bush or be bound by agreements with the Palestinians.

By 2000, Sharon was acutely aware at his relatively advanced age (seventy-two) that to reach the pinnacle of leadership of Israel so late in life he needed to cultivate an image of measured statesmanship. He had to erase the impulsive bulldozer legacy of his earlier years in first the army, then politics. He was elected in February 2001 by a public frightened by the outbreak of the second Intifada and edgy about Ehud Barak's negotiating failures with both Syria and the PLO to the extent of trusting Sharon the aging warrior. But just to be sure, Sharon's TV campaign clips portrayed him cradling a newborn sheep on his farm not far from the Gaza Strip. The message was: gentle, grandfatherly, anchored in the land.

Even more surprisingly, after the lethal Dolphinarium suicide attack in Tel Aviv in June 2001, Sharon, now prime minister, abjured a military response and openly adopted a policy of "restraint is strength." He asked publicly for a mere "seven days of quiet" on the Palestinian side as a pre-condition for negotiating a cease-fire. Despite his loathing of Arafat, he talked with the PLO leader twice by phone and sent his son Omri to the Palestinian leader with personal messages that produced a brief but abortive cease-fire. He consulted with his colleagues and advisers and respected their advice even when he disagreed.

Accordingly, when Tom Friedman first publicly presented Crown Prince Abdullah's peace initiative, Sharon responded proactively. Better, he presumably reasoned, to preempt with two key initiatives and neutral-ize any conceivable pressures on Israel generated by the prospective Saudi peace plan.

One move was to publicly welcome the notion of an Arab Peace Initiative and even, discretely, seek involvement. Thus, as early as February 2002, Sharon began making generalized statements advocating an eventual peaceful settlement with the Palestinians. First, he insisted, the terrorist at-tacks had to stop. And he repeatedly identified Arafat as part of the terrorist problem, not the solution.

On March 23, Sharon actually noted in an offhand remark that he him-self should be allowed to attend the approaching summit, which would start in days. The Arab response to the man held responsible for Sabra and Shatila was instantaneous. Arab League secretary general Amr Moussa stated drily that the Arabs would consider the request, but also weigh whether to allow Sharon to leave Beirut and return to Israel. Lebanese prime minister Rafiq Hariri retorted angrily that Sharon "should stop killing Palestinians, with-draw and sign a peace agreement before talking about something like that."[4]

As we shall see, Sharon was not in the least deterred by the sharp Arab retort. Indeed, Moussa's pronouncement was an intriguing precursor to Sharon's attitude a week later regarding the prospect of Arafat traveling to Beirut—that Arafat could leave but not return.

A second initiative was to create a new post, prime minister, in the Palestinian Authority. Its occupant would be a more moderate and constructive figure than Arafat, who had been elected president when the PA was created by the 1993–1994 Oslo Accords. This would take advantage of Bush's antipathy toward Arafat and give Israel a more positive Palestinian partner to work with. Perhaps that would enable some minor bilateral progress toward reduction of violence and thereby render Arab and American initiatives alike less urgent.

Sharon and his entourage had plenty of ammunition for persuading the international community that Arafat should effectively be nudged aside or "kicked upstairs" by someone more constructive and moderate. Between the signing of the Oslo Accords in September 1993 and the launch of the second Intifada seven years later, the nascent Palestinian Authority had received more than five billion dollars in international aid. Arafat did not apply most of these funds to economic and infrastructure development that might improve Palestinian living standards and generate stability. Rather, he used the money to establish and maintain control over a cadre of supporters, including terrorists. With the exception of a brief period following heavy terrorist attacks on Israelis in early 1996, Arafat never confronted the more extreme organizations such as Hamas and never projected a sense of proper governance.[5]

Two senior security officials took on the task of identifying and crowning a PA prime minister: Efraim Halevy, head of the Mossad, and IDF chief of planning branch major general Giora Eyland (see chapter 3). Indeed, Halevy's activities combined both of Sharon's new missions: confronting the Arab Peace Initiative head-on and persuading the Arab world and the United States alike of the need for a Palestinian prime minister who would be easier to deal with than Arafat. Halevy traveled clandestinely to President Hosni Mubarak in Cairo and to King Hussein in Amman to sell them on the idea. He met with Prime Minister Tony Blair in London and with President Bush in Washington. He even met in Doha, Qatar, under the auspices of the royal family, with the obvious candidate for the job of PA prime minister, Mahmoud Abbas (Abu Mazen), who had spent years in Qatar.[6]

In February 2002 Halevy traveled to the Sultanate of Oman, an Arab country with which Israel, and Halevy in particular, had maintained longtime discreet relations. The British had brought Oman and Israel together. Britain's MI6 had assisted Oman's ruler, Sultan Qaboos, in seizing power in 1970. The crucial moment had been quite dramatic:

Sultan Qaboos bin Said al-Said ascended to power in Oman in 1970 by deposing his father. The British were closely involved in the plot, which involved getting Qaboos out of the detention his paranoid father had kept him in for six years. The father's *diwan* (court) chief, a Canadian named Tim Landon, confronted the father, Said bin Taimur, and told him to turn power over to his imprisoned son and leave the country. The father refused. Landon replied, "Don't you understand you have to do this?" "No, I don't," said the father, whereupon Landon drew his revolver and shot bin Taimur in the leg. "Now do you understand?" he asked.

The British, having witnessed Israel's military capabilities in Yemen and in the 1967 Six-Day War and being wary of the political ramifications back home of their own involvement in Yemen and Oman in an era of decolonization, then proceeded to bring Israel into the picture.[7]

Now, more than a month before the Beirut Arab League summit, Halevy asked a very senior Omani official to support the project of creating a Palestinian post of prime minister. The Omani, in turn, asked that Halevy relay an Arab request to Sharon regarding the Arab Peace Initiative: "We don't expect your prime minister to say yes. But we ask him not to say no." This was not a problem. Sharon, from his standpoint, knew he would have to react constructively if he wanted to blunt possible international pressures generated by the API.

Halevy passed this request on to Sharon from Oman in real time. In response, Sharon told Halevy to ask the Omanis to arrange an invitation for the Israeli prime minister himself to the Beirut Arab League summit, where the API would be discussed. Halevy: "I told the Omani, I have a good proposal for you: invite Sharon to Beirut." The surprised official, quite naturally fearing what Sharon would say in Beirut and presumably affected by Sharon's aforementioned "Genghis Khan" image, turned down the request. Halevy: "The Omani asked me, 'what happens if [a Sharon appearance in Beirut] fails?' 'That's the point,' I said, 'nobody can afford for it to fail.'"[8]

The Sharon/Halevy Beirut initiative indeed got nowhere. Instead, upon Halevy's return to Israel the Omanis relayed a suggestion that al-Jazeera interview Sharon regarding the emerging Arab League initiative. These days there is an al-Jazeera correspondent permanently in Israel; back in 2002, the idea of such an interview was revolutionary. Sharon agreed to the al-Jazeera interview, on condition that it take place face-to-face in Jerusalem. The Qatari satellite station got cold feet and insisted instead on a hookup from Doha, their home studio. In the end, and as anticipated, nothing happened: Sharon was not invited to Beirut and al-Jazeera did not interview him.

But Halevy had delivered a message to the Arab League via Oman and Qatar: Israel's prime minister was well aware of the League's impending peace initiative and would go through all the motions of welcoming it, however cautiously. Indeed, in March Sharon sent an adviser, Danny Ayalon, to Washington to solicit a meeting about the impending API with Adel Jubeir, foreign affairs adviser to Saudi Crown Prince Abdullah. This was the same Jubeir who had brought Tom Friedman to Saudi Arabia to discuss what became the Arab Peace Initiative. According to Ayalon, Jubeir backed out at the last minute.[9]

Sharon went public with his proposal to address the Arab leaders about their initiative on April 8. Barely ten days had elapsed since the Park suicide bombing, the League's endorsement of the Arab Peace Initiative, and the launching of Operation Defensive Shield. Addressing the Knesset, the prime minister commended "first signs of [the Arabs] taking their distance from the prolonged tendency to negate the very existence of the State of Israel. Despite the extreme demands included in the decision of the Arab leaders in Beirut, I welcome the fact that an Arab leader as important as Prince Abdullah of Saudi Arabia has for the first time recognized the State of Israel's right to exist within secure and recognized borders."[10]

Absent a Sharon-Arab summit to talk about it, the Arab Peace Initiative was greeted cautiously but encouragingly by the Israeli security and foreign policy establishment. Uzi Dayan: "The discussion was whether to accept partially, with comments and criticism, or to dismiss. . . . This was not a dramatic change [in Arab demands] but it was de facto recognition."[11] Shalom Lipner recalls a "response along the lines of 'We won't accept diktat, but sure, if they're serious, we'd be happy to test that hypothesis by meeting face-to-face to explore the possibility.'"[12]

Accordingly, Sharon went on to state in his April 8 Knesset speech, "The Saudi initiative comprises a positive component, but the details must be discussed among the parties themselves. We cannot accept diktats in peace negotiations. They must be based on mutual respect and on a sincere effort to reach a compromise. The initiative will remain devoid of content without free dialogue between the two sides regarding details."

After briefly laying out the Israeli position regarding relevant UN decisions and the refugee issue, Sharon stated, "Therefore I have proposed going to Beirut to meet with the leaders of Arab states. Readiness for peace has no meaning without readiness to meet. . . . I am ready to go anywhere, without preconditions from either side, to talk about peace. . . . I beg you to accept my initiative to meet, just as I am prepared to see the positive side of your recent decision and not just the negative."[13]

Sharon's post-Beirut public appeal to the Arab leaders did not resonate any more than did his pre-summit request for an invitation. A few of those leaders presumably recalled Sharon's attempt, via Halevy in Oman, to engage them prior to the events of late March and understood what he meant when he said, on April 8, "Therefore I have proposed going to Beirut." It is fairly certain that none of them understood the impact of the Park Hotel bombing on Israel's militant mood. Sharon's Knesset statement was made at the height of the West Bank fighting, an event to which he devoted the bulk of his speech. At the time, Arab public opinion was incensed over the Israeli West Bank offensive (see chapter 11).

No Arab leader responded. The Israeli public also paid little attention. Israeli Peace Index polls for March, April, and May 2002 did not even bother to ask the public about the API. Remarkably, reliable West Bank opinion polls from the same period registered two-thirds Palestinian support for the Arab Peace Initiative. On the other hand, the Palestinian polls neglected even to inquire about Tony Zinni's mediating effort. Further, they registered narrow majority support for "bombings inside Israel" and 86 percent opposition to the arrest by the Palestinian Authority of those who carry them out.[14] The dissonance between the two publics could not have been more jarring.

Sharon's cynical approach toward the very notion of peace with the Arabs was well known. Inviting himself to Beirut, whether before or after the March 28 summit there, was a throw-away proposal that had absolutely no chance of being taken seriously in view of his image in Arab eyes. Indeed, at the time it seemed to be little more than a cynical gesture made by an embattled leader with a bloody history of fighting and killing Arabs. Now, with Israeli forces overrunning and reoccupying the West Bank, Sharon was taking pains to portray himself unconvincingly and noncredibly as one for whom defeating terrorism would not be an end in and of itself but rather a road to peace?

Here, then, we may pause and contemplate the reaction of Arab state leaders to Sharon's concerted attempts, both clandestine and public, to solicit an invitation to Beirut. Sharon's monstrous "Genghis Khan" reputation in the Arab world was widespread. His record of slaughtering Arabs, or being somehow linked to the slaughter of Arabs in Kibya, Gaza, and Sabra and Shatila, was well known.

What was he thinking? Even assuming Sharon was understood by Arab kings and dictators to be bearing a message of peace and reconciliation—

a doubtful premise—they still have to justify to their publics extreme gestures like welcoming "Genghis Khan." Yet Sharon at the time had no peace plan, no specific gesture to offer the collective Arab League leadership. Under different circumstances, he could and did meet with individual Arab leaders. In June 2003 he even met in Aqaba, Jordan, with Jordan's King Abdullah II, Palestinian prime minister Mahmoud Abbas (see below), and US president Bush to endorse the Quartet's Roadmap (for details see chapter 12, "Sharon, Weissglass, and the American Effort").

Here a comparison to another Israeli hawk who is still around, Benjamin Netanyahu, is instructive. Upon assuming the Israeli premiership for the first time in 1996, Netanyahu visited President Hosni Mubarak of Egypt and King Hussein of Jordan. Egypt and Jordan were then the two Arab states with which Israel had peace treaties and diplomatic relations. Mubarak and Hussein had no problem agreeing to see Israel's fledgling prime minister despite his reputation as a hawk. There was no Arab blood on Netanyahu's hands. They would give him the benefit of the doubt.

After all it was a right-wing Likud leader, Menachem Begin, who had made peace with Egypt in the late 1970s. Perhaps the little-known Netanyahu was cast in his mold. It was not as if Israel's many left-wing leaders who governed from 1948 to 1977 and preceded Begin were understood by the Arabs to be dedicated to peace and compromise.

Netanyahu came to Amman and Cairo and, as noted earlier, offered his hosts profuse promises of an active peace process with the Palestinians. "I'll surprise you" was his slogan. It took a few years and a few more meetings until the leaders of Jordan and Egypt concluded they were dealing with a compulsive liar. Yet even in recent years they have met with Netanyahu—no longer to talk about peace, where he proved totally untrustworthy, but to discuss their shared enemies, Iran and ISIS. Against them, Israel under Netanyahu has been a reliable and valuable ally to the Arabs.

The drive to create the post of Palestinian Authority prime minister proved more successful than the task of soliciting an invitation to Beirut for Sharon. Halevy and other Israelis had sold the idea to President Bush as a means of imposing "reforms" and "checks and balances" on Arafat. PA reform was a precondition for US-sponsored Israeli-Palestinian peace talks. In this endeavor Israel had allies among the donor states that were keeping the PA afloat. The donors, led by the United States and the European Union, insisted on anti-corruption reforms as a condition for further support.

A number of prominent West Bank Palestinians, too, led by Finance Minister Salam Fayyad and by Azmi Shoebi, who headed an important economic committee in the Palestinian Authority parliament, were pushing a division of authority between Arafat and the soon-to-be-created post of prime minister. They met repeatedly with the donor representatives at the Grand Park Hotel in Ramallah. The project of appointing a prime minister and pushing for anti-corruption reforms in the PA seemed to be coming together.

The key candidate for PA premiership was Mahmoud Abbas, who was generally considered Arafat's number two. Abbas had led the Palestinian negotiations of the 1993 Oslo Accords. He had been encouraged by the Israelis and Americans to see himself as an eventual replacement for the problematic Palestinian leader. Abbas outspokenly opposed violence by Palestinians against Israelis. No one could link him to Palestinian terrorism.

This contrasted sharply with Arafat's image. Israeli intelligence believed the *Rais* was either engaged directly in terrorism or was maintaining a terrorist potential. He occasionally took pro forma action against terrorists in his midst but never engaged them in a life-or-death struggle.

Abbas had actually met with Sharon on June 16, 1997, at the latter's northern Negev farm near the Gaza Strip. At the time, Sharon was minister of national infrastructure in a Netanyahu government locked reluctantly in negotiations with Arafat over additional steps in the Oslo process. Sharon was plainly seeking to project a pragmatic and moderate image in order to upgrade his status with Netanyahu. Following that meeting, Abbas told aides and advisers that Sharon was someone he could do business with.[15]

Abbas briefly filled the post of Palestinian Authority prime minister from March to September 2003, before resigning due to Arafat's refusal to give him genuine control over the PA security services. It emerged that Arafat had deliberately divided responsibility for security between himself and Abbas in a lopsided way. Arafat retained control over the more central security agencies: intelligence, the Force 17 presidential guard, and the national security force, the closest thing to a PA army. Abbas was given the leftovers: the police, preventive security and rescue, and a firefighting force.[16] Small wonder Abbas felt helpless when confronted with a major Hamas suicide attack in Jerusalem that August.

Even though Arafat reputedly disliked him, Abbas remained Arafat's chosen successor. After Arafat died in 2004, Abbas was selected to succeed him as president, a position he still held in 2021. The post of prime minister has continued to exist ever since. But Abbas's open rejection of the use of violence and his commitment to Palestinian-Israeli security cooperation have, since 2004 and especially since the Hamas takeover of the Gaza Strip in 2007, rendered the Palestinian prime minister primarily an administrator of internal economic and governance tasks.

10

A KIND OF DEATH TANGO: SHARON AND ARAFAT

In March 2002, the fate of the Israeli-Palestinian conflict and by extension of the Middle East was to a large extent in the hands of two extremely problematic men. Ariel Sharon and Yasser Arafat were a fascinating study in similarities and contrasts. Nearly a decade after the Oslo process began and after Israel and the PLO had officially recognized one another in accordance with international law, the elected leaders of the two peace partners broadly viewed each other as the personification of evil. Each had a proven penchant for violence; each believed in the use of force for tactical-political purposes against a backdrop of a failed diplomatic or political process. The two leaders were locked in what veteran American mediator Aaron Miller called "a kind of death tango."[1]

Both Arafat and Sharon were short and had unattractive high-pitched voices, yet they evinced charisma. Neither was a serious strategic thinker. Indeed, each had barely escaped from a physically dangerous wartime impasse he had recklessly maneuvered himself into: Arafat in Beirut in 1982, Sharon in the fighting against Egypt in the Sinai Peninsula in 1956 and again in 1973.

Both, in person, seemed warm and genuine. They cared about their staff's personal problems. They remembered birthdays.

Both men served until stricken fatally ill. Sharon, dangerously overweight for decades, died of a series of fatal strokes that left him comatose for years. Arafat died of unknown causes. HIV/AIDS and leukemia are two conjectures; a highly sophisticated poison not traceable to his mortal enemy Sharon is another.

Both had problems with the truth. The ramifications were by turns infuriating, amusing, and possibly criminal.

Arafat was judged by many of his Israeli and Western interlocutors to be a compulsive liar. On one occasion in February 1995, he handed US congressmen visiting him in Gaza sloppily forged Israeli ID documents and alleged without blinking that they were genuine. The forgery was obvious upon superficial examination even by an untrained observer. The IDs had, Arafat claimed, been given by the Shabak to Palestinian Islamic Jihad, a Fateh ally. He alleged that they were part and parcel of an Israeli provocation, the Bet Lid double suicide bombing of January 22, 1995, that killed twenty-one Israelis.

On another occasion, at Arafat's Ramallah headquarters in the late 1990s, he was confronted by the testimony of the leader of an American Jewish advocacy organization that CNN had broadcast the exhortation of a Palestinian school teacher to her fifth graders to go out and murder Jews. Arafat feigned shock in an embarrassingly transparent way, then publicly admonished his minister of education to punish the teacher.

When these incidents transpired, you would look around the room and observe Arafat's most senior lieutenants dropping their gaze in embarrassment. A few days after the Ramallah meeting, one of Arafat's most effective international spokespersons, Hanan Ashrawi, remarked that "next time we have to organize the meeting with Arafat better."[2]

One of several international cease-fire-facilitating emissaries relates that Arafat's usual ploy in their meetings in early 2002 regarding suicide bombings was to exploit an obvious loophole in the Oslo Accords. Arafat would insist that the Palestinian perpetrators had entered Israel from Area B, the part of the West Bank that since the mid-1990s had been under Palestinian Authority political autonomy but Israeli security control. Alternatively, they had entered Israel from Area C, which encompassed fully 60 percent of the West Bank and remained under complete Israeli control. Area A (where Palestinians enjoyed civil and security autonomy and where Crooke, Zinni, and others would meet Arafat in the Muqataa in Ramallah) was, Arafat insisted, clean.

In other words, the only party to blame for the suicide bombings was Israel itself. This explanation of Arafat's was presented deadpan to his Western interlocutors. It contradicted massive evidence that the attacks were inspired and planned in Area A and that wanted Palestinian terrorists were holding up there.[3] Tulkarm, bordering on Israel, the town the Park Hotel bomber set out from, was in Area A.

Prior to Oslo, the Palestinian leader had been Israel's bitter enemy for more than three decades. He had led first the Fateh movement he founded, then the umbrella Palestine Liberation Organization, in acts of armed opposition that involved numerous terrorist attacks against Israeli civilians. An engineer who ironically had spent most of his early years not in Palestine but in Egypt and Kuwait, the near-mythological figure of Arafat became a flesh-and-blood peace partner to Israel with the successful conclusion in September 1993 of the Oslo behind-the-scenes negotiation.

Most Israelis who dealt with Arafat face-to-face emerged from the encounter with decidedly mixed feelings. The Israeli-Palestinian agenda was now peace and cooperation. Yet the diminutive Arafat with his grizzly beard, meaty lips, tiny hands, and soft handshake, dressed in an improvised uniform whose stylistic origins were somewhere between Che Guevara and Britain's WWII army, did not seem to project a strategic grasp of the requirements of a peace process. The more implicated he was by Israel's intelligence establishment in presiding over terrorism from the Muqataa in Ramallah, the easier it was to distrust the Palestinian leader.

So much for Arafat and truth-telling. As for Sharon, he was renowned for fudging operational reports early in his career. As an IDF commando officer in the 1950s, he was accused by Prime Minister and Minister of Defense David Ben-Gurion of bending unpleasant facts about civilian Arab deaths incurred in the course of reprisal operations he led. As minister of defense he famously misled Prime Minister Menachem Begin regarding the depth of Israel's planned penetration into Lebanon in June 1982. As we have seen, Sharon also had problems with money and the truth in some shady business dealings.

But that is where the similarities ended. Once enshrined as prime minister, Sharon's obfuscation and fabrications appeared to cease. Remarkably, he changed both his attitude and his politics and became extremely and courageously outspoken on such strategic issues as the two-state solution.

Arafat's handshake was soft and feminine, Sharon's steely. Arafat's subordinates were afraid to contradict him even when he blatantly lied or talked nonsense. Sharon's advisers openly argued with him and often won the day.

Arafat married late in life. First, he was "married to the revolution." Many Palestinians who knew him and worked with him believed his marriage was for reasons of public image, that is, to render him "father of the Palestinian nation." Some hinted that he was a closet homosexual operating in a very conservative culture.

Sharon by his eighth decade was a widower twice over; he married sisters, one after another. He was very much the family man though he never concealed his admiration for attractive women. His famous remark about US national security adviser Condoleezza Rice, "she has nice legs," was the topic of a panicked phone call from Sharon's son and confidant, Omri, to US national security Middle East adviser Bruce Riedel the night of Sharon's election in February 2001. The new prime minister, Omri relayed, was worried lest "Condi" take feminist offense. According to Riedel, she brushed off the remark with a laugh.[4]

Perhaps the most significant contrast between Sharon and Arafat, and the most relevant to our narrative, concerns the ultimate exercise of leadership. When the chips were down and a hard decision was called for, Sharon bit the bullet. He would decide, knowing that the direction he chose would prove critical to the future of Israeli-Palestinian relations yet could alienate an important faction among the leader's supporters. Arafat could not or would not.

The second Intifada and Operation Defensive Shield offer a helpful example. Arafat, as we have seen, consistently denied responsibility for violence against Israelis and deflected blame even when his role was obvious and beyond doubt. Perhaps more important, he simply would not act forcefully against the terrorists in his midst. Sharon, in contrast, relished his leadership role. At one point early in the second Intifada, Sharon presided over a meeting in which Shabak head Avi Dichter complained that the IDF would not provide the Shabak with the "tools" needed for carrying out targeted killings of terrorist leaders. IDF chief of staff Moshe Yaalon argued, "We have the tools Dichter is talking about, but they are for war." Sharon banged on the table, his nostrils flaring, and interrupted: "This is war." The tools were delivered.[5]

Similarly in 2005 Sharon, pressured to take a peace initiative by Bush and by many former comrades in arms in the Israeli security community whom he respected despite having for years rejected their dovish views, embraced his leadership role and opted for a dramatic unilateral withdrawal from the Gaza Strip. He even opted to withdraw from a small part of the northern West Bank as a kind of down payment on a larger withdrawal. In justifying his decisions he remarked to a senior aide, Dov Weissglass, that the Palestinian Authority was in any case already functioning as a Palestinian state[6]—in itself an extremely courageous statement.

Recognizing the de facto existence of a Palestinian state? Dismantling settlements? In Sharon's circles these were considered heretical views. Sharon knew that in so doing he would definitely lose one primary electoral support base, the West Bank and Gaza Strip settlers. And he would probably lose his principal political base, the Likud. He knew he would have to capture the allegiance of a highly suspicious Israeli left-wing camp. The left expected movement toward a negotiated two-state solution and not a non-negotiable fait accompli of withdrawal from Gaza. And he knew he would have to persuade Bush to abandon the last vestiges of the US Roadmap initiative and get behind Sharon's surprising concept of unilateral withdrawal.

Israelis argue to this day about the justice and security-wisdom of the Gaza withdrawal. Justice, in the eyes of the eight thousand or so evicted Gaza settlers and their many allies among West Bank settlers and on the political right in general. Security-wisdom, in the eyes of Israelis targeted from Gaza ever since by Hamas rockets, mortars, and cross-border tunnels. No one disputes that the decision required extreme political courage.

The Gaza withdrawal, along with the minor but symbolic West Bank withdrawal, was a monumental event in Israeli-Palestinian relations. Sharon knew he was exercising courageous leadership. At the time he reportedly told Dennis Ross, a veteran US mediator and troubleshooter for Middle East peace efforts, "My generation is the last one that is not afraid to make big decisions. I fear that the next generation will be led by politicians and they won't decide."[7]

In contrast, Arafat played a double game, balancing violence with cease-fire talks. At a nuanced passive level, he consistently shrank from confronting his archrival for control over Palestinian affairs, Hamas, which was openly dedicated to violence against Israel and rejected Oslo angrily. Fateh's jails were famous for their "revolving doors": Hamas, Palestinian Islamic Jihad, and even Fateh terrorists were occasionally arrested by the PA when it felt compelled to bow to Israeli and American pressure, then quietly released. Perhaps this modulated tolerance for Hamas and other terrorists reflected Arafat's own alleged ideological roots in the Muslim Brotherhood back in his Kuwait days. Hamas, after all, is the Palestinian branch of the Brotherhood.

Years before the Park bombing, Israeli intelligence sources had detected Arafat laying contingency plans for the second Intifada, which erupted in September 2000. An IDF intelligence report from February 2001 quotes Arafat asking Hamas leaders and his own security chiefs, "Why do the Jews not have more deaths?"[8] That was a typical deniable Arafat signal to ramp up the Intifada.

The *Karine A* affair (see chapter 2) was an indisputable instance of Arafat's clandestine preparations for violence. The *Karine A* captain in January 2002 acknowledged that he got his orders from Arafat.

Years later Hassan Yousef, a veteran West Bank–based Hamas leader, would testify to Palestinian al-Aqsa TV's *A Story from History* program concerning the years of the second Intifada. "At the time my office was the [Hamas] Movement's gateway to the PA. . . . everything that the [Hamas] movement wanted I would convey [to Arafat] and we would sit and reach understandings. . . . Arafat would say to us, 'At this stage we want to calm things' and we would calm them. . . . 'This time we want to move together and encourage things.' [We would] prepare the Intifada activities at these [meetings]."[9]

Despite, or alongside, these eyewitness testimonies, there remains to this day a school of thought among Israeli security officials who served during the second Intifada that exonerates Arafat of guilt for premeditating the violence. For example, then head of Shabak Avi Dichter believed the thousands of Palestinian prisoners detained at the time who argued that the Intifada began spontaneously. In contrast, IDF intelligence chief of assessment Amos Gilad believed Arafat was behind everything.[10]

Perhaps Arafat was better at revolution than at governance. At least he was better in his pre-Oslo days at stirring up revolutionary mayhem, insofar as ultimately Fateh's efforts at subversion in both Jordan and Lebanon failed spectacularly, although in Lebanon not necessarily to Israel's advantage. In each of those two countries in turn, both bordering on Israel, Arafat set up Fateh's cross-border guerrilla operations and global terrorist operations against Israel. In both cases Israel responded militarily against not only Fateh but its Arab hosts.

In Jordan in 1970–1971 this led to a civil war so brutal that Fateh fighters preferred to surrender to Israel at the Jordan River border rather than face death at the hands of Jordan's Arab Legion. As for Lebanon, Israel ended up invading in 1982, thereby eliminating Fateh's presence in the country but enhancing that of neighboring Syria. The Israeli invasion and occupation also spurred the emergence of the Iranian-proxy Lebanese Shiite Hezbollah, a consistently destabilizing actor ever since.

Lebanon and Jordan were not Arafat's only failures at strategic thinking. In retrospect it seems clear that in agreeing to the Oslo Accords and to the formation of the Palestinian Authority under his leadership, Arafat was over his head. Did he really think he could negotiate with Israel the emergence of a Palestinian state while tolerating, if not encouraging, brutal acts of terrorism against it?

Sharon's failures at strategic thinking were equally spectacular. Like Arafat, he misread the regional strategic picture with regard to both Lebanon and Jordan. Sharon's concept for Operation Peace for Galilee (the invasion of Lebanon) in 1982 was to engineer Arafat's expulsion from Lebanon via Syria to Jordan. In Jordan Arafat would, with Sharon's blessing, take over and "Palestinize" the country. Once Jordan became Palestine and Lebanon was ruled by friendly Maronite Christians, Israel's hand in the West Bank would be freed.

In the event, Arafat fled Lebanon for Tunisia, the "friendly" Maronites betrayed Israel's trust, and the IDF was stuck in Lebanon for eighteen bloody and traumatic years. An even more grandiose Sharon plan at one point reportedly involved selling the United States on an Israeli land invasion, via Jordan and Iraq, of Islamist Iran.[11]

In the Palestinian Authority after its formation in 1994, Ghassan Khatib was a witness to Arafat's problems in controlling even his own Fateh movement, much less Hamas. Khatib's version of Arafat as elected leader of the nascent Palestinian polity is more nuanced than the Israeli perception.

Khatib was minister of labor in the Palestinian Authority government from June 2002 and minister of labor and planning from 2003. He was affiliated with neither Fateh nor Hamas. He represented the far-left secular Palestinian People's Party in Arafat's government. The People's Party was founded in 1982 as the Palestinian Communist Party. It traces its roots all the way back to 1919, after the Bolshevik Revolution in Russia, when it was founded by Arabs and Jews alike in British Mandatory Palestine. In 1948 when Israel became independent, the joint Arab-Jewish communist party also spawned the Israel Communist Party, which exists to this day.

Fateh, Khatib testifies, was never unified and Arafat was never in total control. The Hamas suicide bombings of the second Intifada were extremely popular with the Palestinian public. They were so popular that some Fateh factions, fearing "losing everything," themselves adopted the suicide bombing tactic in order to compete.

Arafat, Khatib relates, nevertheless tried to maintain Fateh's dual role as the Palestinian counterpart to the Oslo Accords and to a cease-fire with Israel. He had an interest in ending the confrontation. Yet he failed to compel Hamas to comply. In this sense, Hamas was fighting two enemies: Israel and Arafat's Fateh. Charitably, Khatib describes Arafat as "a victim of Hamas." (Khatib's version is not too distant from that presented by several Israeli experts and cited in chapter 2.)

"Maybe he didn't manage well," Khatib adds. "I was not impressed with his management of relations with the Israeli side—not impressed with his government's performance, to say the least."[12]

Sharon, incidentally, appeared to manage his cabinet and staff with great efficiency and tranquility. Anyone entering the shatterproof thick glass doors of the "aquarium" in Jerusalem's Government Quarter—the Prime Minister's Office where his secretaries, aides, and close advisers were quartered—could not help but notice the quiet. Veteran visitors were struck by a decidedly positive contrast with the tensions and raised voices in the very same aquarium under Sharon's immediate predecessor, Ehud Barak.

Recalling Sharon's obsession with removing Arafat from the scene the day after the Park Hotel bombing (see chapter 5), it is fair to say that Sharon was by far not the only Israeli security or political leader who detested Arafat yet hesitated to touch him. During Israel's 1982 siege of Beirut, when an Israeli sharpshooter had Arafat in his rifle's crosshairs, then defense minister Sharon had been ordered by Prime Minister Menachem Begin to desist from targeting the Palestinian leader. Back then, Arafat was deemed an arch-terrorist ideologically distant from any prospect of dialoguing with Israel. It emerges that even twenty years before the Park Hotel suicide bombing an Israeli leader had been worried about the reaction of world opinion if he gave the order to dispatch Arafat.

When in September 1993 Israeli prime minister Yitzhak Rabin joined Arafat on the White House lawn in signing the Oslo Accords, more than one of Rabin's former comrades in the IDF command echelon refused to watch the event, broadcast live to the world. Major General (res.) Aharon Yariv, who headed IDF Intelligence under Rabin and had tracked Arafat for decades, remarked bitterly that he could only imagine what Rabin was going through.[13] The Israeli leader's hesitant body language and contorted smile upon shaking Arafat's hand famously broadcast his mixed emotions of loathing coupled with accepting the opportunity for peace.

★   ★   ★

At the Wye Plantation Israeli-Palestinian peace summit between Arafat and then prime minister Netanyahu in October 1998, Sharon, a minister in Netanyahu's government, was the only Israeli who refused to shake Arafat's hand. US president Clinton, who had convened the conference, tried in vain to bring the two together. So did Jordan's King Hussein. Sharon refused.[14] Arafat did not blink. Even before then, and until his death, Arafat was fond of telling Israeli interlocutors in what may have been a rare display of genuine candor, "You Israelis have the upper hand."[15]

Above: Sharon in the 1973 Yom Kippur War: mistrusted Arabs as peace partners, yet in 2002 sought an invitation to the Beirut Arab League Summit. (Israel Defense Forces Armored Corps Memorial Site)

Left: Yasser Arafat: How complicit was he in launching the Second Intifada? (Wikimedia Commons / Hans Jorn Storgaard Andersen 1999)

Prime Minister Sharon and US president Bush discuss the Second Intifada in 2001. (Wikimedia Commons / Executive Office of the President of the United States)

The Park Hotel in Netanya. (Wikimedia Commons / Dr. Avishai Teicher)

Park Hotel banquet hall after the Passover massacre. (Wikimedia Commons / Israel Defense Forces)

Beirut's Phoenicia Hotel: Hosted ratification of the Arab Peace Initiative the day after the Park Hotel bombing. (Wikimedia Commons / Wuseloo7)

Left: Crown Prince Abdullah of Saudi Arabia: official "father" of the Arab Peace Initiative. (Wikimedia Commons / Cherie Thurlby)

Right: Tom Friedman of the New York Times: Abdullah said to him, "You broke into my drawer. That plan you put out, that was my plan." (Josh Haner / The New York Times)

Left: Nabil Shaath: "The Arab leaders would come and tell [Abdullah] today you are the Arab leader." (Wikimedia Commons / Janwikifoto)

Right: Tony Zinni: The Park atrocity was "Israel's 9/11." (Courtesy of A. Zinni)

The Israel Defense Forces in Jenin: Heavy casualties fighting house to house. (Wikimedia Commons / IDF Spokesperson)

The Muqataa, seat of the Palestinian Authority government, 2013. Arafat in April 2002: "I am under siege." (PalestinianLiberator.tumblr.com)

11

MARCH 29, 2002: OPERATION DEFENSIVE SHIELD AND THE "INNER PALESTINIAN SOUL"

The Park Hotel bombing was the direct trigger for an immediate and massive Israeli invasion of the Palestinian Authority's territory in the West Bank. Operation Defensive Shield (Hebrew: *Mivtza Homat Magen*) involved about forty days of IDF occupation of the entire territory. Prime Minister Ariel Sharon publicly directed the IDF and the Shabak "to enter towns and villages that have become shelters for terrorists, to capture and detain the terrorists and their sponsors, to strike at anyone bearing arms, to neutralize anyone trying to oppose or endanger the actions of our forces, and to avoid injury to the civilian population."[1]

The immediate trigger for the operation was the Park Hotel suicide attack with its highly symbolic timing and heavy and gruesome casualty list. The deeper backdrop was January's *Karine A* capture, which led directly to Arafat, and the bloody month of March 2002. During that month alone, eighty-one Israeli civilians were killed in eleven suicide bombings culminating in the Park Hotel atrocity, and another thirty settlers and soldiers were killed in the West Bank. That on March 8 Sharon dropped his cease-fire precondition of seven days of quiet made no impression on the Palestinians fomenting repeated suicide bombings.

The entire Sharon government of more than thirty ministers approved the operation with the exception of two ministers from the left-wing Labor Party. One of these was Foreign Minister Shimon Peres, who abstained. Peres had been instrumental in generating the Oslo Accords with Arafat some nine years earlier. Now he presumably feared both for the fate of the peace process itself and for the international repercussions of such an extensive reversal of the Oslo dynamic. Regardless of the merits and justice of Defensive Shield, Peres's fears were justified: Oslo never recovered and international condemnation of Israel's tactics was extensive.

The operation commenced with the complete occupation of the Palestinian Authority capital of Ramallah, beginning with a brief battle at Menara Square near the southern entrance to the city. Arafat's Muqataa headquarters complex deep inside the city was now totally under siege. Several buildings in the compound were destroyed, leaving Arafat confined to his office. IDF troops pulled the air conditioners from the Muqataa walls to reinforce Arafat's discomfort.

One IDF commander described the scene as "exceptional and strange: On the top floor [of the Muqataa] we deployed three soldiers in rotation facing three holes in the wall. On the other side, through the hole where their weapons were placed, you could see Arafat's personal corner. . . . A large chair with gold facing, a fancy wooden desk, the smell of cigars."

Another officer was charged with climbing to the roof and firing a laser-guided missile past the window of Arafat's office to send a message to his security detail. IDF soldiers and officers gathered at the Muqataa windows "to watch the hottest movie in Ramallah." The missile hit near the window as intended, causing no Palestinian casualties. The IDF unit occupying nearly all the Muqataa remained there for several more days, hoping in vain for the command to eliminate Arafat.[2]

There remained with the Palestinian leader a number of aides labeled as "wanted" by Israel and a number of officials and advisers who simply happened to be in the wrong place at the wrong time. Eventually, after American intervention, those who were on Israel's wanted list would be delivered to Israeli custody.

For those simply trapped in the Muqataa due to the bad timing of their visits, one recourse was *wasta*, or pull. By the time a similar drama took place a few months later, during the Fall 2002 Jewish holidays, the process was more readily documented by PA minister of labor Ghassan Khatib. Following more Palestinian violence, the IDF had renewed the siege on the Muqataa. Once again, several PA ministers and additional high officials were caught inside the building by the sudden siege. Khatib, Finance Minister Salam Fayyad, and senior PLO activist Hani al-Hassan were among them. Some of the Palestinians began frantically phoning every well-placed Israeli they knew. They called family members who knew well-placed Israelis. Calls to cousins and brothers in the Persian Gulf Emirates bounced back to Tel Aviv and Jerusalem.

Within a day or so, *wasta* was effective. The IDF besiegers were instructed to allow a few select Palestinians, neither terrorists nor "wanted" persons, to leave. Khatib had just returned from Washington, where he had met on Arafat's behalf with the Quartet. He had been invited to the

Muqataa to report on the trip to Arafat. Now he was summoned by name by IDF officers using bullhorns and emerged with his hands raised. He discovered that the car he had used to get to the Muqataa a day earlier and parked outside Arafat's office had been flattened by IDF tanks. He walked home, thoroughly shaken by the experience.[3]

Based on extensive prior intelligence along with information picked up on the fly in captured Palestinian offices and from captured PLO fighters, in April 2002 Israel collected large quantities of weapons in Ramallah. The IDF also captured a number of senior terrorist leaders in the city. Chief among the latter was Marwan Bargouthi, a very senior Fateh leader implicated in terrorist attacks in Tel Aviv. All told, according to then head of Shabak Avi Dichter, the Shabak detained some eight thousand Palestinians during Operation Defensive Shield.[4]

Arafat, incidentally, reportedly thrived in the Muqataa under Israeli attack. "I am under siege," he told Zinni and Miller dramatically when, a week into Defensive Shield, the two US emissaries were permitted by Israel to visit him. The "vibe" Zinni got was that Arafat was defiantly reveling in his own mortality: "Let the next guy make peace."[5] Miller relates his own impression of the beleaguered Arafat: "It took me about ten seconds to understand that he was in his element, automatic weapon on the table, sitting defiantly at its head in his wrinkled Che Guevara outfit. . . . It was the struggle that now defined him, not its outcome."[6] If the idea of spooking Arafat with a siege and the occasional missile fired past his window was to break his spirit, the IDF's mission failed completely. If Arafat had indeed at some point aspired to control Hamas and maintain a cease-fire, that pose was history. Now he was a martyr to the struggle.

Nablus to the north of Ramallah, like Jenin farther north, would prove far more difficult objectives. Indeed, several West Bank towns were fortified and mined in advance by the PLO and Hamas. Nablus alone held more than eight thousand armed Palestinians, many holed up in the winding lanes of the casbah. The IDF deployed three brigades here and in the town's adjacent refugee camps. Israeli paratroops searched more than 80 percent of the town's houses, causing widespread damage.

The Jenin refugee camp witnessed Defensive Shield's bloodiest and most controversial battle. Only here did the IDF encounter serious, organized, armed Palestinian resistance. Many hundreds of booby traps in the camp's narrow lanes forced IDF troops to move from house to house by breaking through connecting walls. When they did try to advance through the camp's cramped alleys in order to limit Palestinian civilian losses, thirteen IDF reserve infantrymen were killed in an ambush. That is when the

Israeli army decided to introduce huge D9 bulldozers, which leveled an entire section of the camp, albeit after calling on the civilian population to evacuate.

Prior to Defensive Shield, Fateh proudly termed Jenin and its fourteen-thousand-strong refugee camp "capital of the suicide bombers." Terrorist activities there were coordinated among the three main Palestinian movements: Fateh, Hamas, and Palestinian Islamic Jihad. Once the IDF moved in, PIJ in particular was dedicated to a fight to the finish. Its combatants detonated gas canisters inside homes where, often, noncombatant residents remained and were, in effect, killed by Palestinian friendly fire.

One explanation for the close Palestinian inter-organizational operational coordination exhibited in Jenin was a kind of circular deal. Syrian funding for Arafat's Fateh was delivered by Palestinian Islamic Jihad, which had better relations with the Damascus regime than did Arafat. In exchange, Fateh relayed early warning of Israeli military movements that had been provided by Palestinian Authority counterintelligence. The latter obtained the information from Marwan Barghouthi's Fateh-Tanzim organization based in Ramallah.

The extensive damage in Jenin inspired and nourished inflated Palestinian claims of thousands of civilian deaths. Israel was hard put to disprove these accusations because for days it prevented the entry of observers and journalists to the Jenin refugee camp due to what it described as ongoing security threats there in the form of booby-trapped ruins and bodies. PLO senior spokesman Yasser Abd Rabo claimed that the IDF had murdered and buried nine hundred Palestinians in the Jenin camp.

The Palestinian claims inevitably led to international condemnation. The United Nations delegated Terje Roed-Larsen to investigate. Roed-Larsen, a Norwegian, had headed an Oslo think tank, Fafo, in the 1990s when he facilitated the Israeli-Palestinian informal negotiations that eventuated in the Oslo Accords. Now, as a United Nations under-secretary general, he visited the Jenin camp, but only after the IDF had kept him waiting for eleven days. There, he dramatically declared he had seen "horrifying scenes of human suffering. . . . Israel has lost all moral ground in this conflict."[7]

Eventually, commissions of investigation from Amnesty International and Human Rights Watch reduced the number of Palestinian casualties in Jenin to less than sixty, nearly half of whom were armed fighters. A UN report delayed until August put the Palestinian death toll at fifty-two, of whom more than half were armed combatants.[8] IDF figures updated to April 16 cited forty-six dead in the Jenin refugee camp, of whom only two were noncombatants.[9] IDF Central Command claimed that its forces had leveled only 130 buildings out of 1,896 in the Jenin refugee camp. According to an Islamic Jihad bomb-maker from Jenin quoted in Egypt's *Al-Ahram Weekly*, "We had more than 50 houses booby-trapped around the camp." A captured Islamic Jihad operative, Tabeat Mardawi, told CNN that more than one thousand explosive devices had been prepared.[10]

Most of this information arrived too late in terms of Israel's standing with world opinion. Nor did any of these clarifications stop Mohammad Bakri from traveling to Jenin shortly after the Defensive Shield fighting ceased and making an hour-long documentary about the death and destruction there.

Bakri is a Palestinian citizen of Israel and a greatly admired actor in Israeli films and stage productions. *Jenin Jenin* is a powerful film that presents a totally one-sided Palestinian narrative of the price paid by Palestinian civilians in the Jenin refugee camp in the course of Defensive Shield. The film features endless shots of destroyed buildings, interspersed with testimony of alleged Israeli atrocities. No atrocities are actually documented. The IDF is represented by brief media clips of tanks, bulldozers, soldiers.

A doctor describes Israeli rockets destroying a hospital. There are no before and after photos. "What harm have these houses done?" asks one elderly man against a backdrop of rubble. He points: "Here was a fig tree, here a lemon tree." "A hundred million Arabs are murdered." Everybody is traumatized. "How could destiny bring us together with such people?" asks one man, referring to Israelis. "We've been through three or four *nakbas*. That's enough!"

Nowhere in Bakri's film is the Park atrocity or Israeli fury over it and earlier suicide bombings mentioned as a factor in the Israeli attack on Fateh's "capital of suicide bombers." No one notes Palestinian fighters having been in the camp at all, only "our resistance." Nor is Israel blamed alone. President Bush, UN secretary-general Kofi Annan, Madeleine Albright, the Arab states, all abandoned the Palestinians. "What good is fighting when no Arab is able to do anything?" asks one seventy-two-year-old man.

Most of those whom Bakri interviews are old men and very articulate young girls, in other words, victims, not combatants. There is a deaf-mute man whose pantomime of IDF soldiers shooting speaks volumes. Palestinians are the morally righteous resistance fighters combating the morally depraved Israelis. That there is scant credible evidence for the film's claims is a testament to its skillful conception and presentation.

Indeed, it is hard after watching and listening to Bakri's witnesses to accept the perpetual Israeli claim, war after war, that "the IDF is the most moral army in the world." And it is hard to justify the then thirty-five-year-long occupation of the West Bank. "After this, coexistence with Jews is impossible," states one man interviewed in the film. "They are the real losers."[11] *Jenin Jenin* is a skillful effort at blackening Israel's image. It is also a testimony to the seeming impossibility of reconciling Israelis and Palestinians.

Jenin Jenin sparked controversy in Israel, where anger at Bakri mounted. IDF reservists who had served in Defensive Shield subjected Bakri to an escalating series of libel charges, appealing all the way to the Supreme Court. Israel's courts determined that the film contained lies and libel, but not libel directed at specific individuals. Hence the film was protected by Israel's freedom of expression laws. In a 2020 interview, Bakri, in the spirit of "fake news" and "alternative facts," readily admits that "no one has a monopoly on the truth. . . . Perhaps someone exaggerated due to trauma and the terrible wound. I'm sure there were exaggerations. But an exaggeration is not necessarily proof of a lie. I tried to portray in great detail the inner Palestinian soul."[12]

The IDF's April 2002 Jenin operation not only involved the loss of twenty-three soldiers. It also clearly constituted an abject Israeli failure at integrating the media into a military operation and explaining Israel's military goals and calculations to the international public.

One additional urban operation of note was in Bethlehem, where 39 armed Palestinians led by Colonel Abdullah Daud, head of PA Intelligence in the town, barricaded themselves in the Church of the Nativity with around 250 civilian hostages, including 46 priests. The IDF wisely backed off from trying to enter the church, merely surrounding it, lest an Israeli attack destroy a major Christian shrine. International mediation, first by the UK's MI6, then by the CIA, was solicited. On May 23 the siege ended with the Palestinian fighters not surrendering but rather accepting exile, either internally or abroad. Another Israeli tactical non-victory.

One particularly troublesome Israeli operation early in Defensive Shield, on April 1, was the occupation and destruction of Jibril Rajoub's security headquarters building in Beitunia, near Ramallah. Rajoub, who for years had worked closely with Israel's security forces, had kept his cohorts out of the second Intifada fighting and had paid a price in condemnation by more militant Palestinians. His Gazan counterpart, Mohammed Dahlan, may have maliciously told Israel that Rajoub was harboring a large number of wanted Palestinians. Dahlan, after all, was also Rajoub's rival for Arafat's attention. In the event, once Rajoub's headquarters was in ruins it emerged that the number of wanted Palestinians there was low.

With or without Dahlan's contribution, the destruction of Rajoub's headquarters testifies to the aggressive mood that gripped Israel's security leaders after the Park bombing. They insisted on total Israeli security autonomy in the West Bank and downplayed the need to locate and work with friendly Palestinian forces. One way or another, Rajoub was a casualty: discredited, humiliated, no longer an active peace advocate.

Operation Defensive Shield was a radically one-sided affair. It pitted one of the world's most battle-hardened and best equipped armies against a ragtag collection of militias and terrorists. All in all, more than a month of combat in the West Bank showed that the Palestinians had no defense against Israeli tanks and D9 bulldozers. On the other hand, to capture terrorists in the narrow warrens of Palestinian towns and refugee camps the IDF had to risk, and sacrifice, the lives of foot soldiers in brief bouts of one-on-one urban warfare.

As veteran Israeli military affairs commentator Ofer Shelah wrote several years later, captured Palestinian fighters alleged that they had not believed Israel would pay such a high price in its soldiers' lives. It was this face-to-face encounter with Israeli soldiers that most convincingly drove home to Palestinians the message of Israeli power. In contrast, Israel Air Force bombings of West Bank targets seemingly only proved to Palestinians that the IDF was afraid to fight. In Palestinians' eyes they also legitimized Palestinian suicide bombings: Since you attack us with weapons we can't oppose, we'll do the same to you.[13]

By mid-May 2002, Israel could claim a dramatic reversal of the momentum of the second Intifada, though not before forty more Israelis had died in suicide bombings. The West Bank terrorist infrastructure that Arafat had built up during more than half a decade of security autonomy was dismantled. Some 1,500 of the 10,000 Palestinians who were detained by Israel would soon be sentenced to long jail terms. Piles of captured documents linked Arafat directly to Palestinian terror operations, including providing the financing. Palestinian sniper fire on outlying neighborhoods of Jerusalem ceased.

From herein, Israeli losses would be considerably reduced though by no means eliminated. The second Intifada would continue for another two years. The most senior Hamas leaders who, by remote control, were behind the West Bank–based suicide bombings remained active in the Gaza Strip. Still, the IDF would from herein enter and roam the West Bank part of the Palestinian Authority at will, including the previously impenetrable casbahs and camps of Nablus and Jenin. The security fence, a parallel outcome of the Park bombing, would further contribute to a reduction in terrorist intrusions from the West Bank.

Uzi Dayan, Sharon's national security adviser, summarized: "If you destroy enough, capture and hurt enough terrorists, damage terrorist infrastructure like workshops that produce weapons or explosives, you show them who's in charge. . . . [Yet] we didn't want to hurt the PA too badly, but rather Hamas, knowing that this would not bother the PA."[14] In other words, Israel still needed a potential Palestinian partner and for the time being that would remain Arafat, warts and all.

Still, the international condemnation was deafening. Even US president Bush, an out-and-out admirer of Sharon, declared on April 5 "enough is enough"[15] and sent Secretary of State Colin Powell to the region. Sharon undertook once again to work with the Americans to achieve a cease-fire with the Palestinians even as, in private, he remained deeply skeptical. He replied in the Knesset to his European and Arab critics with bravado: "If I have to decide between your difficulties with public opinion in Europe and the discomfort of the rulers of countries in the region [on the one hand], and the need to prevent daily acts of murder [on the other], it doesn't take me more than a second to decide."[16]

Looking back on Brigadier Yossi Kuperwasser's futile attempt the night of March 28 to persuade Sharon to give the United States advance notice of Defensive Shield, it turns out that Sharon's refusal was well grounded. Had he given Washington, through Zinni, a heads-up, it is possible President Bush would have phoned Sharon and demanded that Israel, in the interest of a more energetic American mediation effort, not retaliate at all.

Before Defensive Shield began, Sharon would have been hard put to say no to the American demand. Once the operation was underway, it was easier to yield to Bush's entreaties by evacuating smaller Palestinian towns such as Tulkarm and Qalqilya that had been quickly subdued by the IDF. Note that Tulkarm, where the Park bombing originated, was considered by the IDF less threatening to Israeli security during Operation Defensive Shield than bigger West Bank cities such as Jenin and Nablus.

12

SHARON, WEISSGLASS,
AND THE AMERICAN EFFORT

Prior to the Park bombing, and as Palestinian-Israeli violence worsened, the United Nations Security Council on March 12, 2002, passed Resolution 1397. Drafted by the Bush administration, 1397 for the first time supported the establishment of a Palestinian state. This fulfilled a commitment made by Bush earlier, in November 2001, to the UN General Assembly. For all his post–*Karine A* reservations about Arafat and his hesitation and distraction with the spillover from 9/11, this would be Bush's singular contribution to the Israeli-Palestinian peace process. Inevitably, it provided wind in the sails of the emerging API, which was scarcely weeks away.

Bush had actually signaled to Saudi Crown Prince Abdullah earlier, in late 2001, that he would support a viable independent Palestinian state. The idea then was to use the Palestinian issue to shore up US-Saudi relations, which had been seriously challenged by 9/11 and Abdullah's famous threatening letter on the eve of that disaster. Yet Bush was never enthusiastic about the Arab Peace Initiative as an immediate catalyst for Israeli-Palestinian peace. After all, Israel had demonstrated clearly to the US president that Yasser Arafat was deeply involved in arms smuggling to fuel the second Intifada.

Instead, repeated Arab appeals to Bush to intervene more energetically to reduce Israeli-Palestinian violence produced missions to the region by the likes of Zinni, Miller, Vice President Cheney, and his envoy, John Hannah. Secretary of State Colin Powell also got involved. Yet Bush was skeptical and otherwise preoccupied. Indeed, by this time he was far more deeply committed to planning a US invasion of Iraq than to ending Israeli-Palestinian violence or embracing an initiative like the API. UNSCR 1397 would suffice.

Both Israel and the Arabs were aware that the Bush 43 administration was less than fully committed to orchestrating peace between them. Palestinians and Israelis were correspondingly disincentivized to make the painful concessions necessary for progress.

Looking back to previous decades, we find two relevant models of a US role in Israel-Arab peacemaking. One may be described as positive. In the second model, the United States was initially unhelpful and even mounted obstacles to progress.

In the positive model, American leaders such as Henry Kissinger, Jimmy Carter, and the Bush 41/Baker team were very actively committed to Israel-Arab peace. They registered dramatic progress in the form of Israeli-Egyptian and Israeli-Syrian disengagement agreements on two fronts in 1974–1975 following the 1973 Yom Kippur War. The United States also dynamically shepherded the Egypt-Israel peace treaty in 1978–1979. And it organized the Madrid Conference in 1991 in the aftermath of the First Gulf War and the collapse of the Soviet Union, with the aim of advancing a broad Israel-Arab peace process.

The second model appears three times in recent history. Here a willing Israel and a willing Arab partner did not need the United States in order to register a dramatic breakthrough toward bilateral peace. The Sadat trip to Jerusalem of November 1977, the Palestinian-Israeli Oslo agreement of September 1993, and the Jordan-Israel peace breakthrough of mid-1994 all transpired despite US reservations that obliged the Middle East partners to operate behind Washington's back. Indeed, Washington's focus on its own alternative ideas was obstructionist, thus mandating Israeli and Arab secrecy. To be sure, upon registering dramatic progress on their own, the Israelis and their Arab partners sought and received massive American backing.

Israel and the PLO in 2002 did not fit either model. They needed a lot of help from the United States but it was less than forthcoming. And they were incapable of progressing on their own.

Here it is useful to recall that the neocon actors in Bush 43's administration were skeptical about any Israel-Arab process that demanded of Israel territorial concessions. Cheney, his assistant for national security affairs, Scooter Libby, and Elliott Abrams of the National Security Council often went out of their way with last-minute phone calls to demand that Bush's representatives in the region present the Roadmap in public as little more than an idea, a kind of beginning. It must not develop into a territories-for-peace process between Israel and the Palestinians. It must not negatively affect Israel's West Bank settlements.

The neocon pressure on the non-neocon sector of the Bush administration was not gentle. At one point, Abrams admonished US ambassador to Israel Daniel Kurtzer apropos the US call for an Israeli settlement freeze, "We don't quote the president on settlements." At another, an attempt by Powell to leverage a meeting with Arafat into an optimistic press conference was cancelled abruptly at the last minute by Bush himself.[1]

This neocon approach to Israeli-Palestinian relations, coupled with the countdown to the invasion of Iraq, had a dampening effect on President Bush's energy level regarding Israel and the Palestinians. Aaron Miller, the veteran US peace process troubleshooter, is today convinced that Bush had no intention of seriously pursuing an Israeli-Palestinian process.[2]

Certainly not after 9/11, when neoconservative influence on Bush's strategic approach grew exponentially. The US president displayed no serious independent strategic thinking regarding the Middle East or anywhere else in the world. (The sole possible exception was Africa, where Bush shepherded South Sudan's independence and spearheaded the fight against HIV.) Now, under neocon tutelage Bush introduced such aggressive concepts as the Axis of Evil (Iraq, Iran, North Korea). He launched a War on Terror that involved preemptive attacks against terrorist havens.

Bush also prepared to invade Iraq, not a terrorist haven. Cheney and a host of neocon thinkers in the administration favored proactive US military activity, coveted Iraqi oil, and advocated a more passive policy toward that alternative Middle East preoccupation, the Palestinian issue.

Not surprisingly, then, the only concrete innovation eventually to emerge from all this activity was the "Performance-Based Roadmap to a Permanent Two-State Solution to the Israeli-Palestinian Conflict." The Roadmap was unveiled on April 30, 2003, more than a year after the events of late March 2002. Its main distinguishing feature was its sponsorship by the Quartet: the United States, the European Union, Russia, and the United Nations. One may speculate that by bringing into the Roadmap the international community and making the two-state solution an international rather than a specifically American project, Bush and Powell were able to overcome the objections of their neocon mentors.

But the Roadmap would not produce peace. It comprised (see appendix 2) detailed timetables for ending violence, entering into negotiations, and verifying compliance with cease-fire and de-escalation provisions. It made progress toward reducing both terrorism and Israeli reprisals. But it did not significantly advance a new peace process. Ultimately, the Roadmap's collapse coincided with a decision by Sharon to preempt and initiate a unilateral Israeli withdrawal from the Gaza Strip and northern West Bank.

Israel's prime minister, we recall, had previously been deterred by the very notion of negotiating a deal with the Palestinians and was uncomfortable dealing with the Quartet, preferring to talk only with the Americans.

Bush had inherited the second Intifada from his predecessor in the White House, Bill Clinton. This very bloody and extended round of violence began on September 28, 2000, on the occasion of a visit by Sharon, then heading the Likud opposition to the Barak government in Israel, to the Temple Mount in Jerusalem.

True, Sharon's behavior and rhetoric on the Mount were provocative. The timing interfered with Prime Minister Ehud Barak's effort to salvage something from the failed Camp David summit of July 2000. Clinton was as yet working toward proposing his own parameters for peace. But Sharon's provocation was aimed at outflanking his political rivals in Israel—Benjamin Netanyahu at the level of Likud leadership and Barak in anticipation of elections—not Arafat. Besides, Israelis visited the Mount constantly.[3] Sharon's visit ignited the second Intifada because Arafat willed the outbreak of Palestinian violence and Sharon mischievously and conveniently provided both an excuse and good timing. The violence began on the Mount itself and quickly spread.

One link between Clinton's hands-on approach and Bush's half-hearted attitude to the broken peace process and the second Intifada would be the committee appointed by Clinton to look into this latest confrontation. The Sharm al-Sheikh Fact-Finding Committee was chaired by former US senator George Mitchell. The committee report, including recommendations for restarting a peace process, would be delivered in April 2001 to the Bush administration, three months after Clinton left office. Secretary of State Colin Powell accepted the recommendations despite skepticism emanating from the rest of the Bush administration with its heavy neocon presence. There followed the Tenet mission, led by CIA director George Tenet, laying out recommendations for reaching an Israeli-Palestinian cease-fire.

Ambassador Fred Hof was chief of staff of the Mitchell Committee and the principal author of its report. He notes that

> once Sharon took power we had the full cooperation of the GOI [government of Israel]: he told Martin Indyk [until June 2001 US ambassador to Israel], "I don't like this committee, but Israel agreed to it and we're not a banana republic." Both sides praised the report's integrity and balance. But each side wanted the other first to start implementing the recommendations pertaining to it, and the "cooling off period"—

an unfortunate phrase used in the report—gave Israel an advantage in delaying.

Mitchell told Powell, "Colin, our report will not implement itself." Yet the failure of Bush and Powell to follow up instantly helped to produce the disaster brought about by terrorists. . . . the vacuum created by non-implementation was filled within weeks. . . . I think the Mitchell Report was the last shot for a two-state outcome, and that the failure of both sides to engage in timing and sequencing discussions for implementation doomed the effort.[4]

Then came the Zinni mission, which featured two visits to the region between November 2001 and April 2002.

In retrospect, Zinni's mission was a good indicator of the fruitless nature of the Bush administration's Israeli-Palestinian peace efforts. Zinni was charged by Powell with achieving an immediate cease-fire. This was rendered impossible first by the *Karine A* revelations of January 2002, then by the Park Hotel attack, which Zinni labeled "Israel's 9/11 . . . I knew immediately we had come to the end of the road."[5]

In between *Karine A* and Park, after several meetings with Arafat, Zinni became convinced the Palestinian leader was not prepared to order a crackdown on the Hamas and Islamic Jihad terrorist networks in his midst. His skepticism was not muted even when confronted with a concession by Sharon: a troop withdrawal from parts of Area A the IDF had occupied. Nor did Sharon and Mofaz's reluctant acceptance of all of Tenet's security recommendations dispel Zinni's pessimism. Indeed, an always-suspicious Arafat accused Zinni of conspiring with the Israelis regarding the Tenet proposals.

Actually, Bush wanted to end the Zinni mission early, before the Park atrocity, but was prompted to continue by news from Riyadh of the emerging Arab Peace Initiative. Obviously, it would constitute an unnecessary provocation to remove Zinni at the very moment Crown Prince Abdullah, a key US ally, was readying the Saudi initiative.

The Zinni mission officially ended March 1, 2003, nearly a year after the advent of the API, even though Zinni departed the region for good in April of 2002. Already in June 2002, Sharon and Bush both refused any more dealings with Arafat. It was then that Bush's Roadmap to Peace—effectively the next but not the last abortive American initiative in the conflict—was mentioned in a speech by Bush.

By the by, in the emotional hubbub following 9/11, Sharon irresponsibly accused Bush of selling Israel out "Munich style" by not recognizing that Israel, too, had long been a victim of Islamist terrorism. The reasoning behind Sharon's Munich tirade was, according to Deputy Foreign Policy Adviser Shalom Lipner, an "underlying fear that Israeli concessions could be the currency with which Bush might decide to buy his post-9/11 Arab coalition."[6]

Prompted by US ambassador Kurtzer, Sharon quickly apologized to Bush and patched up the damage. He then proceeded to take a major new step, at least in part to conciliate Bush. After April 2002 he began to speak publicly about "ending the occupation," dismantling settlements, and the need to accept a compromise two-state solution. This flip-flop particularly angered the West Bank and Gaza Strip settlers, whose cause Sharon had long championed and who had been his most vocal supporters.

Was Sharon simply trying to placate Bush and keep him on Israel's side? Some Israeli political observers attributed Sharon's newly minted dovishness to Dov Weissglass, Sharon's longtime personal lawyer, who was installed as director general of the Prime Minister's Office in mid-April 2002. This was scarcely two weeks after the Park Passover attack. Weissglass's dovish views were well known.

Eyebrows were raised on the Israeli political right. Some right-wingers now sought to implicate Sharon and his son Omri along with Weissglass in questionable dealings with Austrian tycoon Martin Schlaff and Arafat's Gazan security adviser Mohammad Dahlan. Prior to Sharon's election to the premiership, they had allegedly been involved in a casino project in Jericho in the West Bank and another aboard a ship in Israel's Red Sea port of Eilat.

Somehow, by extension, Sharon's former right-wing settler allies, now vociferous critics, alleged that he had been blackmailed by Weissglass and forced to adopt dovish views regarding a Palestinian state. At a minimum the casino deal with the Palestinians implicated Sharon in a potential conflict of interest that it was Weissglass's job to neutralize. Yet these highly conspiratorial settler explanations for Sharon's growing moderation did justice neither to Sharon's political evolution nor to Weissglass's apparent role.

Weissglass's professional and personal profile and his protracted relationship with Sharon require greater elaboration. Weissglass was a criminal defense lawyer. He represented a number of Israelis with security backgrounds in court cases and in hearings held by the official investigating commissions that inevitably followed upon Israel's more problematic wars: the 1973 Yom Kippur War and the 1982 invasion and occupation of Lebanon. He first came to know Sharon in 1982, twenty years before the Park atrocity and Operation Defensive Shield.

Weissglass represented Sharon before the commission of inquiry that looked into the Sabra and Shatila atrocity that so badly blemished Sharon's record in Israel's First Lebanon War. Weissglass represented Sharon again a few years later when Sharon successfully pressed a libel charge against the American weekly magazine *Time*, which had reported that Sharon had personally encouraged the Sabra and Shatila massacre by a Lebanese Maronite faction allied with Israel.

Between 1982 and 2002, Weissglass argues,[7] Sharon's views on solving the Palestinian issue underwent a transformation. Sharon came to believe that only he was capable of reaching and implementing an agreement with the Palestinians. Sharon's disastrous 1982 experience in Lebanon, Weissglass adds, also made him an extremely cautious military decision-maker. It explains why Sharon refused to launch Operation Defensive Shield earlier than the end of March 2002, despite Israel's heavy losses from Palestinian terrorism prior to then. "Sharon acted with great restraint as one of his lessons from the First Lebanon War" of 1982, Weissglass explains. "He looked for consensus before taking a military initiative."

Aaron Miller was a veteran Sharon-watcher and he concurs with Weissglass regarding Sharon's "post-Lebanon rehabilitation." As prime minister, Sharon knew he had to avoid alienating Washington and to recognize Israel's military limitations.[8] He took his distance from earlier "Jordan is Palestine" schemes (see chapter 10). Hashemite Jordan, he now understood, offered Israel important strategic depth. Together with Israel, it could "sandwich" and deter a West Bank–based Palestinian state.

Weissglass also has a partial explanation for the link between Sharon, his son Omri, Mohammed Dahlan, and Austrian tycoon Martin Schlaff. More than a year prior to joining Sharon's staff officially, Weissglass had tried on behalf of Sharon to negotiate an early cease-fire and an end to the second Intifada. The negotiations were with Dahlan and they centered on the casino Schlaff had built in Jericho in which, apparently, all the principals noted here had a prior financial stake.

Those early negotiations failed. The casino has had a more checkered history. It opened in 1998 in the four-star Oasis Hotel just outside of Jericho. Israeli law prohibits the existence of gambling institutions on Israeli soil. But Jericho was never part of Israel. It was the first autonomous West Bank town under Oslo, and for years it had been relatively peaceful and accessible to Israelis. Hence beginning in 1998, in the heyday of Israeli-Palestinian commercial cooperation linked to the advent of the Palestinian Authority, Israelis hankering to gamble were offered easy access to the Jericho casino. Schlaff and his Israeli and Palestinian partners would make money, and Israeli-Palestinian economic coexistence would blossom. The setup was not very different from that in Native American autonomous reservations that feature gambling. In 2005, after years of second Intifada violence, the casino closed, only to reopen in 2015.

The Jericho casino was not Ariel Sharon's only financially tenuous adventure. His readiness to accept money and financial benefits from a variety of admiring tycoons in return for shadowy "favors" was well known decades earlier. Among the alleged shady dealings was the financing of the land purchase and construction of Sycamore Ranch, Sharon's northern Negev farm and home. There was also a suspicious link to a deal involving purchase by a wealthy Israeli of a Greek island. Throughout, Sharon was shielded by his sons, Omri and Gilad, and by Weissglass's legal maneuverings.

Sharon arrived at the Prime Minister's Office in early 2001 with all this unsavory baggage. Very senior security advisers such as Efraim Halevy and Uzi Dayan could not help but notice. They proceeded, for reasons of ethics and reputation, to take their distance on occasion even at the possible cost of exercising influence within the Prime Minister's Office. Worse, in 2006 Omri Sharon resigned from the Knesset, to which he had been elected in 2003, and submitted to a nine-month jail term for campaign fundraising violations widely attributed to his father.

None of this deterred the elder Sharon, the bulldozer, in the least. We have already noted that he had a strong pragmatic streak. As a totally secular Jew, he lacked any religious-messianic sentiment about the settlements. He supported the settlements because he thought they provided a measure of tactical security against Palestinian aggression. That he found political allies among the ultranationalist messianic settlers was a marriage of convenience, not principle.

Yet that marriage, and the political cynicism behind it, carried Sharon through the 2001 elections. He defeated Ehud Barak for the premiership on the basis of a platform that denigrated the entire Oslo peace effort. Regarding Sharon's professed devotion to the Greater Land of Israel prior to becoming prime minister in 2001, veteran Israeli press and TV journalist Amnon Abramovich testifies: "A few days after Netanyahu established his first government, in 1996, I sat with him for a background conversation. He stated that he intends to implement the Oslo Accords in three phases, three ticks of the clock. That evening on primetime TV news I called them three 'beats' or 'pulses.' After the broadcast, Arik [Ariel] Sharon called and berated me: 'That guy (Bibi) is returning parts of the homeland and your heart throbs? What is your heart beating about? There were heartbeats when we declared the creation of the state, not when we give up its land.'"[9]

Yet as prime minister and as a pragmatist, and when confronted by pressures and emerging realities, Sharon proved perfectly capable of rethinking the settlements. As this fascinating process unfolded, he was fond of quoting to a bewildered public a line from a Hebrew song composed by Yaakov Rotblit and made popular in 1994 by singer Yehudit Ravitz: "Things you see from there you don't see from here." This, he indicated on dozens of occasions and in repeated remarks widely disseminated, explained why becoming prime minister had changed his point of view.

As Halevy and Dayan dropped out of the picture, Weissglass came to play an increasingly prominent role in representing Sharon in dealings with both the Americans and the Palestinians. Sharon was neither the first nor the last Israeli prime minister to discover the advantage of bringing your personal lawyer into your entourage: The lawyer-client privileged relationship ensures maximum discretion and a minimum of leaks.

Thus, with Weissglass now officially on board, after Defensive Shield Sharon began lecturing the public, and especially his fellow Likudniks, on the need for compromise with the Palestinians. This dovetailed nicely with Bush's Roadmap, officially issued on April 30, 2003, and the energetic diplomatic activity surrounding it.

Many of those involved at the time in Israeli-Palestinian peace dealings were highly skeptical of the Roadmap. Halevy privately considered it a "farce" and a "catastrophe."[10] According to Fishere, now seconded by UN headquarters in Jerusalem to represent UN Roadmap interests as a partner in the Quartet, the Palestinians were "cynical about the whole exercise."[11] Zinni said the plan was "stupid" and its timetable "ridiculous."[12] Palestinian security, economic, and institutional reforms within one month? A Palestinian state by December 2003? This was nothing less than magical thinking.

Weissglass, in contrast, took very seriously the prospect of integrating Mahmoud Abbas's elevation to prime ministerial status with Zinni's efforts to permanently upgrade the PA's security performance and its functioning as a genuine polity. This would be the prelude to a Roadmap-based negotiation over a Palestinian state.

There are problematic contradictions in Weissglass's narrative of advancing an Israeli-Palestinian peace process. The Roadmap took note of the API because, according to Weissglass, the United States believed "this would incentivize the Israeli public to accept a Palestinian solution." Yet the public was so unaware of the API that opinion polls never even asked about the Arab League initiative. Fishere argues that it was only UN, EU, and Russian pressure that persuaded a reluctant Washington to mention the API in the Roadmap preamble.

Sharon, Weissglass insists, "believed in 2003 in a process based on the Roadmap." Yet by late May 2003, Weissglass had delivered to Washington a document outlining Sharon's fourteen "reservations" that effectively negated or neutralized the thrust of the Roadmap. For example, one reservation stipulated that Palestinian security and state-building reforms and Israeli territorial withdrawal and other concessions should be sequential, not simultaneous: First the Palestinians would reform and deliver on security; only then would Israel offer concessions. Another reservation conditioned Roadmap progress on "The emergence of a new and different leadership in the Palestinian Authority within the framework of governmental reform." That meant Arafat's removal or at a minimum the neutralizing of his executive authority. Weissglass at one point even demanded in Sharon's name that the API not be mentioned in the Roadmap.

The United States never accepted the fourteen-point document of Roadmap reservations. In fact, the entire Quartet rejected it. Events quickly passed it by.

Was the Roadmap a serious effort as Weissglass argues or a farce as Halevy, Zinni, and Fishere contend? Did Sharon under Weissglass's tutelage become a true believer in a negotiated solution or did he remain a calculating cynic? One way or another, the Roadmap process itself collapsed around late summer of 2003.

Shaul Mofaz was IDF chief of staff during Defensive Shield but now, as a civilian, minister of defense under Sharon. In the summer of 2003, Mofaz negotiated the IDF's withdrawal from Ramallah, the last parcel of Area A it still held in the aftermath of Operation Defensive Shield launched nearly eighteen months earlier. Weissglass believed Sharon was on the cusp of a genuine security achievement that would usher in a peace process. Then, in August, a devastating Hamas suicide bus bombing was perpetrated at Shmuel HaNavi Road in Jerusalem. That atrocity led to the Arafat-Abbas showdown in which Arafat refused to accede to Abbas's demand to be given the security authority the latter needed to take charge of the emerging Roadmap process.

Abbas resigned his short-lived post of prime minister. The Roadmap, which emerged from the events of late March 2002 and was intended to rescue and facilitate the Oslo process, had failed. Sharon was increasingly aware of pressures to find an alternative way to move forward. The pressures emanated both from Bush and from key sectors of the Israeli public, including retired senior security figures whom Sharon respected. He professed to be less moved by the December 2003 Geneva Accord or Initiative, an Israeli-Palestinian virtual peace agreement negotiated by non-accountable dovish retired senior Israeli and Palestinian officials. Yet "Geneva" affected Israeli and international public opinion and that in turn also affected the prime minister.

Sharon needed to act, but he did not want to negotiate. Not surprisingly in view of his overall cynicism regarding peace with Arabs, by 2004 he claimed to be convinced that a negotiated solution chaperoned internationally by means of the Roadmap or something similar would not work. Arafat was too treacherous.

Accordingly, Sharon began to lay plans for the unilateral Israeli act of withdrawal or "disengagement" from the Gaza Strip that took place in the summer of 2005. He could draw on majority public support for such a move dating all the way back to 2002.[13] He and Weissglass sought to coordinate (but not negotiate) this with Washington and even, after Arafat's death in November 2004, with Abbas.

The latter had returned to power as president of the Palestinian Authority and as Arafat's successor at the helm of Fateh and the PLO as well. Sharon believed Abbas was well intentioned but too weak to actually negotiate with. Indeed, Abbas was characterized by Sharon after another unusual face-to-face meeting at Sharon's Sycamore Ranch in the northern Negev as a "plucked chicken."

It was then that Weissglass rashly told *Haaretz* interviewer Ari Shavit: "The disengagement plan . . . is the bottle of formaldehyde within which you place the president's formula [Bush's Roadmap] so that it will be preserved for a very lengthy period. . . . so that there will not be a political process with the Palestinians. . . . We educated the world to understand that there is no one to talk to . . . [until] Palestine becomes Finland."[14]

Weissglass has since expressed regret over his wording. Incidentally, he did not invent the Finland comparison. Wistful demands that Israel's neighbors behave like Scandinavians in order to qualify for a peace process are part and parcel of the Israeli peace and conflict lexicon. That the Finland comparison in particular ignores the Finns' martial profile as recently as World War II simply reflects Israeli ignorance.

Sharon was obliged to provide Bush with a way forward other than the Roadmap. The Israeli prime minister seemingly had radically changed his point of view at this late stage in his life. Accordingly, he opted for unilateral withdrawal from the Gaza Strip and part of the northern West Bank rather than a Roadmap-based negotiating process. He still refused to negotiate the move with the Palestinian Authority, now led by Abbas. But he did attempt to coordinate an international aid effort to facilitate Palestinian state-building in the Strip, post-withdrawal.

Sharon's falling-out with the settlers was final: To them it did not matter if Sharon's betrayal took the form of a peace process or a unilateral dismantling of their homes. In August 2005 Israel withdrew. Sharon personally supervised resettlement arrangements for some eight thousand Gaza Strip settlers who were escorted out of the Strip by the IDF with minimal resort to force.

The Israeli public, including some of the settlers, acquiesced in the Gaza withdrawal in view of overwhelming realities. From a religious standpoint, the Gaza Strip was not part of biblical Israel; it was Philistine territory. From a geographic-demographic standpoint, the Strip's Palestinian population, now nearing two million in an area encompassing only 365 square kilometers (141 square miles), simply dwarfed Israel's settlement effort.

According to Sharon's concept, Gaza would remain fenced off from Israel but with a border crossing into Egyptian Sinai, thereby hopefully convincing the world that Israel had ceased to occupy it. That crossing would be supervised by a European Union force, an idea hitherto belittled by Sharon. The IDF, no longer exposed to Palestinian attacks inside the Strip, would be safer and better deployed. From an international-diplomatic and to some extent a domestic Israeli standpoint, withdrawal from Gaza would satisfy pressures on Israel to "do something."

The Gaza withdrawal, along with removal of four small settlements in the northern West Bank, was a monumental event in Israeli-Palestinian relations. Within three months Sharon could no longer maintain control over a rebellious Likud party that remained dedicated to the settlements and that had broadly opposed the Gaza withdrawal. In November 2005 he gathered his supporters from the right and the left into a newly formed centrist party, Kadima ("Forward"). Shortly thereafter, Sharon fell fatally ill and was replaced by Deputy Prime Minister Ehud Olmert. Olmert had left the Likud together with Sharon and from 2004 on was his point man in designing the Gaza withdrawal and presenting it to the public.

Until President Donald Trump recognized Jerusalem as Israel's capital and moved the US embassy there in 2017, the 2005 disengagement was the last significant strategic development on the ground in the Israeli-Palestinian dispute. In 2007, Hamas proceeded to take over the Gaza Strip—now free of settlements and the IDF—in a bloody coup against Abbas's Fateh movement. The Hamas action—a Palestinian-Palestinian clash—dashed whatever hopes anyone still entertained that the Palestinians would take advantage of an opportunity at state-building in Gaza. Hamas was not impressed with the Strip's internationally agreed boundaries. Nor was it a candidate for the international economic aid that had been promised to Mahmoud Abbas.

In March 2006, Olmert led Kadima to electoral victory on a platform of further withdrawals from the West Bank. That would prove a far more challenging undertaking than the Gaza withdrawal. Hundreds of thousands of settlers remained in the West Bank, the cradle of biblical Hebrew civilization. In 2008, still in coordination with the Bush administration under what used to be the Roadmap and was now called the Annapolis Process, Olmert and Abbas effectively poured out Weissglass's formaldehyde. They held a series of meetings to try to negotiate a two-state solution. This initiative eventuated in an Olmert offer that Abbas turned down.

By this time, Olmert was facing criminal charges for accepting bribes when he was mayor of Jerusalem several years earlier. His legal status quite obviously cast a huge shadow over the negotiations. But the concessions and compromises he offered Abbas were the most far-reaching to date. In 2013–2014, US secretary of state John Kerry tried again to foster a process, inadvertently triggering one of a series of mini-wars between Gaza and Israel generated by Hamas's Islamist hostility to both Israel and Abbas.

Israelis are still debating whether Sharon's unilateral withdrawal from Gaza was a good decision in addition to being a dramatic one. The years since 2005 have witnessed near-endless fighting between the IDF and Gaza-based Hamas and Palestinian Islamic Jihad, most recently in May 2021. Some 100,000 Israelis living in "Gaza periphery" towns and kibbutzim near the Strip bear the burden of Hamas's penchant for targeting civilians with everything from rockets and tunnels to incendiary balloons. Israel's repeated response has been to target Hamas fighters and ordnance. Inevitably and inadvertently, the Israeli armed response also hits Gazan civilians in the highly crowded areas where Hamas locates its bases. Israel has also laid siege to the Strip in both economic and military terms. Its actions draw frequent international condemnation.

★   ★   ★

Summing up the American role in the events of March 2002 and the developments that preceded and followed them is not an inspiring undertaking. To a large extent, that role reflected the conflicted inner nature of the Bush administration. Back in 2002, that inbuilt contradiction was played out in additional high-level US visits by neocon vice president Cheney and by his long-suffering rival, Secretary of State Colin Powell, who unlike Cheney did meet with Arafat (see chapter 17). Cheney appointed his own emissary,

John Hannah, to parallel Zinni. Extreme neocon Elliott Abrams also got in the act on Cheney's behalf. In retrospect, US involvement both before and immediately after the events of late March 2002 featured no clear objective other than achieving a cease-fire and building confidence. It did not project a genuine compromise peace process as the end product because too many figures in the Bush administration did not believe in one.

This half-hearted US involvement quite naturally generated Arab pressures on Powell and National Security Adviser Condoleezza Rice to extract from President Bush a "political horizon" for the Palestinians to match the Tenet and Zinni security horizon. The Roadmap, the political horizon, ultimately got nowhere. As Aaron Miller notes, "In the end, the only real problem with the road map was that neither the Americans, the Israelis, nor the Palestinians were serious about implementing it."[15] Bush, urged on by the neocons, was much more interested in conquering Iraq, while Sharon and Arafat were less than fully dedicated and cooperative.

By and large, the Americans ignored the broad strategic import of the second Intifada suicide bombings, the API, Defensive Shield, the withdrawal from Gaza, and Hamas's Gaza takeover. Zinni's appreciation of the strategic meaning of the Park bombing ("their 9/11") appears to have been the exception.

Dov Weissglass, a skilled lawyer and a genuine dove on the Palestinian issue, valued US involvement. He knew Israel's security chiefs, Sharon included, because he had represented many of them in court. But he never gained their trust in his nonlegal, Palestinian-related strategic wisdom or skills; many found him amateurish. The Sharon-Weissglass flip-flop moved from a negotiated Roadmap-based political solution to "formaldehyde," demands that Palestinians behave like Finns, and unilateralism. It cannot be attributed only to the hiatus between Abbas's resignation from the PA premiership and his elevation after Arafat's death to the presidency. Sharon may have been a total cynic, but Weissglass was not. Perhaps Sharon's lawyer never had a genuine crack at peacemaking.

Still, Sharon's rapid metamorphosis in his final years is stunning. He went from settlement-building hero, to two-state solution advocate who invites himself to Beirut, to unilateral dismantler of settlements. There had been but few comparable reversals of course by Israeli leaders prior to Sharon's. Ben-Gurion's withdrawal from Sinai in 1957 and Menachem Begin and Moshe Dayan's land-for-peace deal with Egypt in 1979 come to mind. As the elder Dayan famously quipped on many occasions, "Only a donkey never changes its mind."

Ben-Gurion, Begin, and Dayan internalized the limits of war and yielded to domestic and American pressures. Sharon's Gaza withdrawal can be understood only against the backdrop of the events of March 27, 28, 29, 2002.

To crown the narrative of ineffective American involvement, a US administration push for Palestinian democratization led, in February 2006, to elections for the Palestinian Legislative Council. They were won by the Islamist and decidedly non-democratic-minded Hamas. Abbas was elected president of the Palestinian Authority a year earlier. No Palestinian elections have been held since then, though periodically Abbas launches an election initiative (most recently, and abortively, for mid-2021). Fateh-Hamas tensions get in the way. The council never convenes.

Needless to say, these futile efforts at democratization left both Israelis and Palestinians skeptical and cynical of US peace efforts. Still, both sides (the PA/PLO restricted to the West Bank alone) continued to cooperate, offer the Americans ideas, and engage US peace facilitators such as John Kerry in 2013–2014. Until, that is, the Trump administration's brutally one-sided "deal of the century" provoked in 2018 a boycott by Abbas of diplomatic contacts with both Washington and Jerusalem.

In 2021 the Biden administration abandoned Trump's initiative. US-PA contacts were renewed, though not energetically.

It is fair to say that back in 2002–2003 the US role was never expressed in a serious commitment that comprised balanced but heavy pressure on both sides in the mode of Kissinger and Baker. Neither the Palestinian nor the Israeli side took Washington's efforts very seriously.

13

THE FENCE

The immediate security outcome of the Park Hotel bombing was Operation Defensive Shield, launched barely a day after the bombing and extending into the month of May 2002. It was a direct response to the cumulative toll of Palestinian suicide bombings against Israeli civilians since the start of the second Intifada in September 2000.

Defensive Shield rolled back Palestinian autonomy, and by extension Palestinian hopes for independence, by establishing the IDF's prerogative to enter Palestinian Authority Area A whenever it deems this necessary. As a corollary, PA security forces have ever since acknowledged this prerogative by stepping aside almost nightly when IDF infantry units enter Area A. They also actively cooperate with Israeli security forces at the intelligence and operational level against extremist Palestinian elements.

A less immediate but clearly linked outcome of the Park bombing was a vastly augmented and accelerated Israeli effort to erect a security fence separating Israel from most of the West Bank. Prior to Park, both Prime Minister Sharon and then finance minister Benjamin Netanyahu were opposed to the idea of building a physical barrier against terrorist penetration of Israel from the West Bank.

Sharon's main objection stemmed from his opposition to defensive strategies. His "bulldozer" reputation was based on his aggressive approach to solving most problems, military or otherwise. Unlike the pragmatic Sharon, Netanyahu at the most fundamental ideological level supported an Israeli claim to all the land west of the Jordan River. He feared that a fence would be perceived as partitioning the land and defining the West Bank as a separate territorial entity. A fence would also cut off or at least redefine territorially and possibly politically those West Bank settlements that lie beyond it, that is, between the fence and the Jordan River. And it was among the settlers and their supporters that Netanyahu, even at that early juncture in his political career, saw a major component of his electoral base.

Sharon paid lip service to this same ideology insofar as he headed the Likud, which broadly speaking supported settlements in the West Bank and opposed a viable two-state solution. Indeed, here and there Sharon advocated fencing based on a concept of security considerations that demanded attaching large portions of the West Bank to Israel. For security reasons related to threats from east of the Jordan River (Iran, terrorist infiltration), Sharon advocated a Jordan Valley fence too. It would attach anywhere from 10 to 30 percent of the West Bank to Israel. A fenced-in Jordan Valley strip of land would be attached to the main body of Israel at Beit Shean in the north and via an east-west corridor to Jerusalem in the south. It would physically separate the valley from the mountain heartland of the West Bank.

But here Sharon was held back by legal and strategic advisers. They pointed out that fencing in the West Bank heartland from both the west (Israel) and the east (the Jordan Valley) would thwart any hope of a settlement with the Palestinians. Moreover, it would be challenged in international tribunals. In a two-state solution, Israeli strategic thinkers agreed, Israel must maintain some sort of security presence in or access to the Jordan Valley in order to be capable of defending itself against enemies from the east, such as Iran. But it could do this without physically or formally separating the valley from the rest of the West Bank.

Then too, whenever the need for a barrier was agreed yet the area being separated from Israel was urban, the fence with its sophisticated contact alarms and remote monitoring became a very high and imposing wall. This remains the case where Israeli-annexed Arab-majority East Jerusalem borders on adjacent villages. A wall is also the concept where Qalqilya and Tulkarm—Abd al-Basset Oudeh's town—border on the green line 1967 boundary, immediately beyond which lies a major Israeli transportation artery, Route 6.

Today, Israel has imposing security fences along its borders with Egypt, Syria, the Gaza Strip, and Lebanon in addition to the West Bank fence. The fence separating the Israeli Negev from Egyptian Sinai was built around a decade ago to keep out African asylum-seekers and labor migrants. Once ISIS established a presence in Sinai following the "Arab Spring" 2011 Arab revolutions, the fence kept that Islamist movement, too, out of Israel. The other fences reflect a security rationale of protecting Israel from armed intruders and terrorists.

Security-purposed fences, by the way, go back a long way to pre-
independence Israel/Palestine. In the late 1940s, British mandatory authori-
ties built the Tegart line, a barbed wire fence linking fortified blockhouses
and stretching across northern pre-Israel Palestine. The objective back then
was to prevent infiltration of fighters and materiel from Lebanon and Syria
on behalf of Palestinian Arabs revolting against the Mandate.[1]

But between mandatory times and 2002, it was not always this way.
The West Bank fence/barrier, in particular, reflects a reversal of the approach to the Palestinians espoused by Defense Minister Moshe Dayan in
the immediate aftermath of Israel's June 1967 Six-Day War conquest and
occupation. Back then, all of Israel's international borders with Arab states
and its armistice boundary with the West Bank and Gaza Strip were not
fenced. They were denoted by the occasional marker and by warning signs.

Dayan wanted open borders and active mobility by Israelis and Palestinians (Gazans as well as West Bankers) in both directions. The West
Bank would become known in Israel as Judea and Samaria, the region's
biblical names. The Israeli and Palestinian economies would be integrated.
Palestinians in need of work could commute to Israel, where the post-1967
economy was booming; Israelis could buy inexpensive goods in the markets
of Nablus, Hebron, and Gaza City. As money flowed to the West Bank,
Israelis would find good food in the restaurants of Ramallah.

In the aftermath of the 1967 conquests, when Israelis drove into these
"territories" they encountered only a warning sign at the border that they
were entering land that was not part of the State of Israel and was under
military rule. The guiding principle held that, pending a political solution,
economic integration would ensure the peace. Note that Arab citizens of
Israel, who have close pre-1948 family ties in the West Bank and are pre-
sumed not to constitute targets for Palestinian terrorists, have enjoyed free
access there from 1967 to this day.

There were, of course, terrorist incidents and states of emergency, but
by and large this fenceless system worked for Israeli Jews, too, for the first
twenty years of occupation. Until, that is, the first Intifada broke out in late
1987. Then a fence was built around the Gaza Strip to the east and north,
where it borders Israel. Entry to and exit from the territories became more
regulated from a security standpoint.

Still, following the Oslo Accords of 1993–1994, and despite the initial
wave of suicide bombings they spawned in Israel's cities, an effort was made
in the interest of peaceful coexistence to maintain mobility between Israel
and the emerging Palestinian Authority. In September 2000, two months
after the abortive Camp David peace summit that failed to reach a final

status agreement and days before the outbreak of the extremely violent second Intifada, an Israeli Jew could still drive an Israel-licensed car from Tel Aviv into the heart of Ramallah. He or she could circle the Muqataa and meet a Palestinian colleague at a local restaurant without encountering fences, roadblocks. or security checks of any kind.

It was the second Intifada with its terrorist threat to civilian daily life in Israel that generated the popular demand for a West Bank security fence to parallel the one encircling the Gaza Strip. Major General Uzi Dayan, Sharon's national security adviser, was pushing the fence project as an antiterrorist defensive measure even prior to Passover 2002. The youthful-looking Dayan, disappointed at not being named IDF chief of staff in the footsteps of his illustrious uncle, Moshe, was not entirely comfortable in his national security adviser job due to reservations about what appeared to be remnants of Sharon's corrupt behavior. He even turned down some tasks Sharon tried to assign him, such as the staff work for a floating casino in the port of Eilat, for fear of being dragged into shady dealings.

The irony here is that Moshe Dayan, a dashing figure with his black eye patch who died in 1981, had his own corruption file in the eyes of the Israeli public. He used his military hero status as a cover for confiscating and hoarding archeological treasures from digs around the country. He was also notorious as a sexual predator among young female soldiers.

Uzi Dayan championed the fence idea, even when Sharon was dismissive. Prior to the Park atrocity, several short sections had been built, albeit without a proper cabinet decision. Sharon preferred to avoid any measure that bound the government to a strategy he did not support.

The location of these brief lengths of fence was a cause of constant tension. The settlement movement in general opposed the fence. But when it got down to the nitty-gritty, settler leaders inevitably lobbied to move the fence eastward so as to encompass to its west as many West Bank settlements as possible. Dayan quotes Ron Nahman, then mayor of Ariel, an urban settlement that lies fully eighteen kilometers east of the green line but houses a large Jewish population. By 2002 Nahman could brag of beginning to build the first (and as yet only) Israeli university in the West Bank. "I'm against the fence," he told Dayan. "But once it exists, I'll do everything to make sure I'm inside."[2] The political left, on the other hand, argued for a green line fence along the old 1948–1967 armistice line between Israel and Jordan as an anti-occupation statement to the effect that this would be the border of a future Palestinian state. By May 2002, two-thirds of the Israeli Jewish public believed that a fence would significantly reduce Palestinian terrorist attacks.[3]

Those who advocated the fence from purely a security standpoint generally asserted that it should protect maximum Israelis on minimal West Bank land. In other words, it should attach to Israel the large settlement blocs immediately to the east of the green line, but not such adjacent Arab towns as Qalqilya and Tulkarm. On the other hand, in planning sessions the Israeli security community played pass-the-buck ping-pong with the fence. Who would be responsible for it, the IDF, the Israel Police, or the Shabak? Put differently, if a terrorist succeeded in breaching the fence and killing Israelis inside Israel, who would bear the blame? Still, all the security services supported the fence idea.

Dayan relates that the Park bombing rendered his advocacy and Sharon's grudging agreement far easier. Shabak head Avi Dichter stated publicly and with striking candor that the Israeli security community was unable to offer the Israeli citizenry the minimal security package it required. Suddenly, all understood that if suicide bombers could enter Israel so readily from the West Bank and do so much damage, a fence would help.

True, even a fence would not be foolproof. The Park bomber, after all, had driven through a secure crossing—a place where there would be no fence—using fake Israeli ID and an Israeli-licensed car. Yet there was no lack of terrorist incidents that involved Palestinians from the West Bank entering Israel by foot or by vehicle across unprotected and unfenced green line agricultural land and boundary-straddling villages. On one occasion a truck laden with explosives had driven from the West Bank across the green line into Israel. It was discovered and defused at the last minute. A fence would certainly have stopped it.

Sharon gave his okay for the fence. Netanyahu grudgingly untied the purse strings. "The main fence effort was a consequence of the Park Hotel attack," notes Dayan.[4] Serious fence construction began. Sharon, having concurred, nevertheless meddled repeatedly with the location of the fence in relation to Arab villages such as Baqa al-Gharbia that are located along the pre-1967 armistice line.[5] This tinkering by Israel's commander in chief was reminiscent of Sharon's earlier placement of West Bank settlements with the objective of separating Bedouin tribes. These were tactical moves devoid of strategic calculation and strategic purpose. Still, after Sharon left the scene, the fence project was advanced enthusiastically by Prime Minister Ehud Olmert and Defense Minister Amir Peretz.

Ultimately, the fence barrier would attach about 8 percent of the West Bank to Israel, mainly including settlement blocs located near the old green line. Not accidentally, this broadly corresponded with Sharon's newfound advocacy of territorial compromise with the Palestinians. The cost would exceed six billion US dollars.[6]

Here we encounter what at first glance appears to be a contradiction between the meaning of Defensive Shield and the meaning of the West Bank security fence for the future of the conflict and a two-state solution. Defensive Shield and its aftermath placed Israel on the offensive. The massive IDF operation gave Israel a fluid and flexible yet permanent military presence inside the entire West Bank Palestinian Authority. This severely constrained autonomy, not to mention independence. That situation prevails to this day.

In contrast, the fence is defensive. Using advanced electronics, video surveillance, and mobile patrols, it has worked fairly well from a purely security standpoint to prevent and thwart terrorist attacks from the West Bank. And from a demographic standpoint, by attaching most of the settlers to Israel, it at least partially answers requirements for a border with a future Palestinian state.

14

RUSSIA

R ussia was not a major Middle East actor in March 2002. It played at best a minor role in the narrative of March 27, 28, and 29. But by the time of this writing in 2019–2021, it had become a central regional actor. Indeed, arguably it is the most prominent external Middle East actor. And by dint of its military presence in Syria, Russia had become a strategic neighbor of Israel and Palestine.

Back in 2002, Russia held a special place in the heart of Ariel Sharon. Going back even further to the Soviet era, Moscow was a key backer of the PLO and the Palestinian cause. That is a shared history neither Russia nor the Palestinians have forgotten. Palestinian Authority president Mahmoud Abbas received a PhD from a Russian university and speaks fluent Russian.

Accordingly, prior to concluding and summarizing our narrative, it is instructive to look briefly at Moscow's approach to and involvement in the region in the early years of the millennium. They set a pattern that remains relevant. Against the backdrop of massive Russian immigration to Israel, the events of late March 2002—Hamas terrorism, the Arab Peace Initiative, and Defensive Shield—represented major input into the molding of Russian Middle East policies as we understand them today.

The collapse of the USSR in 1991 brought about a swift retrenchment of Moscow's foreign commitments and deployments. Soviet forces and military missions in Syria, Yemen, Libya, and elsewhere in the Middle East returned home. It was only in the late 1990s that Moscow launched a modest "return" to the region. The dominant figure in this initial effort was Yevgeny Primakov, an expert on the region and veteran KGB operative in the Arab world back in Soviet days. After the collapse of the USSR, Primakov served Russia first as foreign minister and then briefly as prime minister.

The Soviet collapse culminating in 1991 also ended a near-total absence of ties between Russia and Israel. The USSR had cut relations back in 1967 in response to the Six-Day War, which witnessed Israel's resounding defeat of Moscow's Arab allies. Now the collapse generated mass migration of Jews from the Former Soviet Union (FSU) to Israel. The arrival of more than one million FSU migrants in the space of a few years in the late 1980s and early 1990s and the renewal of Russia-Israel diplomatic, trade, and tourist ties now nourished a positive relationship between Russia and Israel.

Russians and Israelis discovered that Tel Aviv and Moscow were in the same time zone and were separated by a mere three-hour flight. Ariel Sharon recalled his Russian-speaking immigrant parents, the Schneidermans, and began to remember phrases in Russian. Of particular note is the fact that Sharon's mother, Vera, was a Sobotnik who converted to Judaism after her arrival in Mandatory Palestine.

Sobotniks (from the Russian for sabbath) were a small sect of Russian Christians who embraced aspects of Judaism. Persecuted under the czars, they in many cases immigrated to Palestine. Vera's Russian cultural interests influenced the young Sharon, who as a boy played the violin and developed a lifelong interest in classical music, learning entire operas by heart. Vera's tough contrariness also rubbed off on Sharon. In Kfar Malal in the Sharon region north of Tel Aviv, where the young Arik Schneiderman grew up, Vera was constantly at odds with her neighbors. Sharon emerged disdaining authority and belittling displays of emotional weakness by his fellow IDF officers. He himself quickly overcame the loss of his first wife to illness and of his oldest son to a gun accident.

Beginning with his successful campaign for the premiership in early 2001, Russia and things-Russian became factors in Sharon's political calculations. By the time he led Israel's withdrawal from Gaza in 2005 and founded the Kadima party, Sharon and his politics enjoyed a huge Russian-speaking following in Israel. Even his "Genghis Khan" image was approved by the Russian immigrants. Their cultural-political inclination was to respect a tough, battle-hardened leader who had shown no mercy for Israel's enemies. As prime minister, Sharon also not incidentally approved the immigration to Israel of additional Sobotniks.

In sharp contrast, active support for the Palestinian cause effectively vanished in Moscow after the Soviet collapse. Gone was the rhetoric boosting Palestinian resistance. Gone was the KGB's arms and intelligence training for Fateh and allied fighters flown from Beirut to Soviet Bloc capitals such as Prague, Warsaw, and Sofia. Soviet-administered courses in mobile surveillance for Fateh fighters, which began at the ancient Orloj clock at the entrance to Prague's Old Town Square and wound up at the old Charles Bridge, ended abruptly. They were soon replaced by guided tours for Israeli tourists, which also began at Prague Orloj but ended at the haunted old Jewish cemetery that inspired the czar's police to write the Protocols of the Elders of Zion.

Back in Moscow, Vladimir Putin took over in 2000. Like Sharon, Putin quickly took on a tough-guy image. From herein, an increasingly resurgent Russia would be motivated regarding the Middle East by four geostrategic factors.

One was its Chechnya wars against an Islamist insurgency on Russian soil. The First Chechen War, in Boris Yeltsin's day, lasted from 1994 to 1996; the Second, waged mainly by Putin, extended from 1999 to 2009.

A second geostrategic motive for Russia's interest in the Middle East was the need to demonstrate and market its weapons. A third was its interest in Saudi and other Gulf Arab investment. And fourth was the existence in Israel of the largest Russian diaspora in the world, one that could vote in Russian elections and that maintained close ties to family and economic interests in Russia. In parallel, and prior to 2008 when it invaded Georgia and found itself at odds with the United States and Europe, Russia consistently sought to improve ties with the West, then still dominant in the Middle East.

Not surprisingly Putin, like Primakov, was a KGB veteran. It was Russia's residual Soviet-era secret international intelligence establishment that effectively ran Moscow's Middle East policies and generated strategic-thinking capabilities. In this regard, Russia under Putin represents to a large extent continuity.

Putin and Sharon developed an unusual rapport in their meetings. Israeli Russia experts who had begun meeting with Putin well before he became president claim that he harbored a particular respect for two countries: Israel and Germany.

Still, those early years witnessed Russian policy zigzags regarding Israel. On the one hand were pro-Israel sentiments. In the autumn of 2000, when the second Intifada erupted, a visiting Israeli delegation to Moscow was told by the then head of Russia's Security Council, Sergei Lavrov, that the terrorism confronted by Israel was exactly what Russia encountered in Chechnya. Indeed, Russia under Putin at times defended its brutal military tactics in Chechnya against Western criticism by citing Israeli precedents.

On the other hand, in deference to the Arabs, Russia consistently endorsed the Arab Peace Initiative. It did so even before the API was ratified in Beirut. On March 12, 2002, when Moscow voted for UN Security Council Resolution 1397 in which the United States for the first time signed on to an endorsement of the two-state solution, Russia inserted mention that the resolution welcomed "the contribution of Saudi Crown Prince Abdullah." On March 28, 2002, the very day the API was approved in Beirut, the United Nations High Commissioner for Refugees meeting in Geneva heard Russia's ambassador endorse the Arab Peace Initiative.

From herein the API would be cited by Moscow as a basis for Middle East peace alongside such veteran UN Security Council resolutions as 242 and 338. All the while, Putin evinced a readiness to cooperate with cease-fire initiatives presented to Israelis and Palestinians by US envoys Mitchell, Tenet, and Zinni.

But Moscow said little in condemnation of the Park Passover bombing. Indeed, following the IDF's massive entry into the West Bank after the Park bombing, Russia expressed support for the Palestinians. It went on to condemn Israel's security fence, which as noted was built partially on West Bank territory. Interestingly, Chechen issues were cited here, too, but with reverse emphasis. Now Russia believed it needed to curb Arab support for the Chechen rebellion by criticizing Israel.

By March 2003, Russia's Ministry for Foreign Affairs was condemning claims by Palestinian Islamic Jihad of responsibility for an inconsequential March 30 bombing in Netanya in which no Israelis were killed. Was Moscow making amends for its relative silence over the Park Hotel bombing almost exactly a year earlier? In contrast, in September 2003, while hosting Prime Minister Sharon in Moscow, President Putin introduced a resolution to the UN Security Council anchoring the Quartet's Roadmap while pointedly ignoring Sharon's fourteen reservations.

Indeed, that same month of September 2003 the Russians hosted Saudi Crown Prince Abdullah and, in return for his pronouncement that the Chechnya conflict was an internal Russian affair, again endorsed the Saudi-sponsored API. Putin, declaring that "Russia could be regarded as part of the Islamic world in some sense,"[1] now asked that Russia be admitted to the Organization of the Islamic Conference as an observer. As noted by Russian Middle East expert Nikolai Surkov of the Moscow State Institute of International Relations' Oriental Studies Department, Russia may have attacked the Saudis' extreme Wahabi version of Islam, particularly in the Chechen context, but it never criticized Islam itself.[2]

Then came what looked like another reversal. In September 2004 Lavrov, by now foreign minister, embraced an Israeli offer to cooperate in the realm of counterterrorism. This initiative followed upon the notorious

Beslan school massacre by Chechen terrorists in early September in which 334 were killed. It highlights the complex interplay between Russia's own efforts to deal with militant Islam in the early years of Putin's rule and Moscow's attitude toward violent aspects of the Israeli-Palestinian conflict.

By 2006, Putin was inviting Islamist-extremist Hamas to visit Moscow, yet he continued to back the more moderate Arab mainstream's API. By now, too, a new dynamic had been established of expanding Russian arms sales to Syria, Libya, and Algeria. Yet Putin was careful to balance this drive for an enhanced Russian presence in the Arab world and Iran with closer commercial and cultural ties with Israel and with its community of well more than a million Russian-speaking immigrants.

To sum up, it was in the years 2000–2004 that Russia again began to emerge as a power to reckon with in the Middle East, with a carefully balanced and integrated strategy for dealing with both Arabs and Israelis. Not surprisingly, the main formative events in the region underlying this strategy were those of March 2002 and the ensuing months.

15

BEHIND THE EVENTS
OF MARCH 2002

How did it come to this? Palestinian Islamists massacring a Passover Seder in Netanya, Arab diplomats in Beirut adopting a peace plan for Israel, and Israel's troops setting out to reoccupy the West Bank and dismantle Palestinian Authority security institutions—all in three days.

What was the nature of Arab thinking about Israel prior to 2002? And how did Israelis and Palestinians approach each other before the March 27 Park atrocity? Why, since 1936 and earlier, is the Israeli-Palestinian political coexistence story a persistent and largely consistent dynamic of failure? Yet the Israel-Arab story, meaning Israel-Arab peace treaties and clandestine strategic cooperation between Arab states and Israel, is so different. Why have some eighty years of concerted attempts to solve this conflict failed, while many other seemingly equally intractable conflicts were resolved?

A brief retelling of the narrative—or rather, narratives—is in order if we are to fully comprehend the ramifications of the events of late March 2002.

At the outset, it is instructive to go back to 1937, when the British government's Peel Commission report attempted the first learned and reasoned analysis of the key issues dividing Jews and Arabs under Britain's League of Nations mandate. The commission's eloquent summary of its observations remains amazingly relevant:

Chapter XX.—The Force of Circumstances
[Taken from Report of the Palestine Royal Commission: Summary of Report]
The problem of Palestine is briefly restated.

Under the stress of the World War the British Government made promises to Arabs and Jews in order to obtain their support. On the strength of those promises both parties formed certain expectations.

The application to Palestine of the Mandate System in general and of the specific Mandate in particular implies the belief that the obligations thus undertaken towards the Arabs and the Jews respectively would prove in course of time to be mutually compatible owing to the conciliatory effect on the Palestinian Arabs of the material prosperity which Jewish immigration would bring in Palestine as a whole. That belief has not been justified, and there seems to be no hope of its being justified in the future.

But the British people cannot on that account repudiate their obligations, and, apart from obligations, the existing circumstances in Palestine would still require the most strenuous efforts on the part of the Government which is responsible for the welfare of the country. The existing circumstances are summarized as follows.

An irrepressible conflict has arisen between two national communities within the narrow bounds of one small country. There is no common ground between them. Their national aspirations are incompatible. The Arabs desire to revive the traditions of the Arab golden age. The Jews desire to show what they can achieve when restored to the land in which the Jewish nation was born. Neither of the two national ideals permits of combination in the service of a single State.

The conflict has grown steadily more bitter since 1920 and the process will continue. Conditions inside Palestine especially the systems of education, are strengthening the national sentiment of the two peoples. The bigger and more prosperous they grow the greater will be their political ambitions, and the conflict is aggravated by the uncertainty of the future. "Who in the end will govern Palestine?" it is asked. Meanwhile, the external factors will continue to operate with increasing force. On the one hand in less than three years' time Syria and Lebanon will attain their national sovereignty, and the claim of the Palestinian Arabs to share in the freedom of all Asiatic Arabia will thus be fortified. On the other hand the hardships and anxieties of the Jews in Europe are not likely to grow less and the appeal to the good faith and humanity of the British people will lose none of its force.

Meanwhile, the Government of Palestine, which is at present an unsuitable form for governing educated Arabs and democratic Jews, cannot develop into a system of self-government as it has elsewhere, because there is no such system which could ensure justice both to the Arabs and to the Jews. Government therefore remains unrepresentative and unable to dispel the conflicting grievances of the two dissatisfied and irresponsible communities it governs.

In these circumstances peace can only be maintained in Palestine under the Mandate by repression. This means the maintenance of security services at so high a cost that the services directed to "the well-being and development" of the population cannot be expanded and may even have to be curtailed. The moral objections to repression are self-evident. Nor need the undesirable reactions of it on opinion outside Palestine be emphasized. Moreover, repression will not solve the problem. It will exacerbate the quarrel. It will not help towards the establishment of a single self-governing Palestine. It is not easy to pursue the dark path of repression without seeing daylight at the end of it. . . .

The continuance of the present system means the gradual alienation of two peoples who are traditionally the friends of Britain.

The problem cannot be solved by giving either the Arabs or the Jews all they want. The answer to the question which of them in the end will govern Palestine must be Neither. No fair-minded statesman can think it right either that 400,000 Jews, whose entry into Palestine has been facilitated by the British Government and approved by the League of Nations, should be handed over to Arab rule, or that, if the Jews should become a majority, a million Arabs should be handed over to their rule. But while neither race can fairly rule all Palestine, each race might justly rule part of it.

The idea of Partition has doubtless been thought of before as a solution of the problem, but it has probably been discarded as being impracticable. The difficulties are certainly very great, but when they are closely examined they do not seem so insuperable as the difficulties inherent in the continuance of the Mandate or in any other alternative arrangement. Partition offers a chance of ultimate peace. No other plan does.

These were Lord Peel's penetrating insights in 1937. Leaving aside colonialist references to "educated Arabs and democratic Jews," Peel displayed a nuanced understanding of the obstacles. He zeroed in on the very partition solution that has informed nearly all peace proposals ever since.

In this spirit, over the years a number of external actors have mediated between the two sides or facilitated their talks. These include Britain, the United States, Egypt, Jordan, Norway, and the United Nations. Some, such as the United States, tilted toward Israel. Others, such as the Arab states, toward the Palestinians. But we have also witnessed well-meaning outside actors seeking to dictate to the parties the terms of a final status agreement or even to obviate the need for one.

In 1937 the Peel Commission, after listening to the parties, proposed a partition map, as did the United Nations in 1947. From 1967 to 1992, Jordan periodically undertook to negotiate the fate of the West Bank and Jerusalem or to represent the Palestinians in negotiations. Beginning with Israeli prime minister Menachem Begin's negotiations with Egypt, that country has been "offered" the Gaza Strip by Israel. Wisely from its standpoint,

Egypt has backed off. In 2020 Israel and the Palestinians confronted an amateurish and extremely unbalanced offer of a solution by the Trump administration in Washington. Still, even Trump's "deal of the century" envisages a two-state solution.

Seen in this context, the Arab Peace Initiative of 2002 represents an attempt by the Arab League to bypass or supersede earlier instances of participation in the process by individual Arab states as well as plans presented by non–Middle East actors. The API would dictate a set of peace parameters in the name of all Arab states while offering Israel collective Arab incentives to agree.

None of these initiatives has worked. Some (the British-drawn and 1947 UN maps) were accepted by one side, the future Israel, but not by the Arab side. The Arab Peace Initiative has been endorsed by the PLO and the Arab League states but not by a succession of Israeli governments. In the decades following 1967, not only Egypt but Jordan as well realized that reoccupying portions of Mandatory Palestine that they had occupied between 1948 and 1967 would burden them with a problem they would rather Israel bear.

One fairly obvious lesson would appear to be the requirement for a mutually agreed "local" bilateral solution. But prior to 1977, none of the Arabs agreed to negotiate directly and openly with Israel. Prior to 1993, no representative Palestinian institution agreed, nor did Israel agree officially to talk to the PLO. And the legitimacy as negotiator of the PLO, which did then agree, has in recent years been undermined by Hamas.

In other words, if external involvement has failed, so has direct bilateral contact.

The international community has also, again with the best of intentions, created structures and institutions that have actually at times obstructed progress. Here are two examples.

UNRWA was the first. The United Nations Relief and Works Agency for Palestinian Refugees in the Near East was created by the UN in 1949 to provide vital sustenance and support for approximately 700,000 Palestinians who fled or were expelled during the 1948 war. In 1950 the UN created UNHCR, the High Commissioner for Refugees, to deal with all other refugee issues in the world.

This means that there is a disparity in the UN's dealings with Palestinian refugees as opposed to all others. It is explained by the ability of the Arab bloc in the UN, for years backed by the nonaligned and the communist bloc, to fashion a special framework designed to keep the refugee issue alive as a crucial factor in any settlement of the Palestinian problem. Even after the Arab states began making separate peace accommodations with Israel (Egypt 1979, Jordan 1994), they still insisted on maintaining UNRWA. After all, at a minimum it housed, fed, clothed, and educated their Palestinian refugee populations. As the late Lebanese-American Middle East scholar Fouad Ajami wrote regarding the birth of Israel in 1948 and the parallel creation of the Palestinian refugee issue, "It would have been the humane thing to tell the [Palestinian] refugees that huge historical verdicts are never overturned. But it was safer to offer a steady diet of evasion and escapism."[1]

UNRWA does indeed care for needy Palestinian refugees. Israel itself has recognized this by supporting UNRWA's ongoing presence in the refugee camps of the West Bank and Gaza Strip. This begs the question, who would fund the education, health, and housing of the Palestinian refugees throughout the Middle East were it not for UNRWA?

By 2020 UNRWA was hard put to recruit operational funds after the Trump administration cancelled the US contribution of some 25 percent of UNRWA's annual budget. The administration accused the UN body of perpetuating the Palestinian refugee issue. That is true. But in the absence of an alternative route to refugee rehabilitation and resettlement, UNRWA remained the least bad option. (In 2021, the Biden administration restored US funding of UNRWA.)

Still, UNRWA's uniqueness in global refugee annals remains an important negative aspect of the Palestinian problem. Note that, in parallel, Israel has absorbed millions of Jewish refugees and displaced persons—from the Holocaust, from Arab countries—without recourse to UN refugee facilities. And the UNHCR has overseen the resettlement of tens of millions of Indians, Pakistanis, Germans, Poles, South Sudanese, and others displaced by war. Unlike all these instances, UNRWA's mandate rejects resettlement of refugees in the countries to which they fled and where they have resided ever since or in "third" countries that absorb immigration. The Arab countries insist the Palestinian refugees' fate be agreed between Israel and the PLO, yet without "patriation," or permanent settlement in their countries of residence. That principle was enshrined as late as 2002 in the Arab Peace Initiative and has been ratified annually ever since.

Meanwhile, uniquely among global refugee issues, the count of certified Palestinian refugees expands from generation to generation, today nearing six million. It is by now axiomatic among all but the more extreme Palestinians (e.g., Hamas) that Israel cannot possibly repatriate all, most, or even a large fraction of the refugees within a final status framework. Put differently, it is understood that the demand that Israel accept more than five million Palestinian refugees, all but a few thousand of whom were not even born in what is today Israel, is in effect a demand to "Palestinize" Israel. No Israeli negotiator will agree. Yet the demand for universal return, if only in an abstract and principled form, has not been abandoned. Note the API's endorsement of UN General Assembly Resolution 194, which is interpreted by Arabs precisely in that light.

A telling reminder of the centrality of the refugee issue and the UNRWA connection was provided in April 2015. In the midst of the Syrian civil war, Islamic militants conquered the Yarmouk Palestinian refugee camp near Damascus.

Yarmouk was once the largest such camp administered by UNRWA, its population numbering around 350,000, equivalent to half of the original 1948 refugee count. After bitter internal-Syrian fighting, by 2015 there remained only some 18,000 besieged refugee noncombatants. While UNRWA was trying valiantly to bring them vital supplies, Arab citizens of Israel from the Galilee tried to intervene. Some of these Israeli Arabs had distant cousins in Yarmouk Camp, whose original Palestinian population in 1948 was from what became northern Israel. Now they argued publicly that Israel was somehow responsible for Yarmouk's current plight and was obliged to help the 18,000 remaining refugees, nearly seventy years after their grandparents had fled Israel's bitter war of independence.

No one suggested that the mess at Yarmouk was the responsibility of Arab countries. But why should they? Arab countries had been manipulating the Palestinian issue for decades rather than displaying compassion for Palestinians.

During a similar crisis at Yarmouk a year or two earlier, Israeli prime minister Netanyahu had agreed that the Palestinian Authority could absorb Palestinian refugee victims of the Syrian fighting in and around Yarmouk. His sole condition was that those refugees declare that by settling in Ramallah, Jericho, or Khan Yunis (i.e., in the West Bank or Gaza), they had fulfilled "return" and would have no further claims on Israel. Hamas in Gaza refused outright to accept the refugees. Palestinian leader Mahmoud Abbas in Ramallah agreed but rebuffed the demand regarding renunciation of further "return." Rather, he stated that it was better the refugees die in Syria than give up their right of return. Jordan would not let them traverse its territory.

Thus has the Yarmouk Camp in recent years effectively symbolized the intractability of the refugee issue.

A second and very different but problematic UN creation is Security Council Resolution 242 of November 1967. That resolution provided the territories-for-peace formula that guided Israel's peace agreements with

Egypt (1979) and Jordan (1994). UNSCR 242 was even the basis for an abortive agreement between Israel and Lebanon (1983) and an almost-agreement with Syria (1995, 1999). But 242, enacted only months after Israel occupied large Palestinian populations in the West Bank, East Jerusalem, and the Gaza Strip, studiously says nothing about the Palestinians. It mentions "refugees," but not Palestinian refugees.

Resolution 242 was good for peace between Israel and neighboring Arab states whose essential quarrel with Israel has been borders. It was bad for the Palestinian issue, which to this day suffers from the absence of a parallel UN definition of a set of principles for resolving it. True, the PLO eventually endorsed 242, thereby strengthening its claim to represent Palestinians in a territories-for-peace deal after Jordan waived its 242 rights in the West Bank in 1988. And 242 is cited in the API as a foundation for peace.

But this could not entirely negate the logic underlying repeated Israeli government claims that the West Bank and Gaza were not conquered from any Arab country whose sovereignty there had been recognized prior to 1967. Accordingly, Israel argues, the territories were "liberated" and not "occupied" (at least as occupation is defined in international law by the Fourth Geneva Convention), could be settled by Israelis, and 242 did not fully apply to them. Until the advent of the Trump administration in Washington in 2017, no one else in the world recognized the validity of this Israeli argument.

The United Nations itself created Israel from the standpoint of international law. It has policed many truces and cease-fires between Israel and its Arab neighbors and contributed positively to Israel's well-being in numerous ways. But it has also clearly been an obstacle.

Israel could make peace with Egypt and Jordan based on 242. But not with the Palestinians, whose conflict with the State of Israel begins in 1948 with their humiliating flight and expulsion from their homeland. The Palestinians did not fight Israel in 1967 and did not "lose" a war or territory then. Quite the contrary, the 1967 defeat of Jordan and Egypt set the scene for the Palestinians to claim, or reclaim, at least a portion of pre-1948 Mandatory Palestine.

Thus, uniquely in the annals of Israel-Arab peacemaking, the direct Palestinian-Israeli negotiations that commenced officially in 1993 focus on both pre-1967 and post-1967 issues. The former concern both the question of return of some or all 1948 refugees to Israel, and the "right of return" of all. These are two related but different issues that we shall come back to.

The pre-1967 issues also touch on the question of ownership of and control over holy places, and particularly the Temple Mount, or Haram al-Sharif, in the heart of Jerusalem. That issue is not merely pre-1967. In some ways it goes back hundreds and even thousands of years, to the building of the First Temple by the ancient Hebrews and the construction on the ruins of the Second Temple of al-Aqsa Mosque by the early Muslims.

In contrast, the post-1967 issues to be resolved by Israelis and Palestinians parallel those resolved in peace talks between Israel and Egypt and Israel and Jordan: borders, security, the fate of settlements. Even the Palestinian demand for a capital in Arab East Jerusalem may be considered a post-1967 issue insofar as it concerns borders and sovereignty. Here it must be noted that many Israelis would insist that anything touching on Jerusalem is somehow a "narrative," hence pre-1967, issue.

Indeed, increasingly influential hard-liners among the Israeli right-religious political mainstream are in part responsible for undermining the negotiating centrality of the post-1967 issues. They reject the 1967 lines in favor of the demand to annex or at least continue to control the entire West Bank and all of East Jerusalem. Hard-liner minimalists would insist on holding on, at a minimum, to all of Area C, constituting 60 percent of the West Bank, while fragmenting areas A and B into 169 territorial islands.[2] The Trump administration "deal of the century" Israeli-Palestinian peace proposal of January 2020 broadly corresponded with this Israeli nationalist-messianic outlook. It offered Israel 30 percent of the West Bank. This explains Palestinian rejection of the Trump plan a priori.

By and large, direct Palestinian-Israeli final status negotiations have registered an encouraging degree of progress on post-1967 issues. This was the case at Camp David in July 2000 and in the "Annapolis" talks between Ehud Olmert and Mahmoud Abbas in 2008. It characterized discussion of such third-party formulae as the Clinton parameters of late 2000. When these diverse negotiations broke off, there remained narrow and negotiable gaps between the two sides. These concerned the location of the border, the scope of land swaps to compensate Palestinians for Israeli annexation of settlement blocs, the parameters of security arrangements, and even the location of a Palestinian capital in or adjacent to East Jerusalem. The Kerry-led indirect talks of 2013–2014, too, claim to have registered some progress on territorial issues.

This has not been the case in negotiations over the pre-1967 issues. True, the two sides have at times agreed to bargain over numbers of 1948 refugees whose repatriation Israel might accept, albeit with numerical gaps in the tens of thousands. But they never came close to agreeing on a verbal formula that Palestinians would recognize as Israeli acceptance, even if only in principle, of the right of return of well more than five million refugees, most third and fourth generation who were not born in Israel or Palestine and never lived there.

The Palestinian rejection of the Clinton parameters proposed by outgoing US president Bill Clinton in December 2000 focused on a refusal to compromise regarding precisely the pre-1967 issues of refugees and Jerusalem holy places.

These pre-1967 narrative issues derive from the circumstances of Israel's origins as a state and the parallel Palestinian dispersal. The huge and seemingly immovable abyss separating the positions of Israelis and Palestinians on these issues is unique to their conflict alone.

Israelis understand the "right of return" of 1948 refugees as a demand to undermine their country as a Jewish state and to deny its legitimacy. Israel's right to exist was ratified by the appropriate international institutions when the League of Nations ratified the Balfour Declaration after World War I and when the United Nations voted after World War II to establish a Jewish state in Mandatory Palestine. The Arab world challenged that right and that state, launched a war to prevent their realization, and lost. The 1948 war created refugees that by any international standard should long ago have been resettled in the Arab world or in immigration-welcoming countries.

Instead, perpetual refugee status has, in Arab hands, become a means toward the end, generations down the line, of delegitimizing and defeating Israel.

Here a comparison offering historical depth might be useful. Imagine if you will a Jewish girl of nine fleeing the Austro-Hungarian province of Galicia upon the outbreak of World War I in 1914. The Russians were invading from the east. The girl and her family fled their flour mill on the banks of a picturesque stream in the village of Kozlov. After a wartime journey that took months and involved considerable hardship, they reached Vienna. There, the girl's mother died of consumption. Her father, a reserve army medic in the Austro-Hungarian army, had been returned to active duty upon the outbreak of war. He was captured by the Russians in the famous battle of Przemysl, spent the war years in Siberia, and in 1915 was thought dead.

The little girl was by any definition a refugee and was so recognized by the International Red Cross. For the ensuing eighty-two years of her life, could she claim the "right of return" to the family mill, now no longer on land that belonged to the Austro-Hungarian Empire but clearly captured in 1914 as spoils of war? More than one hundred years later can her son, the author, claim the right of return to Kozlov and the flour mill? Can her grandchildren make that claim? Her great-grandchildren?

Of course not. Kozlov was no longer part of Austro-Hungary after the war; it became part of Poland, then the USSR, now Ukraine. Her son and his progeny can claim neither "return" nor refugee status nor compensation. To do so would never occur to them. Their narrative, like that of tens of millions of refugees and refugee-descendants ever since, merely underlines the total uniqueness of the status the world has awarded the Palestinian refugees.

Israelis understand the Arab world's nurturing of successive generations of refugees as support for the Palestinian position. Palestinians understand the right of return as the ultimate affirmation of their narrative that holds that Israel is a foreign implant. Israel was "created in sin" by outside forces in the course of the *nakba*, the disaster of defeat, expulsion, and exile that was visited upon the Palestinians in 1948. Israel does not represent a legitimate Jewish national movement at all. Even Palestinians who concede that actual return is impractical insist on getting what one may term the psycho-historical satisfaction of Israel acknowledging its guilt. And they readily admit that this is the Israel they will present to future generations in school textbooks, thereby perpetuating the conflict.

Regarding the Temple Mount/Haram al-Sharif, Palestinians, in a dramatic reversal of classic Muslim historiography, deny there is a Hebrew legacy there at all. Again, Israelis view this denial as a negation of Jewish national and religious roots in the Holy Land. The two successive temples built and destroyed on the Mount have served as the focus of Hebrew national and spiritual life for two millennia. Note, too, that the PLO recruited a huge anti-Israel majority in UNESCO (United Nations Educational, Scientific and Cultural Organization) to ensure that the entire Temple Mount, much of which consists of open courtyards and gardens that lie above the ruins of the two temples, was declared al-Aqsa Mosque. This renders any Israeli activity there whatsoever a "violation."

The Israeli demand to be recognized as a Jewish state (deliberately using the terminology of UN General Assembly Resolution 181 of 1947 that created the State of Israel) is very much a response to these Palestinian positions. It is championed in Israel not only by the political right. Not surprisingly, an examination of attempts to produce an agreed two-state solution since 2000 (Camp David, the Clinton parameters, Taba, the informal Geneva accords, Olmert-Abbas, Kerry, etc.) indicates that discussions of the pre-1967 issues have produced virtually no narrowing of differences.

Indeed, these issues are not even clearly defined in the agreed 1993 Oslo Declaration of Principles.

It was only in the course of final status talks that the two sides became fully aware of each other's narratives and the differences separating them. For example, when Yasser Arafat and Mahmoud Abbas declared at Camp David in July 2000 that there never was a temple on the Temple Mount. Or when Israel demanded recognition as a Jewish state, a position enshrined and hardened in Israel's July 2018 ultranationalist Nation-State Law. The Trump proposal of 2020, incidentally, simply ignored Palestinian narrative demands while endorsing the Israeli Jewish-state demand.

Interestingly, Israeli and American ignorance of the Arab narrative was not always the case. Here is David Ben-Gurion testifying in a June 1919 speech, nearly thirty years before Israel became a state: "Everybody sees a difficulty in the question of relations between Arabs and Jews. But not everybody sees that there is no solution to this question. No solution! There is a gulf, and nothing can fill that gulf. . . . I do not know what Arab will agree that Palestine should belong to the Jews. . . . And we must recognize this situation. . . . We, as a nation, want this country to be ours; the Arabs, as a nation, want this country to be theirs."[3]

One key issue critical to understanding the Palestinian approach is Palestinian negotiating strategy. It operates as a function of the Palestinians' narrative of victimhood and injustice inflicted upon them by the entire Zionist enterprise. Zionism is understood by Zionists as the expression of the Jewish people's right to self-determination in its ancestral homeland. Yet Palestinian Arab opposition to Zionism has from the very outset rejected every aspect of this statement: The Jews are not a people but rather a community of coreligionists; as a nonpeople, they have no right to self-determination but rather were implanted in Palestine by Western imperialism; Palestine is not the Jews' ancestral homeland but rather the ancestral homeland of Arabs and Muslims. "We've been through three or four *nakbas*. That's enough," cries one of the Palestinian victims of the fighting in the documentary film *Jenin Jenin*.

If you are convinced of the justice of the Palestinian position, then you must consistently reject compromise on the grounds that compromise is inherently unjust. You adjust your narrative accordingly. You assert that there never was a Hebrew temple on the Temple Mount/Haram al-Sharif in the heart of Jerusalem. You erase hundreds of years of your own historiography that asserted that the mosques on the Mount were built on the ruins of the Second Temple around a millennium and a half ago precisely in order to reinforce the claim of Islam to supersede Judaism.

And if, in the late 1980s and early 1990s, you reluctantly conclude that Israel is so strong and so permanent that you have to compromise in order to salvage something for Palestinians, then you come to the negotiating table to discuss final status issues, beginning at Camp David in 2000, with an announcement. You have made the ultimate compromise on your claim to undisputed sovereignty over all of Palestine by recognizing Israel's existence—as a sovereign state albeit not a Jewish state—within the 1948 to 1967 boundaries. Having conceded your claim to 72 percent of the territory west of the Jordan River, you will contemplate no further territorial compromises. From the standpoint of the Palestinian narrative and consequent mindset, 72 percent of the land you believe is yours is indeed a huge sacrifice. Hence the API's insistence on the 1967 lines.

This is where the Hamas movement, which perpetrated the Park suicide bombing, parts company with Fateh, the PLO, and the Palestinian Authority. Hamas rejects any compromise as unjust and vows to fight on, viewing all Israeli civilians as legitimate targets. In contrast, the PLO's compromise is embedded in the Arab Peace Initiative. Note that the API, while enshrining the 1967 lines, offers acceptance, legitimization, and security for Israel. But it does not compromise on the Temple Mount or the right of return; it simply avoids mentioning them specifically. It returns them to the negotiating table, where endless efforts have failed to resolve them.

Then too, Palestinian demands regarding Jerusalem are of necessity linked to those of the Arab and Muslim worlds. Is a Palestinian leader free to make the smallest concession regarding Jewish claims to the Temple Mount without consulting the Arab League and global Muslim groups? Almost certainly not, insofar as a Palestinian state will be beholden to Saudi Arabia, guardian of the two holiest sites of Islam, for long-term financial aid and will want its Haram al-Sharif caretaker status recognized by all Muslims. Besides, the Israel-Jordan peace treaty of 1994 awards the Hashemite Kingdom the primary role of guardian of the Muslim holy places in Jerusalem. This introduces another actor into negotiations regarding the third holiest site in Islam.

Then there is linkage regarding the refugee/right of return issue. In negotiating with Israel, the PLO claims to represent the interests of millions of Palestinian refugees. Some, in Lebanon for example, are stateless and bereft of most rights. But others as in Jordan are citizens of another Arab country. Moreover, the API, to which the PLO subscribes, proffers a formula whereby the refugee issue will be the subject of an "agreed" solution and will be resolved based on UN General Assembly Resolution 194 of

1949. Agreed between what countries, movements, and institutions: Israel, the PLO, the Arab League? The API does not say.

Note that 194 never mentions the term "right of return," yet all Arabs claim to understand it to "mean" the right of return. Then too, the API rejects patriation, meaning naturalization, of refugees in their countries of residence, meaning primarily Lebanon and Syria. The API makes no mention at all of some 600,000 Jewish refugees who from 1948 and well into the 1950s fled violence and persecution in the very Arab countries that constitute the Arab League, most ending up absorbed by Israel.

Given all these Arab third-party conditions and counter-conditions regarding holy places and the right of return, how is even the most moderate and compromise-minded Palestinian leader supposed to navigate these issues in final status talks aimed at ending all claims between Palestinians and Israelis? Little wonder the Arab Peace Initiative says nearly nothing about the pre-1967 narrative issues.

16

2002–2021

In 2021 the Park Hotel, long since repaired and refurbished, was still in business. It still held Passover Seder celebrations in its banquet hall, at least until Passover 2020, when the COVID-19 virus forced a temporary halt to all such gatherings anywhere in Israel. The 2003 Seder, held a year after the Park atrocity, was sparsely attended mainly by defiant celebrants from among the Cohen family and their friends who wanted to make a statement. Since then, attendance has gone up, much as visits to the hotel by "terrorism tourists" have slowly declined toward zero. The sole exception are security trainees from Israel's various war colleges and defense missions visiting from abroad. They are brought to the Park to learn from the country's worst terrorist atrocity.

Outside, Netanya seems to be thriving. In the intervening nineteen years, it has lived down a reputation for harboring Israeli mafia chieftains who periodically stage spectacular turf-war shootings and car bombings. Recently there has been a massive influx of veteran Israeli retirees. New immigrants of the "lite" Orthodox Jewish variety have arrived from France, where Islamist extremism not totally disconnected from Hamas and its credo has forced them out. Laniado Hospital has been impressively upgraded.

In the early years after 2002, Netanya's police and the Shabak held meetings at the Park in a gesture of solidarity. A demand by survivors of the suicide attack and relatives of the thirty victims to turn the Park lobby into a shrine to the fallen was rejected by Netanya's mayor. The Park thirty are not the city's only terror victims. There are many more, some killed before Park and some after. All are memorialized in a single central municipal shrine to the fallen: soldiers, sons and daughters of Netanya, killed in Israel's wars, and the dead from terror attacks.

Abbas as-Sayyid, the Tulkarm-based Hamas commander who engineered the Park attack and additional, earlier bombings in Netanya, is serving thirty-five life sentences in an Israeli jail. He received a life sentence for each person killed by bombs whose provenance could be traced directly to him, at the Park and elsewhere. Upon convicting him, his Israeli judges, fearing some sort of future peace-linked general pardon for Palestinian terrorist lifers, tacked on another fifty years of incarceration for good measure. So it's thirty-five life sentences plus fifty years for as-Sayyid. Israel has no death penalty.

At his trial and sentencing in 2006, as-Sayyid was defiant, handcuffed hands flashing a V-for-victory. Among Hamas terrorists imprisoned in Israel, he is recognized as a leader and source of emulation. In 2019 he led a Hamas prisoners' strike over conditions of their incarceration: cell phone usage, family visits, and so on.

Yasser Arafat, who was held ultimately responsible by Ariel Sharon for the Park bombing and all the other atrocities of the second Intifada and whose death by mysterious causes some attribute to Sharon, is buried in the grounds of the Muqataa. His tomb, guarded in perpetuity by two uniformed Palestinian soldiers, is dignified and impressive. He had predicted to Tony Zinni that neither Egypt's Mubarak nor Jordan's Abdullah would "walk behind" his funeral procession. In fact, Mubarak presided over a Cairo funeral service in 2004 attended by dignitaries from around the globe.

The entire Muqataa building complex, which was besieged and decimated by Israel during Operation Defensive Shield and in another confrontation months later, has been impressively restored and expanded. Mahmoud Abbas, Arafat's successor at the helm of the Palestinian Authority, Fateh, and the Palestine Liberation Organization, continues to administer all three organizations from there. Ramallah street signs direct you to the "President's Office."

Abbas, nineteen years after assuming the presidency and fourteen years after Hamas violently co-opted his authority in the Gaza Strip, champions the international track. He seeks to exercise diplomatic pressure on Israel through condemnation in such tribunals as the International Criminal Court and the United Nations Human Rights Council. Both institutions sport large anti-Israel majorities and Jerusalem can do little to influence them. Abbas's office promotes and encourages the BDS (Boycott, Divestment, and Sanctions) movement that advances economic sanctions against Israel. He has recruited recognition of virtual Palestinian statehood from more countries than have diplomatic relations with Israel.

Because Israel continues to violate Palestinian rights and expand settlements in the West Bank and East Jerusalem, Abbas's strategy has evinced sympathy in several strategically important venues such as the European Union and the US Democratic Party. Yet Abbas, now in his mid-eighties, has to deal with a world and a region that are less and less preoccupied with the Palestinian issue and are increasingly authoritarian and anti-liberal.

Apropos authoritarian, until 2021 Abbas had not had to face Palestinian elections for a decade and a half. He was effectively president for life, with no working parliament to report to either. Then, after Donald Trump's replacement by Joe Biden and the beginning of a thaw in US-Palestinian relations, Abbas in a show of democratic liberalism declared parliamentary elections for May 2021 and presidential elections for July. By April he realized that Hamas was primed to win the elections, and he cancelled them. Through a convoluted series of events, this catalyzed yet another Israel-Hamas conflict in May.

Almost nowhere is Abbas's international campaign translated into effective sanctions against Israel. BDS and international legal pressure appear to have had little or no impact. For good measure, the government of Israel in 2006 established a "Ministry of Strategic Affairs" dedicated to thwarting them.

Marwan Barghouthi, the Fateh leader captured in Ramallah during Operation Defensive Shield and sentenced to life imprisonment in Israel for planning lethal terrorist attacks in Tel Aviv, remains in Israeli jail. Barghouthi, if ever released in some sort of general amnesty, is mentioned as a potential successor to Abbas. Meanwhile, to be on the safe side, he planned to run against Abbas in July 2021. He is visited regularly by Israeli Arab members of Knesset and by a few Israeli Jews who had been involved in Israeli-Palestinian informal dialogues with him prior to March 2002.

Jibril Rajoub and Mohammed Dahlan, Arafat's designated security negotiators with US emissary Anthony Zinni at the time of the Park bombing and Operation Defensive Shield, remain active in the Palestinian cause. Today they have vastly different roles. Rajoub is PA minister of sports and, more important, secretary-general of Fateh's Central Committee, a sinecure that keeps him in the running as a possible successor to Abbas. His rhetoric has become increasingly belligerent and angry toward Israel over the years. Perhaps this befits a candidate for the Palestinian leadership whose Ramallah security headquarters was gratuitously destroyed by the IDF in April 2002.

Dahlan was chased out of the Gaza Strip by the 2007 Hamas takeover. He moved to Ramallah, along with a number of Fateh activists who feared for their lives if they remained in Hamas-ruled Gaza. Then, in 2011 Abbas chased Dahlan out of the West Bank, charging him with corruption and conspiring to carry out a coup. Abbas even accused Dahlan of murdering Arafat, thereby seemingly absolving Ariel Sharon of suspicion.

Dahlan moved to Cairo and the United Arab Emirates, made money from business deals and security services, and seems to have become an international adventurer. He is "wanted" by the PA and Turkey, is accused of selling arms to parties to the Yemeni civil war, and in 2015 obtained Serbian citizenship as a reward for brokering Serbian arms deals with the UAE. He has also improved his links with Gaza-based Hamas and still has a cadre of supporters in the West Bank.

Dahlan, too, is occasionally mentioned as a power broker and possible leader, if and when he can return to Palestine after the departure of the aging Abbas. The UAE's August 2020 "normalization" agreement with Israel appeared to give Dahlan a leg up in the much-anticipated race to succeed Abbas. While the normalization move by the Emirates was heavily criticized in many Palestinian circles because it rewarded Israel without demanding Palestinian statehood, thereby violating for the first time the Arab Peace Initiative (see chapter 17), a few bold Dahlan supporters in Ramallah openly supported it. They organized a pro-Dahlan party for the 2021 Palestinian elections.

The senior Palestinian officials trapped with Arafat in the besieged Muqataa in 2002 have gone their separate apolitical ways, not always willingly. Ghassan Khatib teaches cultural studies and contemporary Arab studies at Birzeit University near Ramallah. Salam Fayyad, PA finance minister then prime minister, campaigned for honest, uncorrupt government until he was forced out by President Abbas. He tried to pursue his cleanup campaign through a nongovernmental organization in Ramallah. Eventually, accused by a paranoid Abbas of embezzlement, Fayyad took refuge in an American think tank. By March 2021, with the prospect of new Palestinian elections on the horizon and the aging Abbas seemingly weakened politically, he was planning his own election campaign to return to the Palestinian Authority parliament.[1]

Hani al-Hassan went on to fill senior positions in the PA and Fateh. When Hamas took over the Gaza Strip in 2007, al-Hassan—who began his career as a Muslim Brotherhood activist in Germany—was accused by Abbas of conniving with the Islamist movement and was relieved of his official tasks. He died in Amman in 2012. One of al-Hassan's unique practices was to send greetings on Jewish holidays such as Passover to the Israelis he knew, among them this writer.

Back at the Park Hotel in Netanya, Eric Cohen is smiling, clean-shaven, fiftyish, knitted kippa on his head and dressed informally as hotel managers go. He still runs the place from a small, crowded back-room office. The Cohen family installed a very modest and dignified photo tribute to one of its own, Amiram Hamami, on a wall near the reception desk. It was Hamami, we recall, who manned the entrance to the Passover Seder hall, checked participants' tickets and table numbers as they entered, and paid with his life. The young Hamami—dark hair and mustache, in some photos playing with his son—is memorialized as a happy person. There is nothing written beneath the photos. Visitors are expected to understand what this exhibit is about.

Looking west from the Park Hotel toward the Mediterranean, or for that matter west from Beirut's Phoenicia Intercontinental Hotel toward the Mediterranean, the specter has changed radically since March 2002. In 2009–2010 Israel discovered natural gas deposits beneath the seabed. By international standards, Israel's gas production is marginal. It is not sitting on a huge gas bubble like, say, Qatar in the Persian Gulf. Still, the country has become self-sufficient energy-wise and is exporting gas to Jordan, the Palestinian Authority, and Egypt. It is collaborating with Cyprus and Greece in further exploration and in the laying of seabed pipelines.

Since Israel's Mediterranean exclusive economic zone (EEZ) borders Lebanon's, it is a near certainty that Lebanon, too, will discover gas deposits and exploit them for its economic prosperity. But Lebanon in 2021 was both governmentally dysfunctional and economically in dire straits. It disputed the location of its EEZ border with Israel and argued that Israel's Tamar and Leviathan fields, both producing, extend into its territory. Though it had previously rejected compromise maritime borders suggested by American mediators, in 2020 it agreed to direct talks with Israel regarding the EEZ delineation issue, held under UN and US auspices.

Lebanon has allocated some maritime drilling zones to global energy firms, but little can start until and unless Beirut gets its economic and diplomatic act together. An initial drilling attempt by three energy giants, France's Total, Italy's ENI, and Russia's Novatek, in Lebanon's "block 4" maritime drilling zone, a nondisputed area thirty kilometers west of the Beirut coast, proved unproductive in February 2020. After that, COVID-19 pandemic panic put a damper on everyone's energy exploration.

In early 2021 you could still see Lebanon's block 4 drilling rig from the twenty-first floor of the Phoenicia Hotel, where the Arab Peace Initiative was approved in March 2002. Or from the still battered and unfinished Murr Tower behind it. The Murr's profile is striking. A few years ago,

Lebanese sculptor Marwan Rechmaoui mounted a model of it in London's Tate Gallery. Both buildings survived the horrendous August 4, 2020, ammonium nitrate explosion in Beirut's harbor that shocked the world and upended Lebanese politics.

One aspect of Lebanon's problem in 2021 is widespread economic mismanagement and huge public protests against corrupt officials. Another dimension is the increasing political power of the Shiite Hezbollah party and the Iranian interests it represents. Hezbollah has threatened to attack Israel's Mediterranean drilling rigs.

This has sparked the Israel Navy to upgrade its relatively small missile boats that normally perform coast guard–type missions. What is emerging is a fleet of far more substantial surface ships that begins to parallel Israel's submarine fleet. The latter reputedly sports a very advanced deep-water second-strike capability designed to deter Iran, Hezbollah's patron, located 1,500 kilometers east from the Israeli and Lebanese Mediterranean coast. The eastern Mediterranean basin has become Israel's security and economic strategic depth.

A short distance south of the Phoenicia, the squalid Palestinian refugee camps are still there. "Patriation" has still not happened. The camp residents remain noncitizens, still barred by Lebanon from working in most trades.

Moving south back to Israel, then south along the coast from Netanya, the Gaza Strip would also like to drill for gas. But the Strip's Hamas rulers are under permanent maritime siege by Israel. And the Ramallah-based PLO doesn't have the physical and political presence in Gaza that would allow it to discuss maritime boundaries and drilling rights with Israel. All it can do for the moment is buy Israel's gas.

Gas, then, has radically altered the geostrategic and economic reality of the Eastern Mediterranean since 2002. Lebanon is in such bad shape that it has failed to join the party. Neither can the Palestinians. In Beirut, Gaza, and Ramallah, they can only watch, beset by the stagnation represented by the Arab Peace Initiative, as Israel does gas deals with its other Mediterranean neighbors. Only an increasingly Islamist Turkey threatens to spoil the party by disputing Cypriot drilling rights.

★   ★   ★

In some cases the fate of the actors of 2002 is ironic. We find Ghassan Salamé, the Lebanese minister of culture who organized the March 2002 Arab League summit in Beirut, laboring fruitlessly on behalf of the United Nations to mediate an end to civil war in tribalized and fragmented Libya.

By 2020 Salamé, fed up with the military interventions of fellow Arab League members Egypt and the UAE along with Russia and Turkey, resigned, citing "ill health." He did not return to Lebanon. He hasn't lived there for years. Rather, he returned to Paris to teach at the renowned Sciences Po, the Paris Institute of Political Studies.

Another irony finds Alistair Crooke, the former MI6 operative and EU representative who tried and failed in 2002 to bridge the gaps between Arafat, Hamas, and Israel, running a Levant-based think tank, Conflicts Forum, which advertises itself as "a small geo-political and geo-financial consultancy." These days, Conflicts Forum broadly advances a point of view that appears to critically and intellectually integrate the *Muqawama* (Resistance) ideological platforms of Iran, Syria, and Hezbollah. Much earlier, sometime in April 2002, Crooke, who had been an advocate of indirectly involving Hamas in the discussions despite Jerusalem and Washington's insistence on isolating the Palestinian Islamist movement, had been pushed out of his job in the West Bank by Anthony Zinni and the CIA.

Then too, the Saudi approach to independent-minded journalists, seen with hindsight, is ironic. The Saudis brought a willing Tom Friedman to Riyadh in early 2002. They believed, correctly, that the Pulitzer Prize–winning journalist's freewheeling reputation could lend credence and gravitas to a Middle East peace initiative designed primarily to restore their standing after 9/11 and resolve rivalries among the royal family. Yet in 2018 a scion of this same royal family, Crown Prince Mohammed bin Salman, presided over a gruesomely botched plot in Istanbul to eliminate a mildly critical Saudi journalist, Jamal Khashoggi, working for the *Washington Post*. MbS, the crown prince, has since sufficed with jailing wayward Saudi journalists.

Note that Khashoggi's slot as Middle Eastern contributing columnist with the *Post* was filled by Ezzedine Choukri Fishere, a far more outspoken Egyptian author and academic whom we encountered at the Beirut Arab League summit of March 2002 and in connection with the Quartet's Roadmap in 2003.

The Quartet, or rather a new Quartet, emerged in early 2020 with the goal of reviving the Israeli-Palestinian peace process aimed at a two-state solution. Egypt, Jordan, France, and Germany have been meeting ever since. Their initiative was a response to US president Trump's "deal of the century" with its acute pro-Israel and anti-Palestine bias. By 2021 they had offered no new peace initiative, but presumably they could happily reconcile their effort with the more balanced approach anticipated from the Biden administration.

And here is yet another contemporary irony. The COVID-19 pandemic of 2020–2021 constituted for Palestinians and Israelis a throwback to the days of March and April 2002 in three curious ways. For one, recall how the Shabak had by 2002 developed a cellular contact-tracing capability that it used to apprehend Palestinian suicide-bombing teams. This came in handy in 2020, when the Shabak tracked Israelis who had been in contact with COVID-19 virus sufferers and saved many Israeli lives. Few Israelis objected to this violation of their privacy.

Apropos, by 2020–2021 there were nearly no suicide bombings. There were occasional suicidal knife attacks and car rammings in the West Bank, mostly against soldiers who then killed the assailant. Yet this reality was not permitted to shatter the Palestinian narrative of resistance by suicide. "Strap on the belt, O daughter of my land, and detonate it in front of the enemies. How sweet is the taste of Martyrdom, I have found none like it" was a fairly typical exhortation of Official PA TV Live in late April and early May 2020.[2] If any determined young Palestinian woman took this seriously and shared her thoughts by cell phone, email, or Facebook, the Shabak would be on to her with the same efficiency with which it tracked COVID-19 contaminators.

Still comparing the West Bank Palestinian present to the past, those who had been forced into curfew by the invading IDF throughout April and part of May 2002 during Operation Defensive Shield experienced a sense of déjà vu in 2020–2021. Now, similarly confined and self-isolating due to the corona scourge, they recalled the lessons learned back then regarding solidarity, homeschooling, and self-control. Now they had Zoom.[3]

Finally, Mohammad Bakri of *Jenin Jenin* fame still lives in Israel. But because he can't get an acting job there, he acts in Hollywood productions such as *Homeland*, which is based on an Israeli series. In January 2021, an Israeli provincial court finally found him guilty of libel. The IDF veterans of the April 2002 Jenin battle had succeeded in identifying one of their fellow soldiers shown hazily in the background of Bakri's film. Now the libel charge was specific and personal and the court accepted it. Bakri was fined about $50,000 and *Jenin Jenin* was banned from being shown in Israel.

Banning a film that can easily be Googled was a largely symbolic punishment characteristic of Israel's increasingly ultranationalist mood. At last report Bakri was planning an appeal. The Israeli military, incidentally, has never published its own official version of the Jenin battle.

★   ★   ★

Defensive Shield was one of two security spinoffs of the Park atrocity. The other was a major boost toward building a security fence separating Israel from most of the West Bank. By 2020 there remained a few areas where no fence or wall had been erected. There are three explanations for this lacuna.

One is a topographic or demographic inability to separate Jewish settlements from adjacent Arab villages. A second is occasional topography that lends itself better to army patrols than to fencing. And a third is deference to settler lobbyists who object to any hint of partitioning the West Bank. As more and more of the West Bank is swallowed up by Israel, these explanations increasingly lose their relevancy.

Seen nearly two decades later, has the West Bank barrier fence strengthened the logic of—and the case for—a two-state solution? Back in 2002 that's what the settlers feared and the Israeli peace camp hoped would happen. After all, most fences built by sovereign states are there to separate them from neighbors.

The answer is a resounding "no." Since the fence was built, the settlement enterprise beyond the barrier has expanded radically, and the settler population beyond the fence has grown apace. In the course of a variety of formal and informal negotiations with Israelis, the PLO has never accepted the fence as the prototype or guide for a political border. Indeed, moderate Palestinians who support a two-state solution were highly critical of the fence from the outset, even where it hugs the green line. After all, Palestinians in the West Bank as well as Palestinian citizens of Israel generally refuse to recognize Israel as a Jewish state, with or without fences. They believe that any territorial resolution of the conflict should be based on open borders between a Jewish-Arab binational Israel and a Palestinian state.

In any event, all negotiating and mediating attempts since 2002 have failed. The West Bank–Gaza Strip political link has been largely severed. Israeli governments are increasingly hawkish and pro-settler. PLO and PA leader Mahmoud Abbas has become more intransigent even as he remains declaratively anti-violence and behaves in a manner far less slippery and deceptive than his predecessor, Arafat. The mainly economic and reduced territorial model of a solution espoused by the US government under President Trump was not representative of the international community and was rejected out of hand by the aging Abbas.

In May 2020 Abbas, confronting Netanyahu's declared intention to begin annexing parts of the West Bank in accordance with the Trump plan, proclaimed he was severing security ties with Israel. He had done so before, yet the security cooperation continued. The Arab world, beset by COVID-19 and Iran, remained largely indifferent. It was only when

Netanyahu cancelled his annexation plan in response to the UAE's normalization offer that the PA officially renewed security cooperation.

Here we note that the Israeli security approach to the West Bank launched by Defensive Shield was a key contributor to this stalemate situation. The fence quickly became little more than an accessory to the achievements of Defensive Shield. Professor Menachem Klein of the Department of Political Studies at Bar Ilan University near Tel Aviv, a prominent veteran two-state solution advocate, explains why.

"It's a mistake to view the fence as a barrier in the sense of partition or border," Klein states. "For the IDF and the Shabak, the fence is a tool of control, nothing more. This stems from their operational concept regarding the fence. It is one more obstacle to entering Israel. The major factor in reducing terror is security cooperation with the Palestinian Authority [and the fact that] our forces enjoy a free hand on the other side of the barrier, including in Palestinian-populated cities."[4] The fence rationalizes the process by which Israel's security forces monitor the entry of Palestinians from the West Bank to Israel—for day labor, medical care, and the like.

Nowadays, the fence at Tulkarm where the Park Hotel attack originated looks sloppy in places, with unrepaired gaps and unlocked gates. In keeping with the security concept described by Klein, it is the IDF patrols on the Israeli side and IDF incursions into Tulkarm that claim to guarantee Israel's security.[5]

Breaches in the fence have also come to serve as a kind of safety valve for pent-up West Bank Palestinian tensions and Israeli manpower needs. Movement of tens of thousands of unlicensed Palestinian laborers through holes in the fence to day jobs in Israel is at times tolerated by the IDF. After all, Israel's agriculture and construction economies need this cheap labor. In August 2020, during Muslim celebrations of Eid al-Adha, thousands of West Bank families traversed these same breaches to spend the day at Israel's Mediterranean beaches while the IDF looked the other way. A public outcry by security-preoccupied Israelis sent the army hurriedly to patch the fence for the first time in years.

There is also one Jerusalem urban area where the city's security wall has made a mockery of the entire security barrier concept. Before construction of the barrier, the village of Kafr Akab, which lies between Israel's capital and Ramallah, capital of the Palestinian Authority, functioned as part of Israeli Jerusalem. Like a number of Arab villages on the eastern and northern fringes of Arab-majority East Jerusalem, it had mindlessly been annexed and attached to Jerusalem by Israel in June 1967. Back then, under the spell of post–Six-Day War hubris and euphoria, a victorious Israel ignored demographic security considerations. But since 2002, for reasons of both security and demography, the fence/wall runs south of Kafr Akab, cutting it off from Jerusalem and in effect annexing it to Ramallah to the north. Yet Israel still insists Kafr Akab is part of its capital.

The result is a large urbanized area comprising tens of thousands of Palestinian citizens of Israel who enjoy virtually no municipal services: sporadic garbage collection, no police. Choked streets are rendered nightmarish by cars driving freely against the direction of traffic. High-rise dwellings built without licenses are fined, then taxed based not on on-site inspections but rather on aerial photographs commissioned by the municipality located in West Jerusalem: government by drone. In early 2021, Israel took the unusual step of allowing Palestinian Authority armed forces into Kafr Akab to deal with a triple murder there:[6] better them than the IDF, which keeps its distance.

One of the routes used for driving from Jerusalem to Ramallah traverses this anarchic, manic no-man's-land. It is a fitting metaphor for the post-Park, post–Defensive Shield, post-API reality of Israelis and Palestinians.

Then too, it is instructive to recall Ariel Sharon's initial impulse to fence off the Jordan Valley so as to separate it from the Palestinian Authority and attach it to Israel. Back in 2002–2003, Sharon was warned off by international legal experts and public opinion. By 2020, the Trump administration's "deal of the century" was briefly offering Israel sovereignty over that same Jordan Valley, along with additional real estate in the West Bank. Trump's ultra-hawks had replaced Bush 43's neocons.

Finally, Russia has come a long way in its interaction with Israelis and Arabs since 2002. Beginning in September 2015 with its military deployment in strife-torn Syria and through into 2021, Russia has returned to the region militarily, diplomatically, and economically and reemerged as a full-fledged superpower. It has established a military presence across the region, from Iran to Egypt and Libya. It has systematically exploited the United States' inclination, first under Obama, then under Trump, and then Biden, to seek a military exit from the region's "endless wars." Russia's July 2019 "Security Concept for the Gulf Area," which sought to bring Iran, Saudi Arabia, and the UAE under a Moscow-sponsored counterterrorism umbrella, was in 2020 being debated seriously in Riyadh and Tehran.

But—plus ca change—as in the 2000–2004 era, Putin is still engaged in a balancing exercise between Arab, Iranian, and Turkish interests, meaning regional Islam, and the interests of Israel. He has met with all the players: Israel's Netanyahu, Iran's Rowhani, Turkey's Erdogan, of course Syria's Assad, whose regime he rescued. He looks the other way when Israel bombs Iranian and Iranian-proxy targets in Syria. Yet his own expeditionary force and Russian mercenaries fight alongside those very same anti-Israel elements to restore Assad's rule throughout the country. Moscow even looks the other way when Iranian proxies advance toward Israel's border with Syria.

Putin applies in Syria localized cease-fire-negotiating techniques perfected earlier in Chechnya. He maintains active ties with two local Islamist movements, Hamas and Hezbollah, even as he helps Assad fight Syrian Islamist insurgents. Russia's energy sector takes an interest in eastern Mediterranean gas deposits, whether Israeli or Lebanese. Only when it comes to Israeli-Palestinian peace issues does this intricately balanced symmetrical activism cease and Moscow maintain a low profile.

Whether Russia's major Middle East investment and energetic balancing act will bear strategic fruit over the long term remains an open question. The Middle East, largely incapable of addressing the long term, has no answers.

17

CONCLUSION: MARCH 27, 28, AND 29 AS A TURNING POINT

The events of March 27, 28, and 29, 2002, did not occur in a vacuum. They were preceded and followed by a host of critical developments. Still, it is the immediate juxtaposition of those fateful three days that, as- sessed in retrospect, appears so profoundly to have affected the course of conflict and coexistence in the Middle East as we know it today. All three events—the Park attack, the Arab Peace Initiative, and Operation Defen- sive Shield—were strategic game-changers in the overall context of the Israel-Arab and Israeli-Palestinian conflicts.

Or were they? It is all too tempting to fasten upon a date in contem- porary Middle East history and argue that far-reaching ensuing strategic events were caused or catalyzed by that date. Veteran Arab-Israel mediator and facilitator Aaron Miller prefers the failed July 2000 Camp David sum- mit between Israel and the PLO as the "critical inflection point."[1] Others might point to the 1967 Six-Day War. Kim Ghattas's recent book *Black Wave* argues that events in the year 1979—the Shiite Islamist takeover in Iran, the takeover by extremists of the Grand Mosque in Mecca, the Soviet invasion of Afghanistan that sparked the first modern-day jihad—were the game-changers that determined the ensuing four decades of developments in the Muslim Middle East.[2]

All of these analogies are valid and useful for understanding the course of events. No one "take" reflects absolute and infallible wisdom. Here, in this concluding chapter, we seek to make sense of the Arab-Israel and Israeli-Palestinian spheres by arguing that March 27, 28, and 29, 2002, con- stituted a turning point. That is not to say there were not additional turning points. Yet the confluence of events that transpired then was unique in a multitude of ways, some even Shakespearean in sweep.

FOUR UNIQUE FEATURES

Four features that characterized the March 2002 events remain unique. For one, we encounter a simultaneous inflection point in both the Arab-Israel conflict (the Arab Peace Initiative) and the Israeli–Palestinian conflict (the Park bombing; Operation Defensive Shield). To view similar phenomena, we have to go back to the events of 1948, 1967, and 1978.

The 1948 war that gave birth to the State of Israel and the Palestinian *nakba*, or disaster of defeat and exile, ended up establishing the geographical and strategic boundaries for both conflicts. That war took the better part of a year. The 1967 Six-Day War radically altered the parameters of Israel's conflicts with neighboring Arab states and neighboring Palestinians in Gaza and the West Bank. It also radically altered the balance of power between Israel and the Arabs. That took just six days.

The 1978 Camp David Accords between Israel and Egypt established two precedents: territories-for-peace guidelines between Israel and its Arab state neighbors and a framework for Palestinian autonomy in the West Bank and Gaza Strip. That took thirteen days to negotiate.

In March 2002 the catalytic events, both violent and diplomatic, transpired in three days.

Secondly, at the time the events described here took place, their broad strategic import was not understood. When in 1948 Israel was born in the midst of the emerging post-WWII Arab world and the Palestinian refugee issue was created, virtually all concerned both globally and regionally understood that a major geostrategic earthquake had taken place. A similar judgment can be delivered regarding June 1967 and September 1978.

Not so on March 27, 28, and 29, 2002. None of the principal Arab, Israeli, or American strategic actors seemed to grasp that in the course of three fateful days something momentous had happened in the Middle East. To this day, learned chronicles of the Middle East conflict, the Arab-Israel peace process, and the Israeli–Palestinian issue seem to manage without mentioning the Arab Peace Initiative or the Park bombing. Nor do they inquire whether and why, for Israelis, the Passover bombing was more traumatic than earlier suicide attacks.[3]

None of these chronicles links the three days as a major regional-strategic turning point. Few scholars seem to have taken note that in late March 2002 the Arab states gave up on making war against Israel and the two-state solution died and that both these phenomena emerged in an interactive dynamic. Uzi Dayan, Ariel Sharon's national security adviser, sums up how Israelis saw the events of March then and now: "In retrospect this was an important milestone. It was not understood as such at the time. [Rather] there's a crisis, we have to deal with it."[4]

A third characteristic of these events is the juxtaposition of the unusual personalities and leadership styles of Ariel Sharon and Yasser Arafat. By this stage in the Oslo process, nearly a decade after it began, each of these two leaders was broadly viewed by the other side as the personification of evil. Each believed in the use of force for tactical-political purposes. Neither was a grand-strategic thinker of note.

At the tactical level only one of the two, Sharon, could "win." He enjoyed huge advantages: a sovereign country, a disciplined army, international legitimacy, a democratic society, and the rule of law. Israel defeated the Palestinian uprising known as the second Intifada. Yet the Arafat-Sharon "death tango" lives on to this day in the very dynamic of the Palestinian-Israeli conflict.

A fourth unique feature of the events of late March 2002 is the hand of fate. The Park Hotel bombers chose their target and the timing of their attack randomly. From Hamas's standpoint it was pure chance that the attack killed thirty Passover celebrants. By the same token, it emerges that the Arab Peace Initiative was intended primarily to satisfy a variety of Arab political needs rather than to end the Arab-Israel conflict. Its approval in Beirut transpired in the absence of many key Arab leaders. Its hodgepodge composition is at times ridiculously formulaic, if not self-contradictory. Note, for example, how it pins a "just solution" of the refugee problem to UNGAR 194, which never solved anything, and for good measure rejects "Palestinian patriation," thereby guaranteeing failure on the refugee issue.

Nor did the Arab League ever make a serious attempt to implement the API or sell it to Israel. Viewed nineteen years later, the API's relative staying power is reflected simply in its capacity to outlast the outcome of subsequent disruptive events that the API neither precipitated nor anticipated. The 2007 fragmentation of Palestinian rule between Hamas/Gaza and the PLO/West Bank comes to mind, as do the 2011 Arab revolutions.

But can the API survive the wholesale violation in 2020 of its key linkage between a two-state solution and Arab normalization of links with Israel—by no fewer than four Arab countries, led by the United Arab Emirates? Note that the Arab states in question continued to pledge their allegiance to the API even as they entered into formal relations with Israel. They even alleged that their ties with Israel would from herein be applied to advancing the Palestinian cause, beginning with Abu Dhabi's success in bringing about cancellation of Israeli prime minister Netanyahu's West Bank annexation plans.

REASSESSING THE ARAB PEACE INITIATIVE

Over the longer term, well beyond the life span of Arafat (died in 2004 aged seventy-five) and Sharon (comatose after January 2006, died in 2014 aged eighty-five), Israel has gained greater Arab recognition and coopera-tion, as suggested by the Arab Peace Initiative. Lest we forget, when the API was enacted in March 2002 Israel already had full diplomatic relations with neighboring Egypt and Jordan—achieved in earlier years without a quid pro quo in the form of a two-state solution. But until August 2020, when the United Arab Emirates announced the advent of a normalization process with Israel, the API acknowledged Israel's permanency and legiti-macy completely informally.

The Israel-UAE normalization deal, brokered by the Trump admin-istration, was ostensibly a trade-off. In return for a "roadmap" leading to normalization of relations, Israeli prime minister Netanyahu backed away from his intention to exploit the Trump "deal of the century" final status map to unilaterally annex all or part of the 30 percent of the West Bank the plan allots to Israel. Note that at the time this was a throwaway concession for Netanyahu; by August 2020 he had in any event backed off from an-nexation due to a complex of domestic dilemmas.

The UAE declaration was quite obviously a violation of the API's offer of normal relations only at the successful conclusion of an Israeli-Palestinian two-state deal. Within months, Bahrain, Morocco, and Sudan had followed suit. True, the UAE was largely formalizing a commercial, hi-tech, and strategic relationship with Israel that had long been a Middle East fact of life. Then too, all four Arab states were incentivized and compensated by Trump administration concessions in the form of economic and diplomatic gestures, and particularly highly sophisticated arms—a wrinkle in Israel's qualitative military edge that Netanyahu acquiesced in because of Iran.

Indeed, the Iranian threat, shared by Israel and the UAE despite a geographical gap between them of two thousand kilometers, was obvi-ously a key factor in UAE leader Mohammed bin Zayed's normalization calculations.

Further, in justifying the formal normalization move in terms relating to the Palestinians, the Emirates leader tried rather lamely to provide an API link. He cited one pillar of the API, keeping alive the two-state solution, in order to justify violating a second pillar, conditioning normal relations with Israel on the emergence of an agreed Palestinian state. In the words of UAE ambassador to Washington Yousef Al Otaiba, a key architect of the breakthrough with Israel, "Fundamentally, the Abraham Accords occurred in order to prevent Israeli annexation of the West Bank and save the two-state solution. . . . The accords were not a betrayal of the Palestinians; rather, they halted the advancement of a one-state solution."[5] Yet they certainly did not uphold the Arab Peace Initiative.

So much for Emirates' sophistry. It hardly concealed the UAE, Bahraini, Moroccan, and Sudanese calculation that in a chaotic Middle East, the Palestinian issue was now less important and less urgent than considerations of arms and interaction with Israel. Would more and more Arab states now follow suit, thereby in effect rendering the API officially defunct? Saudi King Salman, a close ally of the Emirates but unofficially the bearer of the "Saudi Plan" torch, refused and stood up for API orthodoxy. Nevertheless, on August 31 and September 1, 2020, the Saudis did permit an El Al Israel Airlines aircraft to overfly Saudi Arabia for the first time, bearing an Israeli delegation on its way to and from Abu Dhabi.

Assessed in mid-2021, barely months after the Trump-MbZ-Netanyahu coup of normalization, it was striking to note how little commotion the demise of the API caused. It was as if no one in the Arab world had ever taken it seriously as a catalyst for Israeli-Palestinian peace. The Arab world had shunted the Palestinian issue to the margins of regional concerns, long overshadowed by a decade of Arab fragmentation and revolutions and by the combined Islamist threats of Iran and ISIS.

It was striking how easily and cynically the API could be repackaged, ostensibly without being formally discarded. After all, in retrospect it remained many things to many people. "A failed PR attempt," Ezzedine Choukri Fishere calls it: There was no serious follow-up and the timing was terrible.[6] Aaron Miller calls the API an "Arab insurance policy,"[7] seemingly generated by the Arab League in anticipation of all the ensuing events the Arabs were unable to foresee, such as the Islamic State and the Iranian hegemonic drive in the Levant.

Egyptian strategic scholar Abdel monem Said Aly argues ominously that in Arab eyes, the "API did not change the Israeli perspective of the conflict. Actually, Israel's imperial appetite increased. The API was [designed] to make a two-state solution; now we are moving to the Israeli [one-] state solution."[8] One reason for this outcome is the API's failure to seriously address any of the core narrative issues separating Israelis and Palestinians mentioned in chapter 15: the right of return, the Temple Mount, and Israel as a Jewish state.

Recall, too, that the API was born of cynicism. Then, as now, the dissonance between the Park Hotel bombing of March 27 and the next day's approval in Beirut of the API is jarring. The Park atrocity was not only, in terms of fatalities, the worst in the history of the Israeli-Palestinian conflict. It struck at the holiday of national liberation observed for over two thousand years by the entire Jewish people, in Israel and the Diaspora alike. One cannot understand Operation Defensive Shield without comprehending what Park meant for Israelis. This was a strategic terror attack that demanded a strategic response. That response in turn would irrevocably turn back the clock on the Oslo process and alter Israel's view of the Palestinian capability of delivering on Israel's security requirements.

Yet these strategic ramifications were apparently not obvious to the Arab world. The Arab leaders convening in Beirut offered not a word of condolence. The Park perpetrators were Hamas Islamists whose leadership opposed any and all peace initiatives toward Israel. They immediately claimed to be sending an anti-peace message to the Arab League summit itself. Arab state intelligence establishments kept half the Arab leaders away from the Beirut summit due at least in part to serious concerns lest Lebanese Hezbollah target them in acts of terrorism. Yet they were seemingly oblivious to the significance of the Park Hotel attack for Israelis and, by extension, for the Arab world as well. The powerful documentary *Jenin Jenin* was oblivious.

Of course, the Arab leaders gathered in Beirut the day after the Park atrocity could claim retrospectively, in interviews in 2019, that the API itself constituted their resounding response to the Park atrocity. Yet by the time they approved the API in 2002, they had integrated Lebanese and Syrian objections regarding the refugee issue to the extent of rendering their initiative stillborn. In any case, the attitude in Beirut that March toward Palestinian suicide bombings against Israeli civilians ranged from trivialization (Bashar Assad: "a detail in a broader picture") to discomfort with the timing (Ezzedine Choukri Fishere: "Oh, shit").

In retrospect, one can only wonder why it took eighteen years for a handful of Arab states to yield to financial and security temptations and, each for its own price, normalize with Israel. In this sense, the API was momentous not because it catalyzed or generated Arab-Israel peace but because it accepted Israel. It was obvious from a cursory reading that the API was too flawed, too take-it-or-leave-it, too much a patchwork designed to please all Arab states and keep them within the consensus. Besides, as Nabil Shaath notes, each principal Arab actor had their own particular agenda, led first and foremost by Saudi Arabia's Abdullah.

The Saudi crown prince seemingly latched on to Tom Friedman's peace initiative idea with four purposes in mind. First, a Saudi-sponsored peace initiative would exonerate Riyadh for the mess and outrage of 9/11.

Second, Abdullah's sponsorship would cement his status as heir to the Saudi throne and enable him to rebuff challenges from his brother princes. Third, at Beirut he would establish himself as leader of the Arab world despite the ugly legacy of 9/11 and the intractability of the Israeli-Palestinian conflict. And fourth but by no means last, he was truly concerned with the fate of the Palestinians and dedicated to promoting diplomatic measures that would improve their lot.

Shaath, by the way, notes that as PA acting foreign minister, he merely sought Arab League approval for the PLO's two-state agenda; he had no illusions that peace would break out. Only Jordanian foreign minister Muasher, the *New York Times'* Tom Friedman, and perhaps the Saudi Abdullah seem to have believed the API could really generate a viable peace dynamic.

No one else seems to have really expected the API to produce an Israeli-Palestinian territories-for-peace deal. US president George W. Bush was too heavily influenced by his own neocons who opposed any Israeli territorial concessions. Ariel Sharon changed his mind about withdrawing from lands conquered in 1967 too late in his life to affect any Palestinian territory beyond the Gaza Strip. He was flawed by lingering corruption allegations and hindered by poor health. Besides, he did not believe in negotiating peace with the Palestinians. Sharon's remark to the effect that his "generation is the last one that is not afraid to make big decisions" rang truer than ever in Israel in 2021, even if in retrospect Sharon's decisions were not at all as productive as he seems to have hoped.

Yasser Arafat remained a terrorist to the end, boycotted by Israel and the United States and barricaded in the Muqataa.

And yet, without saying so, the API renounced war against Israel by the Arab states. As Said Aly notes, "it redefined the Arab perspective of the conflict. The denial of Israeli existence came to an end. There is an Arab consensus that we are not talking about 1948 [the birth of Israel], we are talking about 1967 [the Six-Day War in which Israel ended up with extended boundaries that the Arabs demand it withdraw from]."[9] Note that Said Aly also puts the March 2002 API in the context of the earlier 1948 and 1967 strategic turning points.

Said Aly's remarks place the UAE's August 2020 normalization move, rationalized by Abu Dhabi as a quid pro quo for Israel's renouncing annexation of parts of the West Bank, in the proper context: preserving the 1967 borders, to which UAE leader Mohammed bin Zayed pointedly remained committed. Indeed, once the API recognized Israel and sanctioned the idea of future normalization, perhaps de facto and then de jure normalization became inevitable.

In other words, the issue after the API is Israel's borders, not its existence. This is momentous. By unanimously recognizing Israel within its pre-1967 borders and armistice lines and outlining a formula for settling all other outstanding disputes, the Arab states have in the course of the ensuing nineteen years relegated the conflict to the halls of diplomacy. Or to the martial whims of the non-state Islamists, particularly Hamas, which brutally opposed the API a day before its enactment. Today Hamas and Hezbollah remain hostile not just to Israel but toward most of the sovereign Arab world as well, while the Arab states repeat the ritual of their API support annually. Considering this ritual, coupled with the Islamist and Iranian threats, the UAE's August 2020 initiative was inevitable.

Here we recall that the original Arab Peace Initiative as formulated by Tom Friedman and the Saudi Abdullah prior to the March 2002 summit was "friendlier" to the Israeli concept of peace and far more straightforward than the final version approved in Beirut. Israel would withdraw to the 1967 lines on all fronts and in return would receive from the Arabs peace and security. There were no complicating references to Jerusalem and the 1948 refugees. There were no crafty formulae for ensuring that refugees leave their host countries. There was no mention of UN Security Council Resolution 194, which Arabs insist gives the refugees the right of return to pre-1967 Israel. UAE ruler Mohammed bin Zayed (MbZ) could in 2020 sign off on this original Saudi formulation of normalization in return for the 1967 borders.

One of the Arab foreign ministers present in Beirut later suggested that inclusion in the API of the term "negotiated" regarding the refugees was the only balancing concession Israel needed in order to accept the final product. On the other hand, this same foreign minister acknowledged in 2019 that "the Arab peace initiative was born amongst events on both sides that almost immediately not just diluted it but tried to kill it."[10] He was referring to Syrian and Libyan opposition to "marketing" the API directly to Israel and to the longer-term effects of the Park atrocity and Operation Defensive Shield. Then too, there was the 2002 Beirut summit's routine reaffirmation of the right of return of some five million Palestinian refugees and their descendants in a separate resolution approved the next day and re-ratified annually since 2002.

There has been, incidentally, an interesting initiative by private Israelis to relate to the API. It coalesced in 2010 as the Israeli Peace Initiative (IPI), an unofficial Israeli response to the Arab Peace Initiative. The principal

IPI organizers were Koby Huberman, a hi-tech entrepreneur, and Yuval Rabin, son of the late prime minister. They were joined by a variety of additional Israelis from the political left and center, including prominent retired security chiefs. Broadly speaking, they recognized that the API did not satisfy all of Israel's basic needs in an agreement with the Palestinians. But they suggested that Israel publicly accept the API and note that it wishes to discuss with the Arab League its reservations.

That appeal brought no positive response from a succession of Israeli governments. Nor did IPI lobbying efforts with Arab governments in Cairo and Amman produce the kind of flexibility that would allow Israel to negotiate details of the Arab Peace Initiative. Direct appeals to the Arab League to open the API to negotiation as Sharon originally suggested in April 2002 rather than treat it as a "take-it-or-leave-it" proposition were also rebuffed.

Only once in the course of nineteen years, in July 2007 under pressure from the Quartet, did the League send the foreign ministers of Egypt and Jordan in a gesture to respond to Israeli requests to discuss the API. Yet these are the two Arab countries that already had diplomatic relations with Israel. The League did not, for example, send a senior Saudi official, a gesture that would have made an impression on the Israeli public.

By the same token, the only concession made to Israel by the Arab League, in a controversial vote in 2013, was to acknowledge that "comparable" and "minor" negotiated territorial "swaps" along Israel's borders with Arab countries were acceptable rather than strict adherence to the 1967 lines. Yet the principle of swaps had long before been accepted by both Israel and the PLO.

In recent years the Israel Peace Initiative morphed into the Israeli Regional Initiative (IRI). Its peace plan rejects some of the API's demands, like rigid 1967 borders and refugee right of return, but it accepts the centrality of Israeli-Palestinian peace to any real progress toward overall Israel-Arab peace. Meanwhile, in the spirit of growing economic and strategic Israel-Arab cooperation, the IRI seeks dialogue with more Arab states in order to involve them in Israeli-Palestinian peacemaking and to highlight to Israelis the immense potential economic benefits of peace. MbZ could be understood to have signed off on this initiative too.

This brings us to the Netanyahu reverse version of the API, which seemingly began to reach fruition with UAE normalization. During the second decade of the twenty-first century, the Israeli prime minister sought to expand Israeli strategic cooperation with Arab states such as the UAE, Egypt, and Jordan that shared Israel's concerns regarding both the Islamic

State and Iranian military penetration of Iraq and the Levant. He proposed a concept that turned the API on its head.

Israel, Netanyahu asserted, "used to say that as soon as peace breaks out with the Palestinians, we can achieve peace with the entire Arab world. . . . I am increasingly convinced that the process can work in the other direction, too, and that normalization . . . with the Arab world can help us to advance toward . . . peace between us and the Palestinians."[11] Thus does Netanyahu seemingly leverage the spirit of the API to avoid even a semblance of a peace initiative with the Palestinians.

By 2021, Netanyahu's normalization deal with four Arab states appeared to offer the first fruits of this approach, at least at the official level. Correspondingly, it signaled the Palestinians that their cause was in danger of being relegated officially to second-tier status in the Arab world's order of business. A PLO initiative to convene a Zoom meeting of Arab League foreign ministers to condemn Israel-Arab normalization was blocked by the normalizing countries. These developments, too, were in a perverse way a ratification of the real meaning of the API: creeping coexistence with Israel; lip service to the two-state solution; de facto descent toward an ugly, conflicted binational Israeli-Palestinian reality.

DEFENSIVE SHIELD IN RETROSPECT

Israel's March-April-May West Bank invasion and occupation, Operation Defensive Shield, was not merely large and extended. It was the IDF's biggest maneuver in the West Bank since the 1967 conquest, and it was far more time-consuming. This was the first time since the beginning of the Oslo process in 1993 that the Israeli-Palestinian peace dynamic was substantially rolled back. Israel erased anything resembling genuine Palestinian security autonomy in Area A, that one-quarter of the West Bank ostensibly under total Palestinian Authority control.

True, Palestinian security autonomy was theoretically restored when the operation ended. But ever since Defensive Shield, Israel has elected to ignore the strictures of that autonomy whenever the security need has appeared to arise. IDF troops regularly enter Palestinian cities and refugee camps, usually in the still of night, and PA security forces step aside.

Perhaps the IDF's destruction in the early days of Defensive Shield of Jibril Rajoub's Beitunia headquarters near Ramallah provides the best metaphor for what happened to the Israeli-Palestinian security relationship in March–April 2002. Rajoub had worked closely with Israel prior to the

Park bombing to combat West Bank–based Palestinian terrorism. If his headquarters could be destroyed, this meant that any vestige of trust between the two sides' security establishments was gone. From herein, Israel would not permit itself to depend on the Palestinians to fight terrorism. Rajoub, for his part, would become at least verbally a far more militant anti-Israel spokesman.

ISLAMISTS, SAUDIS, AMERICANS, AND RUSSIANS

The API was not simply a product of Jordanian and Palestinian lobbying of Saudi Crown Prince Abdullah or of a remarkable initiative by Tom Friedman. Rather, the API owes its immediate genesis to 9/11: al-Qaeda's assault on the halls of American power in New York and Washington some six months before the Arab League Beirut summit.

Al-Qaeda is essentially an Arab organization. Its origins and founding father, Osama bin-Laden, were Saudi. Most of its funding came from wealthy Saudis with Islamist fundamentalist leanings. All of this was well known to American, European, Israeli, and Arab intelligence establishments before September 2001. Once it became clear within hours of the Twin Towers and Pentagon suicide attacks that fifteen of the nineteen perpetrators of 9/11 were Saudi, from nearly every direction fingers were pointed at Riyadh.

True, the George W. Bush administration in Washington was the most understanding of Riyadh's friends and never sought to embarrass Abdullah over 9/11. The United States still needed Saudi oil. And it would need Saudi goodwill for the Afghanistan and Iraq campaigns. Yet the kingdom's leadership under Abdullah understood it had to invoke far-reaching measures and initiatives in order to restore its standing as a reliable and moderate partner of the West.

One dimension of this narrative, then, is about militant Islam. There is the al-Qaeda variety of 9/11. And there is the Hamas variety as displayed in the Park bombing. Then too, there is the tacit, unofficial ideological and logistic support awarded Hamas and Hezbollah in 2002 and thereafter by Syria and particularly Iran in their effort to scuttle the API and thwart any long-term Israeli-Palestinian and Israel-Arab understanding.

A second dimension is the Arab world's image and public relations. The 9/11 attacks were an embarrassing blot on the Arab and Muslim record of friendship with the non-Muslim world. The Arab Peace Initiative, focusing on the Middle East's Jewish state and by extension its many supporters in the United States, was intended to right matters and clean the slate. To some extent it did. Note that all fifty-seven states in the Organization of Islamic Cooperation, Iran and Syria included, also periodically and ritually express support for the API. Yet this gesture, like Arab League re-approval annually, appears to be an ineffectual and cynical PR reflex that reflects few genuine sentiments and impresses few observers.

Another significant dimension is the involvement of the United States before, during, and following the events of late March 2002. From Clinton to Bush, from Obama to Trump, Washington has seemingly tried every approach in its efforts to resolve the Israeli-Palestinian conflict. Yet one disturbing constant of the American role appears to be repeated failure to grasp the significance of key strategic events.

This was particularly evident in the treatment of the events of late March 2002 by US emissaries and analysts. If we take the 2003 Roadmap and the 2002 events leading up to it as both metaphor and template, American peace initiatives are still going nowhere. Indeed, they can even be counterproductive. The July 2000 Camp David conference sponsored by the Clinton administration led, within three months, to the second Intifada. Secretary of State Kerry's 2013–2014 mediation attempt helped produce the Israel-Gaza mini-war of mid-2014.

As for Trump's deal of the century, the jury is still out. It catalyzed the UAE normalization initiative and facilitated it with promises of sophisticated arms to Abu Dhabi and arms and economic and diplomatic aid to three additional normalizing states. For Jerusalem and Abu Dhabi, this was quintessential "economic peace." But it left the Palestinians strategically worse off than ever. Here the verdict certainly won't be peace or prosperity. Indeed, by May 2021 the verdict was violence between Palestinians and Israelis.

General Anthony Zinni, who alone understood immediately the impact on Israel of the Park atrocity ("their 9/11"), was out of a mediating job by the time the Roadmap was approved in 2003. Apropos failed US peace gambits, Zinni cynically calls the Roadmap "Einstein's definition of insanity [repeating the same failed experiment or initiative time and again and expecting a different outcome]. We did touch-and-go diplomacy. Fly in the big guys. Let's all do it in eight to nine months." Washington, Zinni says, should have seen the Arab Peace Initiative as an opening for a long-term process, complete with US-sponsored informal, nondiplomatic discussions among the parties involved. "Engage everywhere. You need to get agreement and then be there for the implementation with a team on the ground."[12]

Was the API seen in Washington, and by extension Jerusalem, as unwanted competition and a nuisance? A nice but ineffective initiative? A problematic last-minute obstacle in the way of the neocon agenda to invade Iraq? Or simply as Saudi Crown Prince Abdullah's attempt to make amends for 9/11 and contribute something to the cause of Palestinian-Israeli peace?

US peacemaking efforts during the Park–API–Defensive Shield period moved from desperate and generally fruitless attempts to arrange Israeli-Palestinian cease-fires early in the second Intifada to the fruitless Roadmap process. A long series of emissaries sent by Washington to the Middle East, from Zinni and Aaron Miller to Colin Powell and Condoleezza Rice, had little inclination to factor the API into their peace strategies beyond a brief one-liner in the Roadmap, and even less inclination to assign it strategic significance.

American background motives for Middle East peacemaking in 2002 were, somewhat like Saudi court politics, riddled with intrigue. Washington infighting, spearheaded by a neocon faction hell-bent on invading Iraq and constraining US diplomatic initiatives in the Middle East, would not produce peace in the region. The counterproductive outcomes the United States did produce are reflected in a brief comparison of two of the most relevant US diplomats, Colin Powell and Elliott Abrams.

Secretary of State Powell was a knowledgeable statesman and a serious authority figure. He was accessible to one and all. He understood the limits of intelligence and policy. But those who worked with him at the time argue that he was badly handicapped by his sense of loyalty and was too prone to defer to the administration's chain of command. He would not stand up to Cheney, much less Bush, on cease-fire and Roadmap issues or, for that matter, on the Iraq issue.

What efforts Powell did make were dogged by such Cheney sidekicks as Elliott Abrams. Abrams, a convicted felon from the Iran-Contra fiasco of the mid-1980s and an unrepentant neocon, seemed to turn up wherever Middle East matters could be made worse: Iran-Contra in the mid-1980s, peace and cease-fire efforts in Israel-Palestine in 2002–2003, and America's disastrous Iraq invasion in 2003. In a conversation in 2004, shortly before the first of a string of US-sponsored elections in a democracy-deficient post-invasion Iraq, Abrams, ever the neocon, expressed absolute certainty that the Iraqi exercise in democracy would bring about a democratic revolution in neighboring Iran: "The Iranians will see how well democracy works and get rid of the ayatollahs' regime."[13] America's neocons and their more recent Trump-era successors are still waiting for that to happen, but by mid-2020 Abrams was in charge of the State Department's Iran file.

Yet more misbegotten US-sponsored democratization efforts in the Middle East were still to come. In February 2006 the United States encouraged all relevant parties to hold an election in the Palestinian Authority that was won by Islamist and antidemocratic Hamas. That was the last parliamentary election held in either the West Bank or the Gaza Strip. Fastforward to Egypt in 2012, when the United States under President Obama, having encouraged the removal of President Mubarak a year earlier, gave its blessing to elections that installed the Muslim Brotherhood in power. The Brethren quickly abused that power and were overthrown a year later by Cairo's current dictator. President al-Sisi's human rights record is even worse than his two predecessors, the Brotherhood and Hosni Mubarak.

Then too, by 2021 Washington—first the Obama administration, then presidents Trump and Biden—was trying to lower its profile and reduce its regional presence. Its approach to the Israeli-Palestinian conflict and the Middle East in general has at times been so skewed as to render it far more harmful than helpful. Russia has moved into the region. In late 2019, Middle East scholar Hussein Ibish nicely summed up the evolution of Russian and American Middle East policy since 2015: "Russia knows what it wants, defines its goals narrowly and acts resolutely to secure its specific interests. The US does none of those things."[14]

Nor, back in 2002, were Israeli and Palestinian leaders particularly helpful. The Mitchell, Tenet, and Zinni plans and the Roadmap were generally treated by Israeli inner policy-making circles as nuisances to be maneuvered around elegantly. Arafat's penchant for violence against Israelis reflects an even more cynical response. In other words, criticism of American peacemakers or even of Saudi initiatives like the API can go only so far: Israelis, Palestinians, and other Arabs displayed an equivalent degree of misunderstanding regarding the requisites of peace. Mitchell, Tenet, and others, all the way through Condoleezza Rice, then John Kerry and on to Trump's peace team and Biden's initial efforts, can hardly be expected to analyze and "solve" the situation better than the protagonists themselves.

MARCH–APRIL 2002 AS SHAKESPEAREAN TRAGEDY

Here the narrative suggested by Daniel Kurtzer is instructive, not to mention entertaining. Kurtzer, who teaches Middle East policy studies at Princeton University, was US ambassador in Israel from 2001 to 2005. Earlier, he was US ambassador to Egypt and headed State Department Intelligence and Research. Going even further back, Kurtzer once served as dean of Yeshiva College, an orthodox Jewish institution of learning in New York. Given this background as a thinker and an academic, it should not surprise us that Kurtzer chooses to describe the events in and around late March 2002 as a Shakespearean tragedy. We already encountered (chapter 8) a comparison of the March 2002 Beirut summit with its many absent Arab leaders to a banquet scene from Macbeth. Kurtzer's narrative is a more Washington-centered version of events than one told from the standpoint of Jerusalem, Ramallah, or the Arab League. It features all five classic acts of Shakespearean tragedy: exposition, rising action, climax, falling action, and denouement.

As seen by Kurtzer,[15] Act I begins with the early suicide bombings in Israel, for example at the Tel Aviv Dolphinarium in June 2001, prior to 9/11, and extends through 9/11 and into US post-9/11 policy. It includes Bush's response to a letter from Saudi Crown Prince Abdullah in which Bush acknowledges the Palestinian right to self-determination. Bush also suggests to Sharon a meeting between PLO leader Arafat and Sharon's foreign minister, Shimon Peres, a veteran dove who shepherded the Oslo process. Peres is a wily politician and a consummate opportunist whom Sharon does not wish to involve in Israeli-Palestinian affairs.

During this act, Sharon is "in a tizzy" over Bush's immediate post-9/11 push for Palestinian rights. When Sharon alleges that Bush's tilt is reminiscent of Chamberlain at Munich in 1938, Kurtzer is dispatched to persuade Sharon to walk back his offensive remarks, which were particularly ill-timed in terms of the crisis facing Washington. Act I ends with Sharon and Bush each learning something about the other.

Act II, leading into March 2002, features relative Israeli and US moderation. Prime Minister Sharon gives an unusually dovish speech at Latrun in September 2001: "The State of Israel wants to give the Palestinians . . . the right to establish a state." Secretary of State Powell backs the two-state solution in a speech in Louisville on November 19, 2001, and announces that he is sending General Anthony Zinni to the region. Sharon learns of API and asks to be invited to Beirut. On the negative side, the *Karine A* incident of early January 2002 persuades Bush and many Israelis that Arafat is not a candidate for a genuine cease-fire and peace process.

Act III, the tragedy's climax, is the Park hotel suicide bombing, followed by Arab League approval of the API and then Operation Defensive Shield—all in three days. Zinni's mission fails. Powell arrives in the region and meets with Arafat in the Muqataa. "I'm the last US official you'll see unless you accept a cease-fire," he tells Arafat. Powell somehow remains optimistic and plans a press conference, which is cancelled at the last minute by Bush, who is constrained by the neocons as they plan for the Iraq invasion. Powell has effectively been stabbed in the back. Bush brushes aside the contradictions by calling Sharon "a man of peace."

Act IV features Bush's Rose Garden speech of June 24, 2002, implying that Arafat has to be replaced in order for a Palestinian state to emerge. Jordanian foreign minister Muasher relays to Bush Jordanian King Abdullah II's call for a multilateral roadmap to peace. Back in Israel and the Palestinian Authority, more Hamas suicide bombings in autumn 2002 trigger a renewed Israeli siege of the Muqataa, this time with IDF D9 bulldozers knocking down walls and flattening cars. US intervention achieves an Israeli pullback. The Roadmap emerges in March 2003 with exquisite timing: more or less as the United States invades Iraq.

Act V begins with the Roadmap and its quick demise. By 2005, Sharon is overseeing "disengagement": total Israeli withdrawal (military and settlements) from the Gaza Strip and, in a token gesture, dismantlement of four settlements in a small part of the northern West Bank. Sharon's plans to continue removing West Bank settlements are blunted by American neocon pressure. The neocons also lobby successfully to ignore the API. There follow more abortive American initiatives. Annapolis in November 2007 was "a farce; only Olmert took it seriously." Kerry in 2013–2014 triggers yet another Israel-Hamas war in and around Gaza. The Trump pro-settlement peace team's efforts from 2017 on effectively award Israel nearly the entire West Bank.

Act V, in Kurtzer's telling, continues to this day.

THE WAGES OF WISHFUL THINKING

An alarming proportion of the Israelis, Palestinians, and Americans who engaged in peace negotiations before and after March 2002 insist that if only this or that event had taken place or been avoided a historic agreement could have been reached, or the second Intifada delayed, or a failed peace process could have been prevented.

If only Rabin had not been assassinated in November 1995. If only Sharon had not visited the Temple Mount in September 2000. If only Powell had listened to Clinton when, on Bush's inauguration day, Clinton blamed Arafat "100 percent" for the failure of Camp David.[16] If only Bush 43 and Powell had embraced the Mitchell Committee recommendations and demanded their implementation in real time. If only Arafat had accepted and ratified Zinni's cease-fire initiative on the eve of the Park suicide bombing. If only PA security forces had intercepted the Park Hotel bomber inside Tulkarm before he set out for Israel on Passover eve. If only Hamas atrocities in Jerusalem had not derailed the Roadmap in 2003. If only Olmert had not been forced to resign in 2008. . . .

Apropos the Park Passover atrocity, there is a traditional Passover song, "Dayenu," that tells God that if he had only done this or that in the Passover narrative, it would have been enough for the Jewish people.

The Israelis, Palestinians, and Americans guilty of wishful thinking ignore, either willfully or out of ignorance, the basic narrative issues that have come to the fore whenever an Israeli-Palestinian peace process has made enough progress to encounter them. Israelis insist on Palestinian recognition of Israel as a Jewish state and of its roots on the Temple Mount in Jerusalem and the legitimacy of its links to the West Bank, the cradle of ancient Hebrew civilization. Palestinians insist that Israel recognize the right of return of the 1948 refugees and acknowledge the Temple Mount as solely a Muslim shrine. Each side's demands are perceived by the other as negating its core existential narrative. No peace process, including Oslo, has even begun to untangle this web of totally contrary religious-historical basic stories.

Those stories were not even on anyone's peace agenda by 2021. Indeed, by the time we get to the Trump presidency in 2017, Israeli, Palestinian, and other Arab leaders appear no longer to be interested or motivated.

There is a broad consensus that American peace efforts like Trump's that naively offer "economic peace" to Palestinians and more territory to Israel are destined to fail abysmally. Further, President Trump's well-advertised adversity to deeper US involvement in the Middle East region seemingly eliminated the United States as a broker of any sort of viable Israeli-Palestinian process. The gathering fear of US withdrawal from the region in the face of Iranian hegemonic designs was yet another reason for the Emirates' MbZ to seek a more official strategic relationship with Israel.

The Arab Peace Initiative emerges as an acknowledgment by the Arab states that Israel is here to stay. Looked at in retrospect, it also made a resounding statement about the Arab problem with Israel: War is not the solution for dealing with Israel, Israel within the 1967 boundaries is legitimate and acceptable, and a Palestinian settlement is not in the cards. From here to normalization by four Arab states in 2020 was not, in retrospect, such a great leap.

Arab acquiescence has become all the more obvious as the Arab world, following the "Arab Spring" revolutions of 2011, has changed. Some leaders represented in Beirut in March 2002 were violently removed: Mubarak in Egypt, Saleh in Yemen, Qaddafi in Libya, and Ben Aly in Tunisia. Another, Syria's Assad, has murdered and exiled nearly half his country's population and mortgaged his country to Iran and Russia in order to hold on to power. Beyond pro forma suspension of Syria from the Arab League, the Arab world has come to terms with Assad's bestiality as it has with Yemen's gut-wrenching scenes of mass starvation. In 2021 this was hardly a club Israel felt impelled to join by exchanging territory for peace with the Arab world.

The UAE normalization initiative of August 2020 is, in its audacity, a ringing indication of yet another emerging Arab truth. For generations, the centers of Arab political, cultural, and strategic life were Cairo, Damascus, Baghdad, and, secondarily, Beirut. Now the center is moving to Abu Dhabi, Dubai, Doha, and additional emerging economic hubs of the Gulf. This is a momentous change in the Arab order of things. It is convenient for Israel, which has never fought the Gulf countries, has no shared border with them, and encounters among them relatively little historical memory of the Arab-Israel conflict.

Israel, meanwhile, has grown strategically. It has the population, more than nine million, of a medium-size country. It is achieving energy independence. It is a hi-tech superpower. In Arab eyes, it is one of the region's few islands of stability.

Does the Arab world still have energies to expend on the conflict with Israel? With Arab states fragmenting and fighting civil wars, is there any point discussing the formation of a new state, Palestine, which itself has for years now been fragmented and divided? Given that the Middle East is flooded with millions of new refugees from the Arab revolutions and civil wars of the past decade, does the Palestinian "right of return" that was insinuated into the API by the Syrians and Lebanese still resonate?

Indeed, is the Arab agenda of 2021 in any way similar to that of 2002? The answer is that what the Arab League enacted on March 28, 2002, actually appears increasingly useful for the disjointed and traumatized Arab world of 2021. Today, conveniently and very undramatically, Arab dysfunctionality keeps the Arab-Israel conflict off the agenda. As one former Arab foreign minister notes, "The Arab Spring has meant that countries like Syria are in no position to talk about the Arab Peace Initiative. They are in the midst of civil war. . . . There is no leader in the Arab world today like Crown Prince Abdullah . . . that can gather all the Arab states together and do something like this. . . . There is no Arab leader of this culture."[17]

In other words, the API today constitutes the ultimate excuse for a dysfunctional Arab world to do nothing about Israel and the Israeli-Palestinian conflict, and for at least four Arab countries to formalize their relationship with Israel precisely in the name of preserving the two-state solution.

In sharp retrospect, the Park Hotel bombing and Operation Defensive Shield emerge as the parameters of Israeli-Palestinian stalemate. There is no two-state solution nor even a productive peace process. Israel exercises security and economic control over what increasingly looks like a one-state reality between the Jordan River and the Mediterranean Sea. With the passage of time, will this one-state reality resemble apartheid or a binational state or some hybrid polity embracing elements of both?

We don't know. The Arab states don't know and, having defined their relationship to the conflict in March 2002, no longer particularly care. They will cooperate with Israel in the security sphere against common enemies: Iran, militant Islam. They will pay lip service to the Palestinian cause while privately berating the Palestinians for stubbornly refusing to compromise more, and publicly ignoring them. Israel for its part is clearly sliding down a slippery slope toward a loss of its core identity components. It will lose democracy in the event of the emergence of an apartheid state. It will lose "Jewish state" status in the event that Israel and Palestine evolve into a binational entity.

This reality is convenient for the dominant Israeli right-religious mainstream, which is determined, with tacit Trump administration support until 2021, to hold on to the West Bank and not negotiate a two-state solution. It seemingly does not care what the outcome will be as long as it can dominate the land between the Jordan River and the Mediterranean Sea. To that end, it seems more than prepared to compromise on democracy and the rule of law.

The Trump "deal of the century" of January 2020 had the merit of not precisely repeating past failed experiments. On the other hand, it involved no American-Palestinian or Israeli-Palestinian talks at all and envisioned the transfer of territory to Israel without any sort of active peace process. And it demanded Arab agreement to conditions regarding territory, refugees, and Jerusalem that diverged wildly from the Arab Peace Initiative. It conspired with the Israeli right-religious mainstream to hammer the final nail in the coffin of the two-state solution.

The Arab League, in an emergency meeting in Cairo on February 1, reaffirmed the API and broadly condemned Trump's deal of the century for ignoring virtually all Palestinian narratives and needs. This is the same Arab

League that in the course of the past decade has proved incapable of dealing with rampant Arab state collapse and civil war. The same Arab League that could not even coordinate an Arab response to the COVID-19 pandemic. The very same organization that in August 2020 refused even to discuss the UAE's brazen violation of the Arab Peace Initiative.

When queried on this and related issues the Arab world, exhausted and exacerbated by its own internal anarchy and dysfunction, can smugly and cynically refer all concerned to . . . the 2002 Arab Peace Initiative.

APPENDIX I: THE ARAB PEACE INITIATIVE AS RATIFIED IN BEIRUT, MARCH 28, 2002

THE ARAB PEACE INITIATIVE

The Council of the League of Arab States at the Summit Level, at its 14th Ordinary Session,

- Reaffirms the resolution taken in June 1996 at the Cairo extraordinary Arab summit that a just and comprehensive peace in the Middle East is the strategic option of the Arab countries, to be achieved in accordance with international legality, and which would require a comparable commitment on the part of the Israeli government.
- Having listened to the statement made by his royal highness Prince Abdullah Bin Abdullaziz, the crown prince of the Kingdom of Saudi Arabia in which his highness presented his initiative, calling for full Israeli withdrawal from all the Arab territories occupied since June 1967, in implementation of Security Council Resolutions 242 and 338, reaffirmed by the Madrid Conference of 1991 and the land for peace principle, and Israel's acceptance of an independent Palestinian state, with East Jerusalem as its capital, in return for the establishment of normal relations in the context of a comprehensive peace with Israel.
- Emanating from the conviction of the Arab countries that a military solution to the conflict will not achieve peace or provide security for the parties, the council:

1. Requests Israel to reconsider its policies and declare that a just peace is its strategic option as well.

2. Further calls upon Israel to affirm:
   a. Full Israeli withdrawal from all the territories occupied since 1967, including the Syrian Golan Heights to the lines of June 4, 1967, as well as the remaining occupied Lebanese territories in the south of Lebanon.
   b. Achievement of a just solution to the Palestinian refugee problem to be agreed upon in accordance with UN General Assembly Resolution 194.
   c. The acceptance of the establishment of a Sovereign Independent Palestinian State on the Palestinian territories occupied since the 4th of June 1967 in the West Bank and Gaza strip, with east Jerusalem as its capital.
3. Consequently, the Arab countries affirm the following:
   a. Consider the Arab-Israeli conflict ended, and enter into a peace agreement with Israel, and provide security for all the states of the region.
   b. Establish normal relations with Israel in the context of this comprehensive peace.
4. Assures the rejection of all forms of Palestinian patriation which conflict with the special circumstances of the Arab host countries.
5. Calls upon the government of Israel and all Israelis to accept this initiative in order to safeguard the prospects for peace and stop the further shedding of blood, enabling the Arab Countries and Israel to live in peace and good neighborliness and provide future generations with security, stability, and prosperity.
6. Invites the international community and all countries and organizations to support this initiative.
7. Requests the chairman of the summit to form a special committee composed of some of its concerned member states and the secretary general of the League of Arab States to pursue the necessary contacts to gain support for this initiative at all levels, particularly from the United Nations, the security council, the United States of America, the Russian Federation, the Muslim States and the European Union.

APPENDIX II: THE ROADMAP FOR PEACE IN THE MIDDLE EAST, APRIL 30, 2003

A PERFORMANCE-BASED ROADMAP TO A PERMANENT TWO-STATE SOLUTION TO THE ISRAELI-PALESTINIAN CONFLICT

The following is a performance-based and goal-driven roadmap, with clear phases, timelines, target dates, and benchmarks aiming at progress through reciprocal steps by the two parties in the political, security, economic, humanitarian, and institution-building fields, under the auspices of the Quartet [the United States, European Union, United Nations, and Russia]. The destination is a final and comprehensive settlement of the Israel-Palestinian conflict by 2005, as presented in President Bush's speech of 24 June, and welcomed by the EU, Russia, and the UN in the 16 July and 17 September Quartet Ministerial statements.

A two-state solution to the Israeli-Palestinian conflict will only be achieved through an end to violence and terrorism, when the Palestinian people have a leadership acting decisively against terror and willing and able to build a practicing democracy based on tolerance and liberty, and through Israel's readiness to do what is necessary for a democratic Palestinian state to be established, and a clear, unambiguous acceptance by both parties of the goal of a negotiated settlement as described below. The Quartet will assist and facilitate implementation of the plan, starting in Phase I, including direct discussions between the parties as required. The plan establishes a realistic timeline for implementation. However, as a performance-based plan, progress will require and depend upon the good faith efforts of the parties, and their compliance with each of the obligations outlined below. Should the parties perform their obligations rapidly, progress within and through the phases may come sooner than indicated in the plan. Non-compliance with obligations will impede progress.

A settlement, negotiated between the parties, will result in the emergence of an independent, democratic, and viable Palestinian state living side by side in peace and security with Israel and its other neighbors. The settlement will resolve the Israel-Palestinian conflict, and end the occupation that began in 1967, based on the foundations of the Madrid Conference, the principle of land for peace, UNSCRs 242, 338, and 1397, agreements previously reached by the parties, and the initiative of Saudi Crown Prince Abdullah—endorsed by the Beirut Arab League Summit—calling for acceptance of Israel as a neighbor living in peace and security, in the context of a comprehensive settlement. This initiative is a vital element of international efforts to promote a comprehensive peace on all tracks, including the Syrian-Israeli and Lebanese-Israeli tracks.

The Quartet will meet regularly at senior levels to evaluate the parties' performance on implementation of the plan. In each phase, the parties are expected to perform their obligations in parallel, unless otherwise indicated.

PHASE I: ENDING TERROR AND VIOLENCE, NORMALIZING PALESTINIAN LIFE, AND BUILDING PALESTINIAN INSTITUTIONS—PRESENT TO MAY 2003

In Phase I, the Palestinians immediately undertake an unconditional cessation of violence according to the steps outlined below; such action should be accompanied by supportive measures undertaken by Israel. Palestinians and Israelis resume security cooperation based on the Tenet work plan to end violence, terrorism, and incitement through restructured and effective Palestinian security services. Palestinians undertake comprehensive political reform in preparation for statehood, including drafting a Palestinian constitution, and free, fair, and open elections upon the basis of those measures. Israel takes all necessary steps to help normalize Palestinian life. Israel withdraws from Palestinian areas occupied from September 28, 2000, and the two sides restore the status quo that existed at that time, as security performance and cooperation progress. Israel also freezes all settlement activity, consistent with the Mitchell report.

At the outset of Phase I:

- Palestinian leadership issues unequivocal statement reiterating Israel's right to exist in peace and security and calling for an immediate and unconditional cease-fire to end armed activity and all acts of violence against Israelis anywhere. All official Palestinian institutions end incitement against Israel.

- Israeli leadership issues unequivocal statement affirming its commitment to the two-state vision of an independent, viable, sovereign Palestinian state living in peace and security alongside Israel, as expressed by President Bush, and calling for an immediate end to violence against Palestinians everywhere. All official Israeli institutions end incitement against Palestinians.

Security

- Palestinians declare an unequivocal end to violence and terrorism and undertake visible efforts on the ground to arrest, disrupt, and restrain individuals and groups conducting and planning violent attacks on Israelis anywhere.
- Rebuilt and refocused Palestinian Authority security apparatus begins sustained, targeted, and effective operations aimed at confronting all those engaged in terror and dismantlement of terrorist capabilities and infrastructure. This includes commencing confiscation of illegal weapons and consolidation of security authority, free of association with terror and corruption.
- GOI [Government of Israel] takes no actions undermining trust, including deportations, attacks on civilians; confiscation and/or demolition of Palestinian homes and property, as a punitive measure or to facilitate Israeli construction; destruction of Palestinian institutions and infrastructure; and other measures specified in the Tenet work plan.
- Relying on existing mechanisms and on-the-ground resources, Quartet representatives begin informal monitoring and consult with the parties on establishment of a formal monitoring mechanism and its implementation.
- Implementation, as previously agreed, of US rebuilding, training, and resumed security cooperation plan in collaboration with outside oversight board (US-Egypt-Jordan). Quartet support for efforts to achieve a lasting, comprehensive cease-fire.
  - All Palestinian security organizations are consolidated into three services reporting to an empowered Interior Minister.

- ◦ Restructured/retrained Palestinian security forces and IDF counterparts progressively resume security cooperation and other undertakings in implementation of the Tenet work plan, including regular senior-level meetings, with the participation of US security officials.
- Arab states cut off public and private funding and all other forms of support for groups supporting and engaging in violence and terror.
- All donors providing budgetary support for the Palestinians channel these funds through the Palestinian Ministry of Finance's Single Treasury Account.
- As comprehensive security performance moves forward, IDF withdraws progressively from areas occupied since September 28, 2000, and the two sides restore the status quo that existed prior to September 28, 2000. Palestinian security forces redeploy to areas vacated by IDF.

Palestinian Institution-Building

- Immediate action on credible process to produce draft constitution for Palestinian statehood. As rapidly as possible, constitutional committee circulates draft Palestinian constitution, based on strong parliamentary democracy and cabinet with empowered prime minister, for public comment/debate. Constitutional committee proposes draft document for submission after elections for approval by appropriate Palestinian institutions.
- Appointment of interim prime minister or cabinet with empowered executive authority/decision-making body.
- GOI fully facilitates travel of Palestinian officials for PLC [Palestinian Legislative Council] and Cabinet sessions, internationally supervised security retraining, electoral and other reform activity, and other supportive measures related to the reform efforts.
- Continued appointment of Palestinian ministers empowered to undertake fundamental reform. Completion of further steps to achieve genuine separation of powers, including any necessary Palestinian legal reforms for this purpose.
- Establishment of independent Palestinian election commission. PLC reviews and revises election law.

- Palestinian performance on judicial, administrative, and economic benchmarks, as established by the International Task Force on Palestinian Reform.
- As early as possible, and based upon the above measures and in the context of open debate and transparent candidate selection/electoral campaign based on a free, multi-party process, Palestinians hold free, open, and fair elections.
- GOI facilitates Task Force election assistance, registration of voters, movement of candidates and voting officials. Support for NGOs involved in the election process.
- GOI reopens Palestinian Chamber of Commerce and other closed Palestinian institutions in East Jerusalem based on a commitment that these institutions operate strictly in accordance with prior agreements between the parties.

Humanitarian Response

- Israel takes measures to improve the humanitarian situation. Israel and Palestinians implement in full all recommendations of the Bertini report to improve humanitarian conditions, lifting curfews and easing restrictions on movement of persons and goods, and allowing full, safe, and unfettered access of international and humanitarian personnel.
- AHLC [Ad Hoc Liaison Committee] reviews the humanitarian situation and prospects for economic development in the West Bank and Gaza and launches a major donor assistance effort, including to the reform effort.
- GOI and PA continue revenue clearance process and transfer of funds, including arrears, in accordance with agreed, transparent monitoring mechanism.

Civil Society

- Continued donor support, including increased funding through PVOs [Private Voluntary Organizations]/NGOs, for people-to-people programs, private sector development, and civil society initiatives.

Settlements

- GOI immediately dismantles settlement outposts erected since March 2001.
- Consistent with the Mitchell Report, GOI freezes all settlement activity (including natural growth of settlements).

PHASE II: TRANSITION—JUNE 2003–DECEMBER 2003

In the second phase, efforts are focused on the option of creating an independent Palestinian state with provisional borders and attributes of sovereignty, based on the new constitution, as a way station to a permanent status settlement. As has been noted, this goal can be achieved when the Palestinian people have a leadership acting decisively against terror, willing and able to build a practicing democracy based on tolerance and liberty. With such a leadership, reformed civil institutions, and security structures, the Palestinians will have the active support of the Quartet and the broader international community in establishing an independent, viable, state.

Progress into Phase II will be based upon the consensus judgment of the Quartet of whether conditions are appropriate to proceed, taking into account performance of both parties. Furthering and sustaining efforts to normalize Palestinian lives and build Palestinian institutions, Phase II starts after Palestinian elections and ends with possible creation of an independent Palestinian state with provisional borders in 2003. Its primary goals are continued comprehensive security performance and effective security cooperation, continued normalization of Palestinian life and institution-building, further building on and sustaining of the goals outlined in Phase I, ratification of a democratic Palestinian constitution, formal establishment of office of prime minister, consolidation of political reform, and the creation of a Palestinian state with provisional borders.

- **International Conference:** Convened by the Quartet, in consultation with the parties, immediately after the successful conclusion of Palestinian elections, to support Palestinian economic recovery and launch a process, leading to establishment of an independent Palestinian state with provisional borders.
  - ○ Such a meeting would be inclusive, based on the goal of a comprehensive Middle East peace (including between Israel

and Syria, and Israel and Lebanon), and based on the principles described in the preamble to this document.

○ Arab states restore pre-intifada links to Israel (trade offices, etc.).

○ Revival of multilateral engagement on issues including regional water resources, environment, economic development, refugees, and arms control issues.

• New constitution for democratic, independent Palestinian state is finalized and approved by appropriate Palestinian institutions. Further elections, if required, should follow approval of the new constitution.

• Empowered reform cabinet with office of prime minister formally established, consistent with draft constitution.

• Continued comprehensive security performance, including effective security cooperation on the bases laid out in Phase I.

• Creation of an independent Palestinian state with provisional borders through a process of Israeli-Palestinian engagement, launched by the international conference. As part of this process, implementation of prior agreements, to enhance maximum territorial contiguity, including further action on settlements in conjunction with establishment of a Palestinian state with provisional borders.

• Enhanced international role in monitoring transition, with the active, sustained, and operational support of the Quartet.

• Quartet members promote international recognition of Palestinian state, including possible UN membership.

PHASE III: PERMANENT STATUS AGREEMENT AND END OF THE ISRAELI-PALESTINIAN CONFLICT—2004–2005

Progress into Phase III, based on consensus judgment of Quartet, and taking into account actions of both parties and Quartet monitoring. Phase III objectives are consolidation of reform and stabilization of Palestinian institutions, sustained, effective Palestinian security performance, and Israeli-Palestinian negotiations aimed at a permanent status agreement in 2005.

• **Second International Conference:** Convened by Quartet, in consultation with the parties, at beginning of 2004 to endorse agreement reached on an independent Palestinian state with provisional borders and formally to launch a process with the active, sustained, and operational support of the Quartet, leading to a final, permanent status resolution in 2005, including on borders, Jerusalem, refugees, settlements; and, to support progress toward a comprehensive Middle East settlement between Israel and Lebanon and Israel and Syria, to be achieved as soon as possible.

- Continued comprehensive, effective progress on the reform agenda laid out by the Task Force in preparation for final status agreement.
- Continued sustained and effective security performance, and sustained, effective security cooperation on the bases laid out in Phase I.
- International efforts to facilitate reform and stabilize Palestinian institutions and the Palestinian economy, in preparation for final status agreement.
- Parties reach final and comprehensive permanent status agreement that ends the Israel-Palestinian conflict in 2005, through a settlement negotiated between the parties based on UNSCR 242, 338, and 1397, that ends the occupation that began in 1967, and includes an agreed, just, fair, and realistic solution to the refugee issue, and a negotiated resolution on the status of Jerusalem that takes into account the political and religious concerns of both sides, and protects the religious interests of Jews, Christians, and Muslims worldwide, and fulfills the vision of two states, Israel and sovereign, independent, democratic, and viable Palestine, living side by side in peace and security.
- Arab state acceptance of full normal relations with Israel and security for all the states of the region in the context of a comprehensive Arab-Israeli peace.

PERSONS INTERVIEWED
FOR THIS BOOK

Eric Cohen, manager of the Park Hotel, Netanya
Uzi Dayan, former national security adviser to Prime Minister Sharon
Ezzedine Choukri Fishere, former United Nations official in Israel
Thomas L. Friedman, *New York Times* columnist
Efraim Halevy, former head of Mossad
Menachem Klein, Department of Political Studies, Bar Ilan University
Ghassan Khatib, former Palestinian Authority minister
Yossi Kuperwasser, former head of IDF Military Intelligence Research
  Division
Daniel Kurtzer, former US ambassador to Israel
Shalom Lipner, former deputy foreign policy adviser to the prime minister
  of Israel
Aaron Miller, former US mediator in Arab-Israel conflict
Bruce Riedel, former US national security Middle East adviser
Abdel monem Said Aly, Egyptian strategic scholar
Nabil Shaath, former Palestinian Authority minister
Gareth Smyth, *Financial Times* correspondent in Beirut in 2002
Nikolai Surkov, Moscow State Institute of International Relations' Oriental
  Studies Department
Dov Weissglass, former chief of staff to Prime Minister Sharon
Anthony Zinni, former head of CENTCOM; US peace envoy in 2002
An Arab former foreign minister speaking not for citation
A former European peace envoy, speaking not for citation
A former political adviser to Yasser Arafat, then to Mahmoud Abbas, speak-
  ing not for citation
A senior Lebanese scholar, speaking off the record

NOTES

PROLOGUE

1. "Reuven Rivlin Has Proven That He Is President of the Real Israel," Rivlin speech at 2015 Herzliya Conference, Asher Schechter, Haaretz.com, June 9, 2015.

CHAPTER 1

1. Roula Khalaf and Gareth Smyth, "Arab Summit in Confusion after Palestinian Exit," *Financial Times*, March 28, 2002; diary kept by Gareth Smyth, *Financial Times* correspondent, some of which was published at ft.com. Original supplied by Gareth Smyth.

CHAPTER 2

1. For background on the Israeli-Palestinian conflict and peace process, see chapter 15, "Behind the Events of March 2002."
2. Peace Index, poll taken March 24–25, 2002, Guttman Center for Public Opinion and Policy Research, Israel Democracy Institute.
3. Yasser Arafat speech, CNN.com, December 17, 2001.
4. Yasser Arafat address to the United Nations General Assembly, 1974, *New York Times*, https://www.nytimes.com/1974/11/14/archives/dramatic-session-plo-head-says-he-bears-olive-branch-and-guerrilla.html.
5. See Yossi Ben Ari, "The Skeleton in the Closet of the Second Intifada," *Haaretz* (Hebrew), September 27, 2020; Ofer Aderet, "The Death of the Terrorist with Nine Lives Was a Turning Point," *Haaretz*, September 29, 2020; Mati

Steinberg, "It's Easiest to Put the Blame on Arafat," *Haaretz* (Hebrew), October 31, 2020.

6. Peace Index, March 2002.

7. Yoni Chetboun, *Under Fire: Commander's Notes from a Battlefield* (Tel Aviv: Yedioth Ahronoth Books, 2016), p. 36 (Hebrew; y. a. translation).

8. Chetboun, *Under Fire*, p. 43.

CHAPTER 3

1. This and following citations from Anthony Zinni interview, Alexandria, Virginia, October 22, 2019.

2. Personal recollection. y. a.

3. *Peace Index*, March 2002.

4. Shalom Lipner email interview, April 16, 2020.

CHAPTER 4

1. Robert J. Brym and Bader Araj, "Suicide Bombing as Strategy and Interaction: The Case of the Second Intifada," *Social Forces*, Vol. 84, No. 4 (June 2006), pp. 1969–86.

2. Saul Kimhi and Shmuel Even, "Who Are the Palestinian Suicide Terrorists?" *INSS Strategic Assessment*, Vol. 6, No. 2, September 2003.

3. For discussion of this distinction in the context of a Hezbollah attack on an American military target, see Frederic C. Hof, "The Beirut Bombing of October 1983: An Act of Terrorism?" *Parameters, Journal of the US Army War College*, Vol. 15, No. 2, 1985.

4. Yoram Schweitzer, Aviad Mendelboim, and Dana Ayalon, "Suicide Bombings Worldwide in 2019: Signs of Decline Following the Military Defeat of the Islamic State," *INSS Insight*, No. 1244, January 2, 2020.

5. Kimhi and Even, "Who Are the Palestinian Suicide Terrorists?"

6. Official Fateh Facebook page, November 22, 2019, cited by Palestinian Media Watch, November 28, 2019.

7. Yohai Ofer, "Can You Identify Terrorists Based on a Facebook Page?" nrg (makorrishon.co.il), March 22, 2016 (Hebrew, y. a. translation).

8. See for example, Amos Harel, "No Terror, No Accords: 20 Years On, Effects of Second Intifada Are Clear," *Haaretz*, September 29, 2020.

CHAPTER 5

1. Efraim Halevy interview, May 1, 2019; Uzi Dayan interview, April 21, 2019.
2. Raviv Drucker and Ofer Shelah, *Boomerang* (Jerusalem: Keter, 2005), p. 215.
3. Reconstruction of the March 28, 2002, cabinet meeting is based primarily on interviews with Efraim Halevy, May 1, 2019; Uzi Dayan, April 21, 2019; and Yossi Kuperwasser, June 17, 2019.
4. Announcement by Prime Minister Ariel Sharon and Defense Minister Binyamin ben-Eliezer after special government meeting following terror escalation and the Pesach Eve attack, March 29, 2002, Government Press Office (y. a. translation).

CHAPTER 6

1. Marwan Muasher, *The Arab Center: The Promise of Moderation* (New Haven: Yale University Press, 2008), chapters 3 and 4.
2. Bruce Riedel interview, October 21, 2019.
3. Bruce Riedel interview, October 21, 2019.

CHAPTER 8

1. Gareth Smyth, "Beirut Summit Diary—Rocky Road to Peace," *Financial Times*, April 1, 2002.
2. Personal interview, April 3, 2019.
3. This and following quotes from Nabil Shaath interview, Ramallah, August 7, 2019.
4. Robert Fisk, "Palestinians Walk Out as Summit Snubs Arafat," *Independent*, London, March 28, 2002.
5. Ezzedine Choukri Fishere, "Happy to Be Proven Wrong," in *The Bitterlemons Guide to the Arab Peace Initiative*, ed. Yossi Alpher, Ghassan Khatib, and Charmaine Seitz (Jerusalem: bitterlemons-api.org, 2011), p. 23.
6. Saud al-Faisal, CNN.com, March 28, 2002.
7. Ezzedine Choukri Fishere interview, Dartmouth College, New Hampshire, October 16, 2019.
8. Fishere interview, October 16, 2019.
9. Diary kept by Gareth Smyth, *Financial Times* correspondent, some of which was published at ft.com. March 25, 2002. Original supplied by Gareth Smyth.
10. Kristian Coates Ulrichsen, *Qatar and the Gulf Crisis* (London: Hurst, 2019), pp. 35–36.

CHAPTER 9

1. Internet interview with Dr. Abdel monem Said Aly, chairman of the board and director of the Regional Center for Strategic Studies, in Cairo, June 25, 2019.

2. Personal conversation with Sharon, Tel Aviv, 1994.

3. This statement has been attributed to Sharon over the years by a number of Israeli politicians.

4. Roula Khalaf and Gareth Smyth, "Arab Summit May Heal Scars—Or Reopen Wounds," *Financial Times*, March 24, 2002.

5. Raviv Drucker and Ofer Shelah, *Boomerang* (Jerusalem: Keter, 2005, Hebrew), p. 15.

6. Interview with Efraim Halevy, *Mabat Malam*, edition 85, December 2019 (Hebrew).

7. Yossi Alpher, *Periphery: Israel's Search for Middle East Allies* (Lanham: Rowman & Littlefield, 2015), pp. 38–39.

8. Efraim Halevy interview, Tel Aviv, May 1, 2019.

9. Raphael Ahren, "Arab Peace Initiative Take 2: Major Development or 'Scam,'" *Times of Israel*, May 1, 2013.

10. Prime Minister Ariel Sharon's address to the Knesset, April 8, 2002, news1 .co.il/Archive (y. a. translation).

11. Uzi Dayan interview, April 21, 2019.

12. Shalom Lipner interview, April 16, 2020.

13. Sharon's address to the Knesset, April 8, 2002.

14. Palestinian Center for Policy and Survey Research (PSR), Ramallah, Public Opinion Polls #4 (May 2002) and #5 (November 2002).

15. Skype interview with former political adviser to Arafat and Abbas, August 30, 2019.

16. Ghassan Khatib interview, April 5, 2020.

CHAPTER 10

1. Aaron David Miller, *The Much Too Promised Land* (New York: Bantam Books, 2008), p. 329.

2. The author witnessed the incidents and was the person Ashrawi spoke to.

3. Interview with former European peace envoy, Europe, June 18, 2019.

4. Bruce Riedel interview, Washington, DC, October 21, 2019.

5. *Mabat Malam*, edition 88, February 2021, p. 17 (Hebrew, y. a. translation).

6. Dov Weissglass interview, Ramat HaSharon, August 19, 2019.

7. Quoted by Tom Friedman, "How the Palestinian-Israeli Peace Process Became a Farce," *International New York Times*, August 22, 2019.

8. Quoted in David Landau, *Arik: The Life of Ariel Sharon* (New York: Knopf, 2014).

9. Al-Aqsa TV, *A Story from History*, July 11, 2019, quoted by Palestinian Media Watch.

10. *Mabat Malam*, edition 88, February 2021, p. 17 (Hebrew, y. a. translation). See also n. 5, chapter 2.

11. Uri Avneri, "You Can't Understand Sharon without Knowing His Mother," *Haaretz*, November 3, 2016. Avneri's claim has not been corroborated elsewhere.

12. Ghassan Khatib phone interview, April 5, 2020.

13. Personal conversation, September 13, 1993.

14. Bruce Riedel interview, Washington, DC, October 21, 2019.

15. Heard on several occasions by the author.

CHAPTER 11

1. Sharon Knesset speech, April 8, 2002, news1.co.il/Archive/0018-D-999-00.html (Hebrew, y. a. translation).

2. Yoni Chetboun, *Under Fire: Commander's Notes from a Battlefield* (Tel Aviv: Yedioth Ahronoth Books, 2016, Hebrew), pp. 54–55.

3. Ghassan Khatib interview, April 5, 2020.

4. *Mabat Malam*, edition 88, February 2021 (Hebrew, y. a. translation), p. 18.

5. Tony Zinni interview, October 22, 2019.

6. Aaron David Miller, *The Much Too Promised Land* (New York: Bantam Books, 2008), p. 343.

7. John Lancaster, "U.N. Envoy Calls Camp 'Horrifying,'" *Washington Post*, April 19, 2002.

8. www.un.org/peace/jenin/.

9. See "Jenin—Capital of the Suicide Bombers," Israel Intelligence Heritage and Commemoration Center (IICC), August 31, 2003, http://www.terrorism-info.org.il/he/245/ (Hebrew, y. a. translation).

10. *MEMRI*, April 24, 2002.

11. *Jenin Jenin* can be viewed at archive.org/details/JeninJenin_201811.

12. "A Refugee in His Country," *Haaretz* Friday Gallery, April 17, 2020 (Hebrew, y. a. translation).

13. See Ofer Shelah, *Maariv* Weekend, December 28, 2008 (Hebrew, y. a. translation).

14. Uzi Dayan interview, April 21, 2019.

15. *Washington Post*, April 5, 2002.

16. Sharon Knesset speech, April 8, 2002.

CHAPTER 12

1. Daniel Kurtzer interview, Princeton, October 10, 2019.
2. Aaron Miller interview, Washington, October 22, 2019.
3. Coincidentally, the author strolled around the Mount and entered its mosques without incident just days before Sharon.
4. Email exchange with Fred Hof, February 2020.
5. Tom Clancy with Tony Zinni, *Battle Ready* (New York: Penguin, 2005), p. 463.
6. Shalom Lipner interview, April 16, 2020.
7. All quotes that follow except those attributed to *Haaretz* are from Dov Weissglass interview, Ramat HaSharon, August 19, 2019.
8. Aaron Miller interview, October 23, 2019.
9. Amnon Abramovich conversation with Sima Kadmon, *Yedioth Ahronoth* Passover Supplement, p. 13, April 8, 2020 (Hebrew, y. a. translation).
10. Efraim Halevy interview, May 1, 2019.
11. Ezzedine Choukri Fishere interview, October 16, 2019.
12. Tony Zinni interview, October 22, 2019.
13. Peace Index, May 2002.
14. "The Big Freeze," Ari Shavit interview with Dov Weissglass, *Haaretz*, October 7, 2004.
15. Aaron David Miller, *The Much Too Promised Land* (New York: Bantam Books, 2008), p. 352.

CHAPTER 13

1. Clive Jones, *The Clandestine Lives of Colonel David Smiley: Code Name "Grin"* (Edinburgh: University Press, 2019), p. 16.
2. Uzi Dayan interview, April 21, 2019.
3. Peace Index, May 2002.
4. Uzi Dayan interview, April 21, 2019.
5. Raviv Drucker and Ofer Shelah, *Boomerang* (Jerusalem: Keter, 2005, Hebrew), p. 267.
6. Shaul Arieli, "Bennet's Terrorist Attack," *Haaretz*, January 18, 2020 (Hebrew, y. a. translation).

CHAPTER 14

1. Quoted by Radio Free Europe/Radio Liberty, October 16, 2003.
2. Nikolai Surkov interview, Moscow, October 8, 2019.

CHAPTER 15

1. Quoted in Yossi Alpher, *No End of Conflict: Rethinking Israel-Palestine* (Lanham: Rowman & Littlefield, 2016).
2. Shaul Arieli, "Bennet's Terrorist Attack," *Haaretz*, January 18, 2020 (Hebrew, y. a. translation).
3. Quoted in Alpher, *No End of Conflict*.

CHAPTER 16

1. Daoud Kutab, "Salam Fayyad's Return to Palestinian Politics," *Al-Monitor*, March 11, 2021.
2. *Palestinian Media Watch*, May 10, 2020.
3. See Raja Shehadeh, "Stay Vigilant, Says a Curfew Veteran," *International New York Times*, March 26, 2020.
4. Menachem Klein telephone interview, June 2019.
5. Gideon Levy and Alex Levac, "Live Fire from an Ambush on Laborers Seeking Work in Israel," *Haaretz* Twilight Zone, January 3, 2020 (Hebrew, y. a. translation). See also Nachum Barnea, *Yedioth Ahronoth* Weekend Supplement (Hebrew), p. 3, August 14, 2020, and Amira Hass, "Why I Didn't Write about the Hole in the Fence," *Haaretz* (Hebrew), August 11, 2020.
6. Nir Hasson, "Israel Lets Armed PA Forces into E. J'lem after Triple Murder," *Haaretz*, January 3, 2021.

CHAPTER 17

1. Aaron Miller interview, October 9, 2019.
2. Kim Ghattas, *Black Wave: Saudi Arabia, Iran and the Forty-Year Rivalry That Unraveled Culture, Religion and Collective Memory in the Middle East* (New York: Henry Holt, 2020).
3. See for example, Marwan Muasher, *The Arab Center: The Promise of Moderation* (New Haven: Yale University Press, 2008), which barely mentions the Park bombing, and Aaron David Miller, *The Much Too Promised Land* (New York: Bantam Books, 2008), which omits any mention of the API, as do Raviv Drucker and Ofer Shelah in *Boomerang* (Jerusalem: Keter, 2005, Hebrew).
4. Uzi Dayan interview, April 21, 2019.
5. "US Policy toward Arab States, Palestinians, and Israel: Ideas and Approaches for the Biden Administration," *WINEP* Policy Forum Report, February 3, 2021.
6. Ezzedine Choukri Fishere interview, October 16, 2019.
7. Aaron Miller interview, October 9, 2019.

8. Abdel monem Said Aly interview, June 25, 2019.

9. Abdel monem Said Aly interview, June 25, 2019.

10. Interview, April 3, 2019.

11. Excerpt from a July 2016 speech to the Israel National Security College, Mazal Mualem, "Netanyahu's New Worldview," *Al-Monitor*, August 12, 2016. Cited in Yossi Alpher, *Winners and Losers in the "Arab Spring": Profiles in Chaos* (Abingdon, UK: Routledge, 2020), pp. 71–72.

12. Tony Zinni interview, October 22, 2019.

13. Personal conversation, Israel, 2004.

14. Hussein Ibish, "The US Is to Blame for Its Foreign Policy Paralysis over the Past Decade," *National*, December 29, 2019.

15. Narrative that follows, quotes included, from Daniel Kurtzer interview, October 10, 2019.

16. Bruce Riedel interview, October 21, 2019.

17. Interview, April 3, 2019.

SELECTED BIBLIOGRAPHY

Aderet, Ofer. "The Death of the Terrorist with Nine Lives Was a Turning Point." *Haaretz*, September 29, 2020.

Ahren, Raphael. "Arab Peace Initiative Take 2: Major Development or 'Scam.'" *Times of Israel*, May 1, 2013.

Al-Aqsa TV. *A Story from History*, July 11, 2019.

Alpher, Yossi. *No End of Conflict: Rethinking Israel-Palestine*. Lanham: Rowman & Littlefield, 2016.

Alpher, Yossi. *Periphery: Israel's Search for Middle East Allies*. Lanham: Rowman & Littlefield, 2015.

Alpher, Yossi. *Winners and Losers in the "Arab Spring": Profiles in Chaos*. Abingdon, UK: Routledge, 2020.

Arieli, Shaul. "Bennet's Terrorist Attack." *Haaretz*, January 18, 2020 (Hebrew).

Avneri, Uri. "You Can't Understand Sharon without Knowing His Mother." *Haaretz*, November 3, 2016.

Barnea, Nachum. *Yedioth Ahronoth* Weekend Supplement, p. 3, August 14, 2020 (Hebrew).

Ben Ari, Yossi. "The Skeleton in the Closet of the Second Intifada." *Haaretz*, September 27, 2020 (Hebrew).

Brym, Robert J., and Bader Araj. "Suicide Bombing as Strategy and Interaction: The Case of the Second Intifada." *Social Forces*, Vol. 84, No. 4 (June 2006), pp. 1969–86.

Chetboun, Yoni. *Under Fire: Commander's Notes from a Battlefield*. Tel Aviv: Yedioth Ahronoth Books, 2016. Hebrew.

Clancy, Tom, with Tony Zinni. *Battle Ready*. New York: Penguin, 2005.

Drucker, Raviv, and Ofer Shelah. *Boomerang*. Jerusalem: Keter, 2005. Hebrew.

Fishere, Ezzedine Choukri. "Happy to Be Proven Wrong." In *The Bitterlemons Guide to the Arab Peace Initiative*. Jerusalem: bitterlemons-api.org, 2011.

Fisk, Robert. "Palestinians Walk Out as Summit Snubs Arafat." *Independent*, London, March 28, 2002.

Friedman, Thomas L. "Memo to: President Hosni Mubarak, Crown Prince Abdullah, King Abdullah, President Bashar al-Assad and the Rest of the Arab League, from: President Bush." *New York Times*, February 6, 2002; "An Intriguing Signal from the Saudi Crown Prince." *New York Times*, February 17, 2002; "How the Palestinian-Israeli Peace Process Became a Farce." *International New York Times*, August 22, 2019.

Ghattas, Kim. *Black Wave: Saudi Arabia, Iran and the Forty-Year Rivalry That Unraveled Culture, Religion and Collective Memory in the Middle East*. New York: Henry Holt, 2020.

Haaretz Friday Gallery. "A Refugee in His Country," April 17, 2020 (Hebrew).

Harel, Amos. "No Terror, No Accords: 20 Years On, Effects of Second Intifada Are Clear." *Haaretz*, September 29, 2020.

Hass, Amira. "Why I Didn't Write about the Hole in the Fence." *Haaretz*, August 11, 2020 (Hebrew).

Hasson, Nir. "Israel Lets Armed PA Forces into E. J'lem after Triple Murder." *Haaretz*, January 3, 2021.

Hof, Frederic C. "The Beirut Bombing of October 1983: An Act of Terrorism?" *Parameters, Journal of the US Army War College*, Vol. 15, No. 2, 1985.

Ibish, Hussein. "The US Is to Blame for Its Foreign Policy Paralysis over the Past Decade." *National*, December 29, 2019.

Israel Intelligence Heritage and Commemoration Center (IICC). "Jenin—Capital of the Suicide Bombers." August 31, 2003 (Hebrew).

Jenin Jenin (film). archive.org/details/JeninJenin_201811.

Jones, Clive. *The Clandestine Lives of Colonel David Smiley: Code Name "Grin."* Edinburgh: University Press, 2019.

Kadmon, Sima. "Conversation with Amnon Abramovich." *Yedioth Ahronoth* Passover Supplement, p. 13, April 8, 2020 (Hebrew).

Khalaf, Roula, and Gareth Smyth. "Arab Summit May Heal Scars—Or Reopen Wounds." *Financial Times*, March 24, 2002; "Arab Summit in Confusion after Palestinian Exit." *Financial Times*, March 28, 2002.

Kimhi, Saul, and Shmuel Even. "Who Are the Palestinian Suicide Terrorists?" *INSS Strategic Assessment*, Vol. 6, No. 2, September 2003.

Kutab, Daoud. "Salam Fayyad's Return to Palestinian Politics." *Al-Monitor*, March 11, 2021.

Lancaster, John. "U.N. Envoy Calls Camp 'Horrifying.'" *Washington Post*, April 19, 2002.

Landau, David. *Arik: The Life of Ariel Sharon*. New York: Knopf, 2014.

Levy, Gideon, and Alex Levac. "Live Fire from an Ambush on Laborers Seeking Work in Israel." *Haaretz* Twilight Zone, January 3, 2020 (Hebrew).

Mabat Malam. Edition 88, February 2021 (Hebrew).

MEMRI. April 24, 2002.

Miller, Aaron David. *The Much Too Promised Land*. New York: Bantam Books, 2008.

Mualem, Mazal. "Netanyahu's New Worldview." *Al-Monitor*, August 12, 2016.

Muasher, Marwan. *The Arab Center: The Promise of Moderation*. New Haven: Yale University Press, 2008.

Ofer, Yohai. "Can You Identify Terrorists Based on a Facebook Page?" nrg (ma korrishhon.co.il), March 22, 2016 (Hebrew).

Official Fateh Facebook Page. November 22, 2019, cited by *Palestinian Media Watch*, November 28, 2019.

Palestinian Media Watch. May 10, 2020.

Peace Index. Polls taken March 24–25, 2002, May 2002. *Guttman Center for Public Opinion and Policy Research*, Israel Democracy Institute.

Public Opinion Polls #4 (May 2002) and #5 (November 2002). *Palestinian Center for Policy and Survey Research* (PSR), Ramallah.

Schechter, Asher. "Reuven Rivlin Has Proven That He Is President of the Real Israel." Rivlin Speech at 2015 Herzliya Conference, Haaretz.com, June 9, 2015.

Schweitzer, Yoram, Aviad Mendelboim, and Dana Ayalon. "Suicide Bombings Worldwide in 2019: Signs of Decline Following the Military Defeat of the Islamic State." *INSS Insight*, No. 1244, January 2, 2020.

Sharon, Ariel. Address to the Knesset, April 8, 2002, *news1.co.il/Archive* (Hebrew).

Shavit, Ari. "The Big Freeze," interview with Dov Weissglass. *Haaretz*, October 7, 2004.

Shehadeh, Raja. "Stay Vigilant, Says a Curfew Veteran." *International New York Times*, March 26, 2020.

Shelah, Ofer. *Maariv* Weekend, December 28, 2008 (Hebrew).

Smyth, Gareth. "Beirut Summit Diary—Rocky Road to Peace." *Financial Times*, April 1, 2002.

Steinberg, Mati. "It's Easiest to Put the Blame on Arafat." *Haaretz*, October 31, 2020 (Hebrew).

Ulrichsen, Kristian Coates. *Qatar and the Gulf Crisis*. London: Hurst, 2019.

"US Policy toward Arab States, Palestinians, and Israel: Ideas and Approaches for the Biden Administration." *WINEP* Policy Forum Report, February 3, 2021.

INDEX

193

ABOUT THE AUTHOR

Yossi (Joseph) Alpher is a consultant and writer on Israel-related strategic issues. He is the author of *And the Wolf Shall Dwell with the Wolf: The Settlers and the Palestinians*; *Periphery: Israel's Search for Middle East Allies*; *No End of Conflict: Rethinking Israel-Palestine*; and most recently, *Winners and Losers in the "Arab Spring": Profiles in Chaos*. His books have won the Yitzhak Sadeh Prize, the Chechik Prize, and the Chaikin Prize in Israel.

Alpher served in the Israel Defense Forces as an intelligence officer, followed by service in the Mossad. From 1981 to 1995 he was associated with the Jaffee Center for Strategic Studies at Tel Aviv University, ultimately serving as director of the center. From 1995 to 2000 he served as director of the American Jewish Committee's Israel/Middle East Office in Jerusalem. In July 2000 (during the Camp David talks) he served as special adviser to the prime minister of Israel, concentrating on the Israeli-Palestinian peace process. From 2001 to 2012 he was coeditor, with Ghassan Khatib (until recently vice president of Bir Zeit University), of the bitterlemons.net family of internet publications.